Mazes and Labyrinths

Nigel Pennick is a writer and lecturer on ancient and modern mysteries, and is an authority on geomantic practices and labyrinths. For fifteen years he worked as a marine microbiologist and published papers describing eight new species previously unknown to science. A founder and co-ordinator of the Institute of Geomantic Research, Nigel Pennick organized the five Cambridge Geomancy Symposia, and has co-ordinated an international conference on labyrinths. He has written many books including *Geomancy, The Cosmic Axis* and *Labyrinths – Their Geomancy and Symbolism*. With Paul Devereux he is the author of *Lines on the Landscape: Leylines and Other Linear Enigmas*. His practical work includes geomantic design on an architectural competition entry for the La Villette Park project in Paris; remedial geomantic work in England and Germany; and the laying-out and supervision of the construction of the first permanent stone labyrinth in North America. He constructed a series of ten different temporary labyrinths as a demonstration at *Art in Action* at Waterperry House, Oxfordshire, and has also built labyrinths in Austria and Ireland. He lives in Cambridge.

Mazes and Labyrinths

Nigel Pennick

ROBERT HALE · LONDON

ISBN 0 7090 5508 0

Robert Hale Limited
Clerkenwell House
Clerkenwell Green
London EC1R 0HT

Printed and bound in Malta
by Interprint Ltd.

Contents

Illustrations

FIGURES

PLATES

Between pages 80 and 81

Between pages 128 and 129

PICTURE CREDITS

Figures

All line illustrations were drawn by Nigel Pennick, except where noted. Author's collection: Figs. 1.8a, 1.10, 2.2a, 2.3c, 2.6, 3.4. *Caerdrois* Project: Figs. 1.2d, 2.9, 2.11, 3.2. After Paul Devereux: Fig. 3.8. K. Frank Jensen: Fig. 4.1. Cambridgeshire Collection: Fig. 2.8. Cumbria County Record Office: Fig. 2.11. After Jeff Saward: Fig. 4.8.

Plates

Bo Stjernström, 1983: 1. Jeff Saward, 1983, *Caerdroia* archives: 2, 5. Nigel Pennick: 1979 – 22; 1987 – 3, 17; 1988 – 8, 19; 1989 – 4, 7, 20, 23; collection of – 12-14, 16. Reproduced with the permission of the Controller of HMSO, Crown Copyright/M.o.D.: 6, 18. Cambridgeshire Antiquarian Society: 9. Cambridgeshire Collection, Cambridgeshire Libraries: 10. Nottinghamshire Libraries: 11. Paul Devereux: 1975 – 15; 1986 – 21.

Acknowledgements

Many people have helped me in various ways in the production of this work. I would like to thank the following for various assistance: Jeff and Deb Saward, Adrian Fisher, John Kraft, Bo Stjernström, Michael Behrend, Mike Taylor, Colin Dudley, Jonathan Mullard, Paul Devereux, Stephen J. Best, K. Frank Jensen, Piotr Rypson, Marco Bischof, Professor Peter Schmid, Professor Waltraud Wagner, Adrian von Aesch-Hoppler and Rupert Pennick. Also I thank the staffs of the university libraries at Cambridge and Zurich; the County Library at Nottingham; the Cambridgeshire Collection at the Central Library, Cambridge; Huntingdon Library; the Caerdroia Project Archives and the County Record Offices of Cambridgeshire, Cumbria, Hampshire, Huntingdonshire, Kent and Nottinghamshire, for assistance and valuable information. Finally, I would also like to acknowledge those who have helped me in my practical labyrinth constructions: The International Labyrinth Team, 1988: Rosemarie Kirschmann, Ursula Schmitz and Mona Miksicek; also Eleonore Schmid and others, unnamed, who have joined in with me on the great labyrinth adventure. Should I have missed out anyone from this list, I wish them to know that my gratitude to them is in no way diminished.

An art that has life does not restore the
works of the past. It continues them.

Auguste Rodin

Introduction

Some run the Shepherd's Race – a rut
Within a grass-plot deeply cut
And wide enough to tread –
A maze of path, of old designed
To tire the feet, perplex the mind,
Yet pleasure heart and head;
'Tis not unlike this life we spend,
And where you start from, there you end.

Bradfield, *Sentan's Wells*, 1864

The maze or labyrinth is perhaps the most complex of all of the symbols which have been used by human beings. Although it can take a myriad of forms, it is recognizable immediately. It has a remarkable distribution throughout the world, and also through time, having been known and used from antiquity until the present day. Labyrinth patterns are known as far back in time as the northern European Bronze Age and, historically, from the Twelfth Dynasty period of ancient Egypt.

The first recorded labyrinth in history was built in Egypt at Harawa in the Fayum district, at the time of King Amenemhet (1842–1797 BCE). It was a building which, according to Herodotus, consisted of 'twelve courts, all of them roofed, with gates exactly opposite one another'. The rooms were ' ... half underground, half above ground, the latter built on the former. The whole number of these chambers is three thousand.' This labyrinth was a massive building complex, which appears to have been part tomb, part shrine, part initiatory complex and part storehouse. After this, the most famous labyrinth of antiquity, which may have been a similar building, was that of Knossos on Crete, built for King Minos around 1600 BCE. The legend of this labyrinth, which contained the horrendous Minotaur, has been

1.1. Coins of Knossos. From these the name 'Cretan' came to be used for the Classical labyrinth, though Scandinavian ones may well predate the Cretan civilization.

the base material for labyrinth lore ever since. But at the same period, or perhaps earlier, the people of Sweden were also building stone labyrinths for ritual purposes.

Labyrinths have been used as ornament or magical protection on a remarkable variety of human artefacts. In prehistoric times they were carved on rock faces. One is painted on an Etruscan wine jug. They were stamped on Cretan coins, whilst jewels engraved with labyrinths are known from the time of imperial Rome. A wooden basket from the Caucasus has a design which parallels the patterns in the traditional basket-weaving of Arizona. Labyrinths were engraved upon a church bell and a stone cross, both from Scandinavia. A wooden mangle-board used in laundry from Gotland, dating from 1800, has an eleven-circuit Classical labyrinth design. Various stones, some with a magical function and others of unknown use, have been found in Ireland, the Isle of Man and Cornwall. Labyrinths appear on medieval church floor tiles at Châlons-sur-Marne and Mirepoix in France. Around the year 1500 the labyrinth was used as a printer's device by the Italian Gian Giacomo Benedetti, who worked under the Latin name Johannes Jacobus de Benedictis. The labyrinth is a motif of perdition and salvation in didactic prints of the Renaissance. They appear as graffiti in an abandoned stone mine in southern England.

Labyrinths carved or painted on door-posts or above entrances are known to have existed in many places in Europe and Asia. The church at Taaning in Denmark has one, whilst two labyrinth-like coils once existed over the door of a house in Marmeke in the Sauerland district of western Germany. On a larger scale, labyrinths have been cast in bronze, made of pebbles and boulders, cut into turf, formed of mosaic tesserae, inlaid in stone with lead, laid as gravel or brick pathways and marked with hedges, walls, wooden fences or wire mesh.

Wherever they have existed, the basic theme of the labyrinths has been that of impenetrability and entrapment. This may be taken literally, in that any person entering the maze is lost. Entering the labyrinth, the individual is 'amazed' by the profusion of pathways, and the faculty of rational thought is obliterated. On a more esoteric level, labyrinths have been used magically for the trapping of

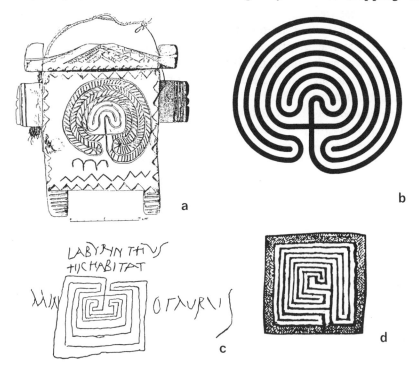

1.2. Classical labyrinths – a: Caucasian wooden basket (after von Richthofen); b: Classical labyrinth design, of the Dalby turn maze; c: Graffito from Pompeii, with inscription 'Labyrinth. Here lives the Minotaur'; d: Classical labyrinth variant: Roman masaic from Saint-Come-et-Maruéjols, France.

malevolent spirits. But whatever its use, the unique quality of any labyrinth is that it can be made large enough for people to walk in, or small enough to be a talismanic jewel. Where mazes have been constructed large enough for human entry, various materials have been employed. The puzzle hedge maze may be most familiar to many readers, yet this is but one of the options. Labyrinths can be made from pebbles and boulders, they can be cut in the turf, laid as mosaic floors or constructed from such materials as wire mesh, bricks or concrete blocks.

Whatever the material of construction may be, there is no generally agreed system of maze and labyrinth classification. However, there are certain well-defined categories. Basically, mazes and labyrinths can be divided into two forms, the unicursal, in which there is a single pathway, with no deviations or dead ends, and the multicursal, where there are many paths, which may include dead ends. Clearly, whilst there are limitless possibilities for multicursal mazes, the more limited unicursal patterns are more likely to be classifiable. Indeed, this is the case, with a small number of basic patterns recognizable and named. These are the Classical, Rad-type, Roman, Otfrid and medieval Christian forms.

One of the most ancient of these, and the most widespread in time and geography, is known as the Classical labyrinth. This is sometimes called 'the Cretan labyrinth', as the pattern is encountered on the coins of Knossos. However, it is known also from stone labyrinths in Scandinavia, as turf mazes in England and on buildings in central Europe. Because the former may predate the Minoan civilization on Crete, the name Classical is preferred as not prejudging the possible origin of the pattern. In its basic form, the Classical labyrinth is derived from the basic meander pattern, which is 'bent' to create seven circuits with a cross at the centre. More complex forms are possible by producing more loops, creating eleven- and fifteen-turn varieties.

Perhaps derived from this is the Rad-type pattern, in which there is a pair of entrances which access the centre by way of the same back-and-forth pathway. Anciently this type is known from Germany and Scandinavia. Another derivation of the Classical labyrinth is the Otfrid pattern, which is a series of rings through which the path meanders from the outside to the inside. The Roman labyrinth is related geometrically to the meander pattern, being composed of a series of four arranged in a square or circle. The pathway proceeds through the four quarters in strict progression before reaching the centre. Derived from this by way of late antique pavement labyrinths is the medieval Christian labyrinth, whose best-known example is in the nave pavement of the cathedral at Chartres in France, which was adopted for outdoor turf mazes in England.

This work deals with every historic and notable maze and labyrinth in the British Isles, from the prehistoric period to the present day. But whilst it is concerned primarily with mazes and labyrinths in Britain and Ireland, it is impossible to discuss them in isolation from their cultural context, which is one of the wider European tradition. This is true even from the earliest times: the type of prehistoric rock carvings which may have given rise to the labyrinth design can be found in Italy, Austria, Switzerland, Spain, Sweden and Ireland as well as in Britain itself.

1.3. Derivation of the Classical labyrinth form from the meander pattern by bending it into a circle.

The oldest surviving mazes in Britain are Roman mosaics, derived from the Mediterranean tradition, and most probably made by Italian craftsmen. Tradition asserts that the later turf mazes originated in Denmark which at one time, under the rule of King Canute, had the same monarch as England. The parallels which survive in the magical lore and folk customs associated with turf and stone mazes show that the British labyrinths are part of the same folk tradition as that of Scandinavia and Germany. To unravel some of the magical lore of labyrinths, we must turn to Scandinavia, where detailed knowledge survived some generations longer than it did in Britain. The medieval pavement labyrinths of France are part of the Christian tradition that existed simultaneously in England. At one period, floor tiles from a manufacturing centre in France were being supplied to churches in northern France and southern England. This was quite natural as the dukedom of Normandy was within the kingdom of France. Later the first hedge mazes were made in France and Italy, and their ideas and techniques were imported into Britain. Many early designs were direct copies of French models. Finally, the inspiration for the modern revival of the symbolic maze, since 1970, can be traced to the Mediterranean legend of Theseus and the Minotaur.

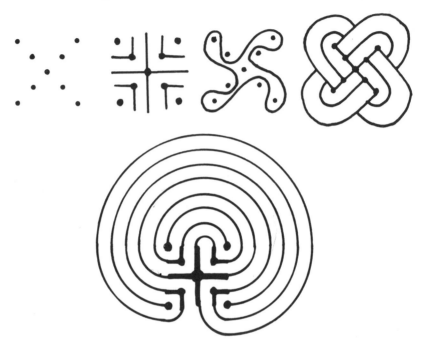

1.4. The nine-dot pattern, basis for the Classical labyrinth, and its geometrical derivatives used in traditional ceremony and magic.

Historically, walk-through labyrinths have proved to be rather more transient than buildings. Turf mazes have been overgrown and lost through neglect: they have been ploughed out, covered with tarmac and built upon. Hedge mazes have also suffered destruction in periods when they were no longer fashionable. They have become overgrown through lack of maintenance and have been rooted up when gardens have been taken for building development. Documentary evidence for even the well-known labyrinths, such as the surviving turf maze at Wing, Leicestershire (formerly Rutland), is often minimal, and for those which are destroyed there may be little more to go on than a stray reference in a document. But, fortunately, research over the past ten years, co-ordinated by the Caerdroia Project, has shed much light on a hitherto-obscure subject, so that it is possible now to gain a more comprehensive overview of mazes and labyrinths in Britain and of their place in the wider context of European culture.

Nigel Campbell Pennick
Bar Hill
October 1989

— 1 —

Ancient Rock and Stone Labyrinths

Ancient Classical Labyrinth Carvings

Ancient rock-carvings of the Classical labyrinth are far from common. Despite the abundance of other carvings of the periods, no indisputable neolithic or Bronze Age rock-carved labyrinths in the British Isles have yet been discovered.

Over the years there have been suggestions, on stylistic grounds, that the labyrinth pattern may be derived from the cup-and-ring rock carvings of the late neolithic–early Bronze Age. Indeed, there are several important carvings of this type which do resemble labyrinths but, tantalizingly, there seems to be none which is a true labyrinth. Many cup-and-ring carvings consist of a central depression surrounded by concentric rings, or part-rings. Often these are joined to a straight line that connects the centre with the outside of the rings.

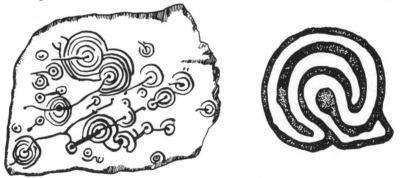

1.5. Left: Cup-and-ring marks on a rock at Old Bewick, Northumberland. Right: Rock carving at Ballygowan, Kilmartin, in the form of a simple labyrinth.

Carvings such as those at Old Bewick, Northumberland (map grid reference NU 075216), and at Roughting Linn (grid reference NT 984367) are good examples of this. A notable series of cup-and-ring and related marks can be found on Ilkley Moor in Yorkshire. The series of carved stones includes the Panorama Stone (map grid reference SE 115473) and the Swastika Stone on Woodhouse Crag (map grid reference SE 094470). This latter stone bears a fylfot or Celtic Rose carving, a pattern related closely to the Classical labyrinth. Scotland, too, has several remarkable series of cup-and-ring carvings which resemble labyrinths. Among these are the Kilmartin complex in Argyll, which contains a large number of rock-carvings. The slab known as Ballygowan has a much-weathered pattern which may be interpreted as a simple three-ring labyrinth.

Elsewhere in Scotland there is a remarkable spiral carving on a rock ledge overlooking the sea at Knock, Wigtownshire (map grid reference NX 364402). But the largest collection of cup-and-ring marks in Britain can be seen at Achnabreck, mid-Argyll (map grid reference NR 856906) on a pair of rock outcrops near a farm 3 km (1¾ miles) from Lochgilpead. At Cauldside Burn, Kirkcudbright-shire (map grid reference NX 528572), to the north of the main cairn, there is a whinstone rock in which is incised a large spiral. Carvings in Ireland, such as those in Cairn T at Loughcrew, County Meath (map grid reference N 585775), and at Newgrange, approximate labyrinthine forms. This is true especially of the famous 'blocking stone' at the entrance to the neolithic chambered cairn of Newgrange (map reference O 007727), which is carved with carefully executed spirals whose form resembles that of the centre of some Scandinavian stone labyrinths.

But the Classical labyrinth is found nowhere in the British Isles as an indisputably prehistoric carving. Furthermore, the precise meaning of these prehistoric sigils (hieroglyph) has been lost for many centuries. There is a hint in the ancient Welsh text known as *The Triads of Britain*, which has a reference to the stones of Gwydden-Ganhebon, from which the initiated 'could read the arts and sciences of the world'. Also, the tomb-slab of the ancient Welsh astronomer Gwydon ap Don, at Caernarfon, was 'a stone of enigmas', carved with ancient symbols unintelligible to the uninitiated. A rock north of Knappers on Clydebank, studied by the Glaswegian antiquary Ludovic MacLellan Mann, contained many loops and straight lines which resemble the labyrinth. He claimed that they symbolized the orbital cycles of the planets. But despite these legends and suggestions, we can only speculate on the meaning which their makers intended them to convey.

Where they occur in the British Isles, the handful of carved labyrinths which do exist are all found in a Celtic context. The total number known comprises one on a boulder in Ireland, one in a castle at Craigmillar in Scotland, and two together on a rock face at Tintagel in Cornwall. Elsewhere in Europe they are widely spread. Four Swedish examples exist carved on rocks on islands in the outer archipelago east of Stockholm, five are known from Val Camonica in Italy, and others from Pontevedra in north-west Spain. Another important example is at Machcesk, North Ossetian, in the USSR. The fylfot or Celtic Rose pattern accompanies the labyrinths among the carvings of Val Camonica, Italy (where they are dated to the early Iron Age period IVc). At Val Camonica it occurs along with Classical labyrinths. It is also found on a rock face at the Bronze Age site at Tossene in Sweden. A neolithic tomb at Luzzanas, Sardinia, known as the 'Tomba del Labirinto', dated to 2500 BCE, would make this carving, if contemporary with the tomb, the oldest known Classical labyrinth.

The largest carved Classical labyrinth in the British Isles is in Dublin. In 1908, near Hollywood, in County Wicklow, Ireland, during a hunt for a weasel, huntsmen overturned a large boulder under which the animal had taken refuge. On the underside of the rock they discovered a carving. This was examined by the antiquary Goddard H. Orpen, who in 1911 was of the opinion that, 'It is plain that the motif is a cross.' At that time, there was simply no awareness of the labyrinth pattern among Irish antiquaries. Later P.J. Lynch (see Nance, Bibliog.) thought that it was a 'Game of Troy'. However, this cross interpretation, which mystifies us now, was the official view and remained the view until the publication of William Matthews' *Mazes and Labyrinths* in 1922, when it was realized suddenly that the pattern was not a cross at all but the broken remains of a well-executed and clearly incised Classical labyrinth. In 1925, the boulder was removed from its original location and taken to the National Museum in Dublin. On the flat face, where the labyrinth is carved, it measures about 0.9 by 1.15 metres (3 feet by 3 feet 9 inches).

As with the Rocky Valley carvings at Tintagel, described below, the Hollywood Stone has been attributed to the Bronze Age. This is because of the supposed similarity between the Classical labyrinth and cup-and-ring petroglyphs. Commenting on the Hollywood Stone, Professor MacAlister (see Nance, Bibliog.) was under the impression that the conventional labyrinth ' ... closely resembles a type of petroglyph common in this country, consisting of a series of concentric circles surrounding a separate cup hollow with a single radial groove'. The gapped-circle designs at Knowth and the carving classified as number K51 at Newgrange, for example, have been adduced as evidence for this connection. But none of these patterns has the correct number of rings, nor the characteristic 'cross and corners' of the Classical labyrinth design, and the resemblance, if not fortuitous, is superficial.

The Hollywood Stone's finding-place was in Upper Lockstown, 6.5 km (4 miles) to the south-east of Hollywood (map grid reference N 99-03-). Its location was close to an ancient trackway, used by pilgrims, known as St Kevin's Road. This linked Hollywood with the sacred place of Glendalough. This early Celtic monastic connection was one of the reasons why it was believed to be a cross when first discovered. It is possible that it was a marker for the pilgrims' path, a possibility reinforced by the fact that the labyrinth has long been a symbol of pilgrimage in the Christian tradition. St Kevin founded the monastery around the year 550, and the labyrinth carving may date from a similar period. The labyrinth carved on the Hollywood Stone, like those at Tintagel, was made with a hard-edged metal tool, giving a sharp appearance qualitatively different from the carvings, for example, within Newgrange or Cairn T at Loughcrew. Its hard-edged tool carving technique makes this far more likely than the neolithic or Bronze Age hypothesis. Being a Classical labyrinth form need not preclude its Christian use either, as the medieval Christian form, used later in cathedrals and in the church of St Laurence at Rathmore in County Meath, had not been developed at that period. Several Scandinavian churches have or had painted Classical labyrinths, four in Sweden and a famous one at Sibbo in Finland. One Swedish church bell has a labyrinth pattern cast into it. The Hollywood Stone, as it is known, was exhibited at the World's Fair in New York, 1964–5, where it generated much interest.

In 1948 two Classical labyrinths were discovered on a rock wall next to a ruined watermill in Rocky Valley, 1.6 km (1 mile) north-east of Tintagel in Cornwall (map grid reference SX 073893). They each measure 23 cm (9 inches) in diameter, though one is more elliptical than the other. Close by now is a metal official notice which states that the inscribed labyrinths are 'Bronze Age, 1800–1400 BC'. Unfortunately, although many people have taken it at face value, this assumption is without foundation, having been arrived at by supposed stylistic similarities with cup-and-ring markings, as Professor MacAlister did for the Hollywood Stone. However, like the Hollywood Stone, on close examination the carvings appear to have been incised with an edged metal tool. Likewise the level of erosion from 1800 BCE should be much greater than the labyrinths have suffered. Another theory, forwarded in the early 1950s, applied the then-fashionable diffusionist theory of culture that a culture in one part of the world might be derived directly from another, and it was suggested that the labyrinths were Cretan in origin. (At about this time, a Cretan-style dagger carving was noticed on a megalith at Stonehenge, and this was taken as evidence that the stone circle was not of indigenous construction.) However, again, nothing but supposed stylistic similarities were taken as the evidence for the labyrinths as graffiti left by Mycenaean explorers. Tellingly, protagonists of this theory omitted to mention that no comparable rock-carved labyrinths are known from the Mycenaean culture. Another suggestion is that the labyrinths date from the early sixth century, when a Celtic monk who was known as St Nectan is said to have lived in a hermitage further up the valley by the waterfall known now as St Nectan's Kieve. This would parallel the Hollywood Stone connection with the Celtic monk St Kevin. But, unfortunately for this theory, the name Nectan is suspicious, for it is connected with pre-Christian water shrines and is clearly a version of the name of the Celtic pagan divinities Nudd, Nodens and Nechtan. Rivers sacred to this deity included the Neckar in Germany and the Neckinger, a Southwark tributary of the Thames, now a sewer. Furthermore, as a 'Nixie' is a water spirit and a 'Nicor' a water monster, the saint may be the folk-memory of a pre-Christian spiritual presence at the place rather than an actual human being.

Another possibility is that the Rocky Valley labyrinths were used for magical purposes during the medieval or Reformation period. By way of comparison, the seventeenth-century chalked labyrinths found in the abandoned Chaldon Bottom stone mine come into this category (see below). Finally, the Tintagel mazes have been connected with the mill itself, whose owner was reputed to have been, although illiterate, a brilliant natural mathematician. Whatever their origin, they can be reached by walking from Tintagel by the coastal path towards Boscastle, or from the B3263 road by a path from the Trout Farm.

The only other ancient carved Classical labyrinth in Britain can be found far from Tintagel, at Craigmillar Castle (map grid reference NT 285709), close to the Scottish capital city of Edinburgh. This is now almost obliterated, but it can just be discerned as a worn carving on a stone bench in the recess of the south window of the Great Hall. It measures about 25 cm (10 inches) across and probably dates from the late sixteenth or early seventeenth century, when the hall's windows were reconstructed. The nineteenth-century *Notes and Queries* correspondent Joseph Robertson (see Nance, Bibliog.) remarked on the connection between this carving and the then-popular children's game 'the Walls of Troy' – mazes drawn in the seaside sand or on school slates.

A stone closely connected with the Rocky Valley labyrinths is kept in the Witchcraft Museum at Boscastle, coincidentally close to Tintagel. This is a Classical labyrinth carved on an irregular piece of slate measuring about 45 cm (1 foot 6 inches) long and about 15 cm (6 inches) wide. The stone came from a farm at Michaelstow, a village south of Boscastle, having been a ritual object in the wisewomen's tradition of the Northern Tradition. In 1950 the stone was donated to the museum by the daughter of the famous 'wise woman' Kate 'The Gull' Turner. It had been handed down to Kate Turner by the Manx wise woman Nan Wade, who in turn had had it from Sarah Quiller from Ballaveare, Port Soderick, also in the Isle of Man. She had acquired it from an earlier wise woman, and it had been handed down through many generations. The stone is called a 'Troy Stone'. It was used for gaining states of altered consciousness. The wise woman would trace her finger over the labyrinth, back and forth, whilst humming a *galdr* (ceremonial call), until the transcendent state was reached. Another Troy Stone was destroyed in 1958 when a local wise woman died. As stipulated in her will, it was smashed and the pieces were disposed of. Clearly these stones are part of a tradition, and it is probable that there are other hereditary Troy Stones still in use today. They obviously have a parallel in Indian women's magic, where a labyrinth-shaped *yantra* magical diagram) known as *Chakra-Vyūha* is used in childbirth to assist an easy delivery. The *yantra* is consecrated by a priest at the appropriate hour; he tells the woman who is giving birth to enter mentally the entrance at the top of the pattern and to follow its winding pathway in deep concentration; after having completed the journey to the centre, she must find her way out again. According to Tantric theory, the mental circumambulation of the labyrinth makes the woman do the same to her own womb, helping her to use the powers of concentration to assist the birth. It is possible that in former times these carved labyrinth stones had a similar function, as it was customary for local wise women to be the village

1.6. Labyrinths from India. Left: *Chakra Vyūha* for concentration in childbirth. Centre: *Kota* (the fortress) used in south India as a threshold protection pattern. Right: Labyrinth design as in the *Mahabharata*.

midwives.

Allied to these carved labyrinths is the series of chalk drawings found in 1981 by speleological researchers in the abandoned stone workings at Chaldon in Surrey. During explorations of this extensive mine system, the Unit Two Cave Research and Exploration Group found a number of graffiti chalked on the walls and ceiling of the mine. The Chaldon Bottom mine was the source of a stone known as Chaldon Firestone. In 1387 the mines were producing stone for the reconstruction of Westminster Abbey, and they were still being worked in 1580. The mine was abandoned in the early 1700s, since when few people have had the courage or ability to enter the workings. The graffiti include a hanged man, in soot, and five labyrinths. These are all of the Classical pattern, ranging in diameter from 30 to 62 centimetres (12–25 inches). Associated with these are four Celtic Rose patterns, ancient protective symbols related geometrically to the construction of the Classical labyrinth. It is clear that the labyrinths were drawn by the 'cross, corners and dots' method (see below). Along with these are chalked and carved inscriptions, in the script of the period, the earliest of which is dated 1609. Others date from the 1720s and 1760s. It is possible that the labyrinths are the sole remains of some magical cult connecting miners' or others' mysteries with the labyrinthine, initiatory depths of the mine. The Chaldon mine is not open to the public, and it is extremely dangerous for anyone to enter it unequipped and without observing the standard safety rules of speleology.

The Classical Labyrinth Pattern

The Classical labyrinth design can be drawn easily, beginning with a pattern of nine dots which is developed into the 'cross, corners and dots' pattern. The labyrinth is developed from the nine dots firstly by making a cross centred on the middle dot, then by drawing right-angled 'corners' from the next four dots. The final four dots eventually become the 'loose ends' of the labyrinth walls. This pattern is sometimes known as the 'basic cross'. The labyrinth itself is constructed by drawing loops from the end of the line or dot to its corresponding opposite point. When all these points are joined, the labyrinth is complete. This is the simplest technique for constructing a Classical labyrinth without using formal geometrical methods of straight edge and compasses.

The nine-dot pattern is the basic pattern for producing several cognate designs or sigils, which include the form known as 'the Farmer's Fylfot' or 'Celtic Rose' and the 'Shield-Knot'. These sigils are all ancient and were used as magical protection or ornament in many lands. The basic pattern can be seen on a fourth-century BCE *pelike* in Apulian red-figure ware showing Eros in pursuit, preserved in the Fitzwilliam Museum in Cambridge (catalogue number GR 5a 1896). It shows the 'cross, corners and dots' pattern enclosed in a circle. The pattern was still being used in England in the eighteenth century, as shown by the surviving and dated graffiti in the Chaldon mine in Surrey referred to above. At Chaldon the connection between the Classical labyrinth pattern and the Celtic Rose is explicit, this pattern being drawn directly below some of the labyrinths and believed to signify the cycle of the seasons. Apart from its prehistoric occurrences, mentioned above, it is known also in the medieval context in graffiti in churches at Sutton, Bedfordshire, and Little Waltham, Essex. At Sutton the pattern is drawn on the chest of an ecstatic dancer, perhaps indicating the costume worn at some long-forgotten traditional festival.

A meaning of this pattern was recorded by the antiquary J. Romilly Allen, who was an authority on ancient rock and stone carvings all over the British Isles. He noted that the Fylfot pattern was part of a children's riddle in his time (early twentieth century): 'Four rich men and four poor men have their houses situated symmetrically at the corners of two squares, one within the other, the houses being in two straight lines and at right angles to one another. The houses of the rich men are outside; in the centre is a pond of spring water, and the houses of the poor men between the houses of the rich men and the water supply. The rich men desire to build a wall, which, although giving them free access to the water, shall exclude the poorer neighbours. How is it to be done?' The pattern generated by this riddle is the Celtic Rose.

An alternative view of the origin of the labyrinthine basic pattern was put forward by L.J.D. Richardson, who thought that it was derivable from a single upright line and placed between two pairs of dots. This was thought to represent, in ancient Cretan terms, 'a cult object between the horns of consecration', symbol of the goddess of the household. From this pattern, the double axe (*labrys*) can be drawn, and from that the unicursal Classical labyrinth pattern. As early as 1892, M. Mayer (see Knight, Bibliog.) put forward as significant the etymological connection between λαβρυσ (*labrys* – double axe) and λαβυρινφοσ (*labyrinthos* – labyrinth), and Richardson's theory was based upon this.

On a strictly geometrical level, the Classical labyrinth can be drawn with compasses centred on certain points of a square. Half of the labyrinth is composed simply of concentric semicircles, whilst the other portion is composed of the cross, corners and dots pattern connected to the semicircles by quadrants of various radii. With five pegs and string marked out by knots into regular divisions, a labyrinth can be laid out upon the ground. As Jeff Saward explained at lectures in 1981/2, simply, the Classical labyrinth pattern is a modification of the meander pattern found in ancient Greek art. Topologically, it is identical with the Classical labyrinth design. The diagram here shows the conversion of one into the other. It is also the basis of the typical Roman labyrinth form, where four meanders are put together to make a fourfold maze. There may be some direct connection between the meander pattern and the apparent annual motion of the sun through the sky. In the book titled *Soft-Tech*, published in 1978, the artist Charles Ross documented his 'Energy to Image' project. This was the result of solar experiments he conducted in New York between the autumnal equinoxes of 1971 and 1972. During this period, Ross recorded the pattern made by the sun. He erected a large stationary lens, and each day he placed a plank of wood at its focus. When the sun shone, the rays concentrated by the lens burned what he called the 'day's signature' into the wood. This was a pattern which reproduced as a mirror image the apparent motion of the sun across the sky, recording the times when clouds obscured the sun, and the sun's intensity as experienced at that place. The patterns that Ross recorded are of relevance when we consider the solar connection of the labyrinth in mythology as discussed by Ernst Krause. In Ross's experiment, each day the sun burned an arc whose radius was related to the length of day and the sun's apparent elevation in the sky. Over the year, from 23 September 1971 until 22 September 1972, he collected the sequential array of these burnt arcs. When he had assembled the whole year's 'burns' to make a continuous pattern, he noticed that the curvature of the patterns varied with the seasons, gradually curving from almost straight near the beginning of autumn and spring, and reversing from winter to summer.

Because the planks laid end-to-end would measure around 535 metres (1,635 feet), Charles Ross photographed them and reduced their images to manageable proportions. When assembled, the whole pattern was seen to be a volute, beginning with an opening spiral which opened out only to close in again with a reverse spiral at the other end. This continued to a point at which it began to open out again in reverse. Ross concluded that the solar year shape was a double spiral which closes down rapidly to a circle around the time of the winter solstice. Then it opens out again, straightening into springtime. The specific degree of curvature and the amount by which it changes from day to day are related directly to the apparent angle of the sun to the Earth's surface at the place of viewing. During wintertime in the northern hemisphere, this angle is more oblique, which is reflected in the tighter spiral of the winter pattern than the corresponding summer one.

The whole 'year pattern' bears a resemblance to the meander pattern that is at the geometric heart of the Classical labyrinth, and also resembles the opened-out medieval Christian pattern. It is possible that the various turnings and returnings of the labyrinth pattern represent the daily path of the sun. Even if the pattern is a coincidence, it is a remarkable instance of how similar patterns occur in the apparent motion of the sun and in the solar-related labyrinth.

At Knossos, the single-square spiral sign was a hieroglyph for a palace, whilst the double-meander hieroglyph is believed to have signified a crenellated enclosure – a castle. Both of these designs have been found on pottery 'soul houses' from burials. Related to this design is a steatite (soapstone) plaque found by the eminent Egyptologist Sir Flinders Petrie at Memphis, which bore a squared multicursal labyrinth pattern with five dead ends.

Pebbles and Boulders: Stone Labyrinths

The earliest antiquarian mention of stone or boulder labyrinths was in *Atlantica*, written by Olaf Rudbeck and published in 1695. One, a strange design with two entrances, is illustrated. Subsequently individual labyrinths were mentioned by various authors.

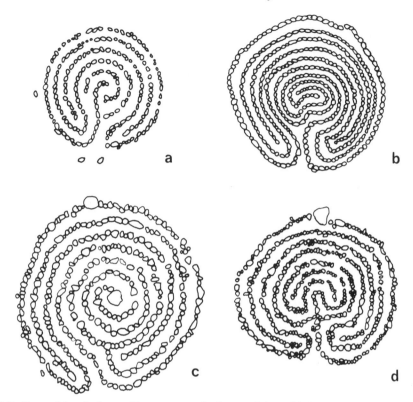

1.7. Stone labyrinths: a: Troytown at St Agnes, Isles of Scilly, in 1983, before reconstruction (after Jeff Saward); b: Great Hare Island, Solovecke Archipelago, White Sea, USSR (restored); c: Kuleryd, Sweden (after John Kraft); Revonsaari, Sweden (after John Kraft).

One of the first researchers to attempt to make some sense of them was C.E. von Baer. Speaking before the St Petersburg Academy in 1842, von Baer described stone labyrinths in the Russian north which he had visited whilst sailing in the Gulf of Finland in 1838. His attention was drawn to labyrinths on Wier Island, where he found the rather corrupted form of labyrinth illustrated here. He saw other labyrinths in the Russian part of Lapland: one near a small, uninhabited bay called Vilovata, and two near the village of Ponoy. These were composed of rounded stones which ranged in size from pebbles to boulders, defining the meaning of the stone labyrinth. Since his time, many stone or boulder labyrinths have been discovered and documented. Stone labyrinths comprise the greatest number of surviving ancient mazes anywhere, and the vast majority of these are in Scandinavia. John Kraft has documented more than 535 stone labyrinths: over 300 in Sweden, 150 in Finland, sixty in the USSR, twenty in Norway, four in Iceland and one (dating from the eighteenth century at the latest) in the British Isles.

The majority of Scandinavian stone labyrinths are not particularly ancient. That is to say, they are medieval or post-medieval. However, it is very difficult to date a stone labyrinth, as there is nothing in them which is susceptible to radiocarbon dating or any of the other scientific techniques available to the archaeologist. Some labyrinths are associated with datable archaeological features. Labyrinths in Åland are associated with prehistoric cairns, and on the summit of the Storberget, an ancient holy mountain south of Piteå, a labyrinth lies among Bronze Age cairns. In Sweden and Denmark, there is evidence that at least some of these labyrinths are of considerable antiquity. It is thought that at least twenty Swedish stone labyrinths were in existence in pagan times (before 1100). Several lie in ancient pre-Christian grave-fields, whilst others are associated with ancient towns and churches in the areas of the oldest settled agricultural land in the country. It appears that these labyrinths were associated with ancient cult-centres which were taken over by the Church and became the nucleii for towns. The distribution of the few known Danish sites also associates them with pagan sacred places. A replica of one was constructed at the ancient religious centre of Lejre in 1987.

Most of the Scandinavian stone labyrinths can be dated to the Christian era; most are close to the sea; many are on small islands. The majority are associated with fishing-settlements: sometimes they have been found with the foundations or ruins of huts used by these seasonal workers; some are located close to fishermen's sheds or lighthouses. Those on the shores of the Gulf of Finland and along the coasts of the Gulf of Bothnia are on land which was beneath sea-level in pagan times, a thousand years ago. Along the coast of Estonia and Finland, the labyrinths have the same distribution as the medieval Swedish-speaking settlements. But around the White Sea and Barents Sea their distribution corresponds with the ancient seasonal coastal hunting and fishing-settlements. Soviet archaeologists have excavated some of the sites and have dated them back to 1000 BCE. John Kraft suggests that they were built by Lapps, who presumably received the tradition and knowledge from the fisher-people of the Gulf of Bothnia.

Although the labyrinths of Estonia and Finland are found almost exclusively along their coastlines, in Sweden and Denmark several are located inland. These inland labyrinths are usually located on small hills, with their entrances orientated towards the west. In Sweden a number of these labyrinths were or are situated in or close to churchyards. These are believed to predate the church, which was built nearby in order to Christianize what had until then been a pagan religious site. A stone labyrinth of Classical design stood close to the church at Enköping, whilst on the labyrinth-rich Baltic island of Gotland there is a stone labyrinth in the churchyard at Fröjel. (The name of this place shows that it was once a sanctuary of the goddess Freyja.) The maze was restored in 1974. Also on Gotland are labyrinths close to churches at Othems and Fleringe. Near the church of Horn in Västergötland were two labyrinths, destroyed in the nineteenth century. One was a seven-circuit and the other an eleven-circuit labyrinth. These church-associated labyrinths are paralleled in England by the turf mazes at Boughton Green in Northamptonshire, Sneinton in Nottinghamshire, and St Catherine's Hill, Winchester, all of which were associated with their corresponding chapel.

During the last century it became popular for school-teachers to build stone labyrinths as a demonstration to their students of the ancient technique. John Kraft believes that about twenty per cent of Swedish labyrinths come into this category. There is a notable group of them on the island of Gotland. The custom has existed elsewhere: the former turf maze at Eberswalde in Germany was reputed to have been made by a school-teacher. Similarly the Mizmaze at Winchester is connected with Winchester public school, whilst the last turf maze to be destroyed in England was in the schoolyard at Comberton near Cambridge.

The possibility that making stone labyrinths is an Indo-European tradition of great antiquity has been inferred from the fact that stone labyrinths are known also in India. A notable example existed near the city of Kundini at Hosur Taluq in Salem District, Madras Province, India. It had an entrance like a Classical labyrinth, ending inside with a spiral. According to John Layard, ' ... the spaces between the lines were about two feet wide. The spirals were laid out with beautiful regularity. Nearby were a large number of *Pandava Gudi*, temples of the Pandavas ...' The form of this labyrinth is the standard Indian design recorded in the epic saga of the *Mahabharata*, where it has mythological similarities to labyrinth legends from Europe.

The St Agnes Labyrinth

The labyrinth on the most westerly Scilly island of St Agnes is the only ancient boulder labyrinth known in the British Isles, and also the closest to the sea of any. Known as 'Troy Town', it is located close to Troy Town Farm (map grid reference SV 876078). Its design is known to have changed over the years, probably starting as a Classical labyrinth but in later years having lost an outer ring and been altered into a different pattern. According to tradition, Amor Clarke, the lighthouse-keeper of St Agnes, who married into the Hicks family on the island, is reputed to have made the labyrinth in 1729. This is supposed to have been done as nothing more than a pastime, but Scandinavian labyrinth lore suggests otherwise, as some stone labyrinths are associated with lighthouses there also, where there is a tradition of ceremonial and magical use.

The closeness of the labyrinth to the sea and its uniqueness in the British Isles indicate something special, probably a Scandinavian influence. In Sweden and Finland there are several hundred similar boulder labyrinths on small islands close to the sea. These were used in fishermen's magic, whilst fishing on the herring banks of the Baltic and Kattegat. They were used for raising the wind magically, giving protection against the perils of the sea and also increasing the catch. These Scandinavian designs are always of the Classical labyrinth pattern, as at St Agnes, never of the medieval Christian design.

There was a royal visit to the maze in 1921, when it was tidied up for the regal footsteps. When Jeff and Deb Saward of the Caerdroia Project labyrinth study group visited the maze in 1983, they made an accurate record of its design. At that time it was a broken-down version of the Classical labyrinth visible in earlier photographs. By 1986 an additional ring of stones had been added to the labyrinth, but the central paths remained the same. Before this, the maze measured 4.8 metres (16 feet) in diameter. But in 1989 it was totally rebuilt by some dowsers, who took away the original turf and stones and replaced them with others brought from some distance away. In the process they altered the design to one which they claimed was shown to them by their divining-rods. Unfortunately this radical reconstruction was done without making any archaeological excavation, and consequently any underlying remains which might have been there were disrupted or destroyed. This incident emphasizes the unfortunate fact that ancient labyrinths are not yet fully scheduled as ancient monuments and consequently are not afforded proper protection and care by responsible authorities.

Labyrinth Names – A Key to Their Mythology

The names of Scandinavian stone labyrinths are an important key to unravelling something of their origin and meaning. On the Åbo peninsula and in Åland, they are Trojaborg (Troytown) and Rundborg (Round Town). Elsewhere in Finland, there are Jatulintarha (Giant's Fence), Jätinkatu (Giant's Street) and Kivitarha (Stone Fence). Additionally, there are a number of city names: Jerusalem, Nineveh, Jericho and Lissabon. Similar names are given to Norwegian and Swedish mazes. Widely occurring are versions of the Troy name: Trojeborg, Trojenborg, Trojin and Tröborg. Others are called Jungfrudans (Maiden's Dance), Steintanz (Stone Dance), Nunnetarha (Nun's Fence), Trelleborg (Troll's Castle) and Rundborg (Round Castle). Icelandic mazes, some of which were made of earth or turf, are known as Völundarhus (Wayland's House). The authority on Scandinavian stone labyrinths, John Kraft, notes that in addition Jericho, Jerusalem, Nineveh, Babylon, Konstantinopel, Trondheim and Viborg are known as labyrinth-names. Trondheim and Viborg are important Scandinavian cities, and the name Lissabon (Lisboa – Lisbon) may commemorate, in the seeming tradition of naming them after overthrown cities, the Portuguese capital's destruction by earthquake in 1755.

But the most widespread name refers to Troy, as in Trojeborg (The Castle of Troy). The connection of Troy with the Classical labyrinth pattern goes back at least 2,500 years, as shown by a sixth century BCE Etruscan wine jug found at Tragliatella in Italy. this fascinating relic depicts riders on horseback connected to a Classical labyrinth in which is written in North Italic (Etruscan) script the word Truia Troy.

John Kraft points out that the Troy name demonstrates that the popular labyrinth traditions of Nordic countries have ancient links with the Mediterranean area. In southern Europe, the word 'troy' may have had the meaning of 'fortified place' or 'defended camp' originally. But the names Trojeborg and Trojaburg or their English equivalents, Troytown and The Walls of Troy also has an interesting etymological connection. 'Troy' is cognate with the Old German verb *drajan*, the Gothic *thraian*, the Celtic *troian*, the Anglo-Saxon *thrawen*, the Middle English *throwen* and the modern English *throe*. It is also linked with the Dutch and Low German word *draien*, the Danish *dreje* and the Swedish *dreja*. All these words mean 'turn', referring to the twists and turns of the layout. The Welsh labyrinth name '*Caerdroia*' means 'The Walls of Troy', but this is believed to be derived from

'*Caer y troiau*', 'The City of Turns'. As a parallel, some turf mazes in Germany were known as *Windelbahn* (coil-track). Connected with this idea of turning are the Swedish labyrinth names Trinneborg, Trinteborg and Trilleborg, which are connected with *trill*, a small wheel, and *trind*, round. Further ideas of circularity comes from Rundgård (Round Court), Ringeborgdstad (Ring-fort-town), Rundborgastad (Round-fort-town) and Ringboslott (Ring-castle). Also it is possible that the name Wunderberg, used in the March of Brandenburg in the German Democratic Republic is a corruption of an earlier name, Wenderberg, in which case the word *wenden*, meaning 'to turn', would be the origin. There is also a connection between Troytown and the Low German word *traaje* which denotes a deep wagon track, a rut. As a verb, it means 'to track' – that is, to follow in the track of another. Clearly this can extend to the tracks, dug in the earth or formed by dancers, which make up the pattern of the Troytown. This is especially true of the rutted paths between the boulders of stone labyrinths, also the German turf mazes, and some English ones, where the track or pathway is composed of ruts in the ground, sometimes filled with gravel. Other Swedish names bring in further connections: Trädenborg is from *träda*, to walk, whilst Gångborg means Walk-fort.

In pagan times, the city of Troy was taken as marking the centre of the world; after the introduction of Christianity, this honour was transferred to Jerusalem. This idea was taken directly from Jewish mysticism.

The city names Babylon, Jerusalem, Jericho and Nineveh, as well as Troy, have been applied to labyrinths. All of these are famous ancient cities from Mediterranean culture, Classical and biblical. Each of these ancient cities was seen as possessing the archetypal form of the Holy City: surrounded by seven walls and with a major shrine at the centre. Because of this, the walled city motif in labyrinth design can be seen throughout the history of labyrinths, ranging from the names of stone ones to the towers and crenellations that surround Roman pavement mosaics, and the explicit connections of labyrinths in Christian cathedrals of the Middle Ages.

It is an emblem widely known from manuscript illustrations. There are several important examples of this motif which survive in libraries as treasured relics. A ninth-century manuscript in the Badische Landesbibliothek at Karlsruhe, Germany, shows the city of Jericho as a rectangular Classical labyrinth. An eleventh-century Syrian Maronite manuscript in the Bibliothèque Nationale in Paris shows the seven walls of Jericho as a circular labyrinth, whilst a twelfth-century manuscript in the Bayerischer Staatsbibliothek at Munich explicitly shows Jericho in the form of a moon-shaped Classical labyrinth. The tradition continued for a long time. For example, a Hebrew manuscript from Casale Monferrato, Italy, dated 1598, has a version of the 'Otfrid'-type labyrinth, titled 'The City of Jericho'. This wide spread in time and geographical terms makes dating a Jericho or similar-named labyrinth very difficult. It can only date to a period after the introduction of the Christian religion, yet it is possible that pre-Christian structures were given the new name at some time. In Finland, stone labyrinths have also been known as Pietarinleikki (St Peter's Game). The latter name refers to a traditional numerical sequence which appears to be related to the lunar cycle. It is known from rock carvings and ancient Scandinavian calendars and as an anti-semitic folk-tale.

The names of Scandinavian stone labyrinths have a direct relation to the traditional names used in Britain in association with megaliths. For example, an old name for Stonehenge was 'The Giant's Dance', referring to a legend that the stones were really giants who had been petrified for dancing on a Sunday, a clear reference to Christian influence.

The Virgin in the Labyrinth

In his travels during the 1870s, J.R. Aspelin noted that the Finnish peasants were usually of the opinion that the stone labyrinths were for what he called 'recreation'. But clearly they had a deeper symbolic meaning of which he was unaware. Typically this 'recreation' was in the form of a ceremonial game. A young woman would stand in the centre of the maze, and the young men of the village would try to reach her by running the paths in a correct manner according to certain rules. In his masterly 1985 dissertation *The Goddess in the Labyrinth*, John Kraft unravels this long-suspected connection. Like Aspelin, he notes the significance of Scandinavian games and tales in which a girl is at the centre of the labyrinth whilst the youths have to enter the winding gyres in order to free her from her labyrinthine prison.

This connection is emphasized in Finland, where some labyrinths are called *Jungfrudanser* (Virgins' Dances). A fifteenth-century wall-painting in the church at Sibbo in Nyland, Finland, shows a woman standing at the centre of a labyrinth. Perhaps this has some reference, now lost, to the labyrinth name Nun's Bower. According to an account by A.O. Freudenthal published in Helsinki in 1874, in the labyrinth ceremonies a virgin would take her place at the centre of a stone labyrinth, and the young men danced inwards towards her, following the maze's gyres. Another version of this was reported in 1930 from Malax in the Vasa district in western Finland. Here a virgin stood at the centre whilst a young man ran through the maze so that he could dance with her once he had reached the centre. This is very similar to a recorded English custom practised in former times at the turf Town Maze at Saffron Walden in Essex, where ' ... it was used by the beaux and belles of the town, a young maiden standing at the centre ... while the boy tried to get to her in record time without stumbling' (Saward, *Saffron Walden Town Maze*, 1981).

The latest recorded Finnish report of the custom was received in 1985 by Åbo Academy. It came from Munsala, 55 km (34 miles) north-east of Vasa. Here the story was more detailed, having been reported by an 80-year-old woman who had played it as a child. In this version of the labyrinth game, a girl stood at the centre whilst a boy tried to reach her. He had to do this without making any false steps, such as standing on the stones or losing his balance whilst walking the maze. Various symbolic objects were placed on the pathway as the ceremony was enacted, such as an old horseshoe for luck. As this was going on, spectators stood around, clapping their hands and singing. Once at the centre, the boy had to pick up the girl and carry her out of the labyrinth. If he was successful in doing this, the girl belonged to him. The old woman who reported it noted that the ceremony was conducted by children, who thought it important to keep it secret from parents and other adults. In order to participate, she had had to promise not to reveal the secret at home.

In the nineteenth century J.R. Aspelin was puzzled by the observation that, whilst some of the mazes were provided with one and others with two 'goals', others had no obvious 'goal', so that one left the maze after walking all the paths. However, in 1978 at Köpmanholm in the archipelago north-east of Stockholm, an old man told John Kraft of the former use of the labyrinth there called the *Jungfruringen* (Virgin's Ring). A girl stood at the centre, and then two boys raced from the two entrances to see who would reach the girl first. This seems to explain one of the uses of mazes with more than one entrance – the Rad type.

The motif of the woman or goddess in the labyrinth is one of the great labyrinthine myths. Like the Minotaur legend, it involves the labyrinth as a place of capture and defence. In his book *The Rudiments of Paradise*, the sculptor and maze-maker Michael Ayrton wrote of this twofold function of the labyrinth. It is a means to arrest an intruder by means of confusion, whilst simultaneously it protects the centre from penetration by any intruder. Constructionally, it uses the technique of the enfilade, allowing those inside to shoot those who enter. The woman in the labyrinth motif can be divided into two types of legend: one tells of the woman who is abducted and imprisoned in the labyrinth, who has to be liberated, whilst the other involves a young woman who has to be reached by the young man.

The German writer Haye Hamkens noted a legend, recorded first by Ernst Krause in his book *Die Trojaburgen Nordeuropas*, from what is probably the most famous stone labyrinth, that at Visby on the Swedish island of Gotland, in the Baltic. According to tradition, the Visby labyrinth originated with a king's daughter who was held prisoner under the *Galgenberg* (gallows hill). Every day she placed one stone against another, until, on her release, the Troy Town was complete. Helen's abduction to Troy, the cause of the disastrous Trojan Wars, is clearly part of the same mythological motif, as the name Troy is such a widespread labyrinth name.

These stories of abduction and imprisonment are paralleled in the ancient Indian epic the *Ramayana*. Ramana, the demon, abducted Sita, wife of Rama, the hero of the tale, and imprisoned her in the castle of Lanka. In a manuscript book about India written by the Iranian astronomer and geographer Al-Biruni, dating from *c.* 1045, this castle of Lanka is depicted as a Classical labyrinth. Rama attacked the castle with an army of apes, killed the demon and liberated his wife. On leaving the successfully stormed castle, Rama circles the ramparts seven times in Ramana's stolen chariot.

Each winter it was customary in Sweden to re-enact the elements of a similar tale in temporary snow and ice labyrinths. This was the story of the hero Grimborg. To enact this mythic drama, large mazes built to the Classical labyrinth pattern were made, with paths wide enough to allow people to ski along them. At the centre of the labyrinth was a girl who stood for the bride of Grimborg, the hero of the legend. On the final turn before the centre was reached, a guard was placed, and the man representing the hero Grimborg skiied from the outside whilst the spectators sang 'The Song of Grimborg'. The song tells how Grimborg has to break through fences of iron and steel to reach a king's beautiful daughter, whom he wishes to marry.

The best-known but most complex of labyrinth legends, re-worked

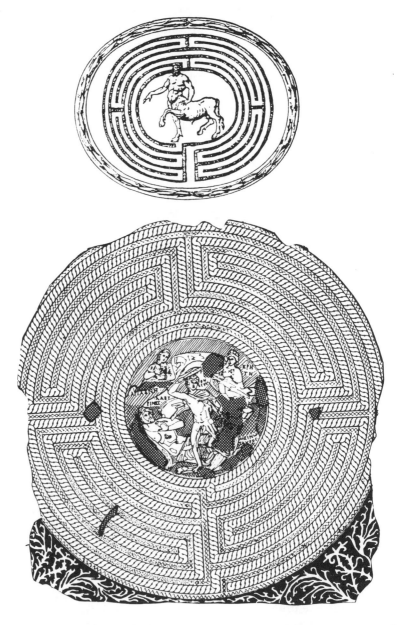

1.8. Above: Late imperial Roman jewel, showing centaur/minotaur at the centre of a labyrinth (from P.A. Maffei, *Gemmae Antichae*, 1709); Below: Mosaic labyrinth, Kato Paphos, Cyprus, *c*. 350, depicting Theseus, the Minotaur and Ariadne.

by many eminent authors over the centuries is that of the Cretan labyrinth. The basic elements of the tale are as follows.

At the time of Theseus, son of Aegeus, King of Athens, Minos ruled the Cretan kingdom of Knossos, the most powerful nation in the Mediterranean. During his travels in Attica, Androgeos, Minos's son, was believed to have been murdered. As recompense for this crime, Minos decreed that every nine years a tribute should be paid by Athens to Knossos. This tribute was to consist of seven young men and seven young women, who were to be taken to Knossos for sacrifice. At Knossos was a labyrinth, constructed by the technician Daedalus, so complex that, if anyone should enter, it was impossible for him or her to get out without a guide. Minos had ordered Daedalus to design and build this labyrinth as a dwelling-place for the Minotaur. This monstrous being was the half-man and half-bull son of Minos's wife, Pasiphaë. This unfortunate result of Pasiphaë's bestiality with a white bull was a ferocious monster which would kill any human being whom he encountered in the labyrinth. As revenge for Androgeos' death, Minos would send the Athenian maidens and youths into the labyrinth, one at a time, to be torn apart and perhaps devoured by the Minotaur.

When he went to see Aegeus, Theseus, having been brought up away from the royal Court, was dismayed at his father's sadness. When he discovered the reason for it, he volunteered immediately to be one of the fourteen young people sent to Knossos as tribute. He vowed that he would be the man to slay the monster and thereby lift the burden on Athens. Finally Aegeus consented to the proposal, insisting that if Theseus were to be successful in his mission, he should, on his return voyage, use a white sail in place of the black one with which it was equipped. Theseus sailed for Knossos with the thirteen other 'sacrifices'. Before he was due to go to the labyrinth, he met Ariadne, Minos's daughter, who fell in love with him and arranged that he should be provided with a clew (ball) of thread and a sword before entering the labyrinth. One end of the thread was attached to the entrance of the labyrinth, and Theseus entered. Coming across the Minotaur, he engaged it in combat and finally dispatched it with his sword. Having slain the monster, he used the thread to find his way out again. He liberated the other hostages, took Ariadne and regained his ship, in which they set sail for Athens. On the way they dropped anchor at the island of Delos, where they celebrated their escape by performing the *Geranos*, the Crane Dance which reproduces the pattern of the labyrinth. Ungratefully, Theseus then abandoned Ariadne on the next island, Naxos, and sailed to Athens. But on the voyage back, he forgot to hoist the white sail, and Aegeus, seeing a black one, assumed that his son was dead and promptly committed suicide by drowning himself in the sea which is now named after him – the Aegean.

Daedalus and his son Icarus escaped from the labyrinth, in which they had been imprisoned, by fashioning wings from feathers and wax. But Icarus flew too high, dangerously close to the heat of the sun, which caused the wax of his wings to melt, and so he fell to his death in the sea. Daedalus, better aware of the nature of his materials, completed the flight successfully and landed at Cumae, place of an oracle known as the Cumaean Sibyl. There he built a temple dedicated to the solar deity Apollo. He then went to Sicily, where Minos, who had been pursuing him, caught up with him, only to be slain. Finally Daedalus voyaged to Sardinia, where he instituted the craft of metal-working and after some time died.

The once-popular story of Fair Rosamond is another version of the labyrinth legend. It tells that King Henry II of England, who lived from 1133 to 1189, had a mistress, Rosamond Clifford. In order that his wife, Queen Eleanor of Aquitaine, should not find out about his lover, he ensconced Rosamond within a maze which he had built on his estate at Woodstock in Oxfordshire. However, the queen found out about Henry's affaire and managed to reach Rosamond's bower within the labyrinth. There she forced her rival to choose between death by poison or the knife, and so Rosamond committed suicide with poison. Rosamond's death is dated at the year 1176, and she is said to have been buried in front of the high altar in the monastic church of Godstowe. This was an unlikely burial-place for a suicide, and her body is said to have been exhumed and reburied in the chapter-house. Whatever the truth of this sad tale, it became part of literary lore and was recounted by many authors, including Michael Drayton, John Aubrey and Samuel Croxall; the latter did not understand archetypal themes and was dismissive, with, 'What have we of this story, but a copy of Ariadne's clue and the Cretan Labyrinth?' As if historic events do not re-create continually the elements of myth!

We have a hint of the mythological and symbolic nature of the story through the Latin epitaph which is said to have adorned Rosamond's tomb:

Hic jacet in tumba Rosa mundi, non Rosa munda;
Non redolet, sed olet, quae redolere solet.

This was translated in the eighteenth century as:

Rose of the World, not Rose the peerless Flow'r,
Within this Tomb hath taken up her Bow'r.
She scenteth now, to nothing Sweet doth smell
Who erst was wont to savour passing well.

The rose was a widespread symbol for the Virgin Mary in medieval Christendom. 'The Mystery of the Rosary' is an important connection here but, being Catholic, died out in later British symbolism. It has re-emerged in the twentieth century in at least two English mazes, at Wyck Rissington and at Kentwell Hall, Suffolk.

The motif of the woman in the labyrinth is known from Afghanistan, where again it has a royal connection. The Afghan tale explains the legend of Shamaili's House. This was a house whose entrance was hidden, and only the Princess Shamaili knew how to get inside. She was the daughter of King Khunkar ('The Bloodthirsty'), who promised his daughter's hand in marriage to any man who could find his way in. Unfortunately the penalty for failing to find the way in was death by hanging. Seven sons of King Namazlum attempted to reach the princess, but the first six failed and were hanged. Finally the youngest prince, Jallad Khan, tried his luck. Being cleverer than his late brothers, he used deception. Disguised, he obtained an apprenticeship as assistant to the royal sculptor. The sculptor fashioned a hollow model in which Jallad Khan hid himself, and the statue was brought before Khunkar, where, to his amazement, it danced for him. Princess Shamaili, fascinated by the animated statue, brought it to her room in the impenetrable labyrinth. When she was sleeping, Jallad Khan got out and placed a ring on her finger. The next night she spoke to the statue: 'Whoever you are, barber, weaver or anyone else, come out and be my husband.' Jallad Khan came out and, after he had spent ten nights with her, went to King Khunkar. Keeping his word, the king allowed them to be married. Here the motif of the sculpture parallels Daedalus's craft as metal-caster, and its hollowness the Trojan Horse, both labyrinth-related themes. When Jallad Khan acceded to the throne of his country, he defeated Khunkar and had him blinded in retribution for having killed his six brothers.

Another version of the labyrinth myth comes from Africa. An Ethiopian tale of King Solomon, from whom the monarchs of that country claimed descent, describes the labyrinth as Solomon's palace. Solomon is supposed to have built a palace in the form of a labyrinth, in which he kept his many wives. But a man called Sirak got into the labyrinth by building a tunnel to the centre, from which he absconded with one of Solomon's wives.

In his *Die Trojaburgen Nordeuropas*, Ernst Krause suggested that the legend of the woman in the labyrinth, and the annual re-enactment at certain significant times, was symbolic of a solar myth. He believed that the labyrinth was the place where, each spring, a hero had to fight and overcome a demon of winter in order to liberate the sun. The sun was represented by the sun virgin, a version of the old Germanic and Norse sun goddess Saule or Sól. She is trapped in the castle of the labyrinth and must be freed in order that the summer can arrive.

Labyrinths in Folk Magic

In the last century, J.R. Aspelin surmised that, as Scandinavian stone labyrinths (and the British one) occur only by coastlines but seldom near settlements, it could be expected that they have some connection with sea travel. Clearly he did not have access to people who at his time were still building labyrinths for magical purposes. Today it is known that at least some of the existing surviving stone labyrinths were connected with wind magic. Until the advent of mechanically powered vessels, the knowledge and use of the wind were matters of life and death to sailors and fishermen.

In his painstaking researches into Scandinavian labyrinth lore, John Kraft has assembled several traditions of labyrinth magic. He notes that J.A. Udde, a local historian from Haparanda in northern Sweden, has been told that the labyrinths of the archipelago outside Haparanda, Luleå and further south were built to lay strong winds. In the early 1970s Eva Eskilsson from Härnösand recounted that a former ships' pilot had told her that, when held up in harbour by bad weather, sailors would make stone labyrinths, so that the wind would become caught in them and thereby would reduce in ferocity. Elsewhere, in Husum parish, labyrinths were used to control the wind magically. In Estonia too, the fishermen used labyrinths to allay bad weather and storms. In Norway, a labyrinth called Truber Slot, which existed at the mouth of Oslo Fjord, was reputed to have been built by a virgin and was used to ensure favourable winds for sailors. Wherever it was used, the labyrinth was believed to appease the weather gods, especially him who rules the north-westerly wind.

If a labyrinth is a seven-circuit version (that is, with seven rounds), it is traditional to walk it seven times. An eleven-circuit labyrinth has

1.9. Binding-knot from *The Book of Kells*.

to be walked eleven times. According to tradition, walking to the centre and out again without faltering will bring success, but bad luck will follow if the walls are jumped or the maze-walker puts a foot wrong. In some parts of Sweden, fishermen would walk a labyrinth before examining their nets. Gunnar Westin, the provincial antiquarian of Umeå, stated that labyrinths were used to improve the catch in fishing. The mechanism of this was explained as a means of ridding themselves of bad luck. The fishermen believed that there were *smågubbar* ('little people' or 'gremlins') who accompanied the fishermen on board the fishing-boats to disrupt the catch. The labyrinth was a means of preventing their getting aboard. Because they accompanied the fishermen into the boats, they would also accompany them into the centre of a labyrinth. But once there, they became confused, giving the fishermen the chance to run from the labyrinth and get on board ship before the gremlins could follow them. Elsewhere this was interpreted in terms of the exorcism of evil spirits. In either case, the labyrinth figure was used as a form of binding-magic similar in intent to the interlace patterns of Celtic and Hiberno-Saxon artwork. In ancient Ireland, when such patterns, known as *Luaithrindi*, were painted on a warrior's shield, they were believed to provide magical protection against harm. The Ulster hero Cuchulainn had such a shield. Sometimes *Luaithrindi* were drawn on the ground in front of an opponent, a parallel with threshold patterns (see below). A knot pattern known from eighth-century *Book of Kells* and used to denote All Saints' Day on the wooden calendars known as Clog Almanacs, is related in English country magic to the direction north-west, the direction invoked by Swedish labyrinth magic.

Sometimes this quality of binding evil spirits or the wind in a magical way was extended to other spheres of human need. The labyrinth of Fridlevstad in southern Sweden, probably laid out around 1870–80, was reputed to cure mental illnesses. Children were discouraged from running it for fun, as it had a specific purpose. The actual use of this labyrinth and also the small portable ones used in trance magic in Britain and the Isle of Man might repay further investigation by practitioners of alternative medicine.

Labyrinths were also used as binding magic against physical foes. At Hedared, near Borås in the south-west of Sweden, there is a tradition that the labyrinth there was used by shepherd boys as a protection against wolves, which were supposed to be confused by the twisting pathway. A similar tradition existed in Lappland, where labyrinths were used for magically protecting the reindeer herds against wolverines.

A labyrinth at Revonsaari, by the River Torne in northern Sweden, is reputed to have been built by a local 'cunning man' in the early nineteenth century. Before undertaking any important action, he would walk the labyrinth as a preparation. These traditions have survived into modern times. An old fisherman from Södermöja told John Kraft that in 1955 he sailed to Kuggören, where he saw an old man running through a stone labyrinth. As he ran, he spat on his hand and threw the spittle backwards over his shoulder. This was done in order to ensure good luck in fishing. Unfortunately the old man died in 1963, before John Kraft could meet him. Clearly he was the local 'cunning man', as often he was requested to cure sick animals. Sadly, although he wanted to hand on his knowledge, his sons were not interested, and he died without having transmitted his knowledge to an apprentice. John Kraft believes that he might have been the last labyrinth magician in northern Europe.

In his analyses of Mediterranean labyrinth mythology, Michael Ayrton pointed out the similarity between the labyrinth's many gyres and the appearance of an animal's or person's entrails. It has been suggested that one of the possible origins of the labyrinth pattern was in the pattern made by the disembowelling of animals or human beings for divinatory purposes, which was a common practice in Babylon and ancient Greece and among the Etruscans. Several carved stones from Babylon, showing labyrinthine entrail forms, are known. In Scandinavia several notable labyrinths have been discovered close to gallows hills, known as *Galgenberg*. Here the labyrinth served the place of the dead, as with those located in cemeteries. This connection is widespread, for the Afghan legend of Shamaili's House involves hanging as a means of execution. The clew of thread and the coil of rope used to hang people appear to be connected here.

In addition to the labyrinths themselves, many gallows hills had a spiral pathway from base to summit. A notable *Galgenberg* at Meldorf in Ditmarschen, Germany, had a spiral form, and traces of this pattern can be seen on comparable mounds in Britain. A mound in the grounds of the hospital at Harlow, Essex, for instance, is still a perfect example of this, with a 3½-turn spiral. In legend, we find the spiral hill motif in connection with the Northumbrian folk-song 'The Lambton Worm'. This saga of serpent-slaying tells of a hill around which the greatly feared destructive beast coiled nine times. Legends connected with German turf mazes tell how a shepherd who was about to be executed made a labyrinth with his crook. Perhaps the condemned was forced to walk the labyrinth as a final act before he was hanged at the *Galgenberg*, symbolizing the release of the soul.

As in Babylonia, the use of the executed in divination was known in northern Europe too. *Hávamál*, an ancient Norse collection of sayings attributed to the god Odin, contains a section on the use of the runes in a series of magical charms. One of these runes is for communicating with the spirit of someone hanged on a tree:

> I know this, the twelfth:
> If I see aloft in a tree, a corpse swinging from a noose,
> Thus I carve and I paint the runes,
> So that the man steps down and speaks with me.

Odin was hanged on a tree for nine days and nine nights, resulting in his obtaining the runes for the use of human beings. The nine circuits of the sun around the tree reflect the nine coils of the Northumbrian serpent-hill, which itself may have been a labyrinth.

It has often been stated that labyrinths mark burials, and in Scandinavia several are in pagan grave-fields or Christian churchyards. The nineteenth-century labyrinth researcher C.E. von Baer believed that the labyrinths were constructed as monuments and, as evidence, quoted an event during negotiations over the ownership of Lappland. In 1592 Russian envoys went to Kola to define the frontier. They asked the locals for ancient place-related tales and received the following reply: 'Among the Karelians there once lived a famous lord, called Valit or Varent, a vassal of Great Novgorod, and a man of uncommon strength and bravery. He invaded Lappland in order to win the Murmansk region for himself. The Lapps appealed to the Norwegians for assistance, but Valit defeated the Norwegians too on the banks of the Varanger Fjord, where, as a memorial down the centuries, he set up a massive stone over a fathom tall, building around it a twelvefold wall, which he called Babylon. This stone is still called Valit's Stone.' The twelvefold walls around the central megalith were single rows of stones, making a labyrinth pattern that marked the place where the Norwegians were defeated and, presumably, buried.

The Seven Circles of Heaven

The Classical labyrinth pattern, which is the form of the vast majority of carved and boulder labyrinths, has seven circuits. This is highly significant, as traditionally the number seven is the 'lucky number'. But it is much more than that. The geocentric Western tradition of

1.10. The seven planets, celestial spheres, rainbow colours, and the notes of the *syrinx* are embodied in Pan, whose horns and human/animal nature link him with the dreaded Minotaur of Crete.

pre-Copernican cosmology tells of seven spherical envelopes that pass above the Earth. These spheres contain the sun, the moon, the planets and the stars. Musically, these are the seven tones sacred to the great god Pan. The seven days of the week are ruled by the seven astrological 'planets'. The Sun rules Sunday, the Moon, Monday; Tuesday is ruled by Mars, Wednesday by Mercury, Thursday by Jupiter and Friday by Venus; Saturday is under the rulership of Saturn. Likewise the English-language days of the week are named after the Anglo-Saxon equivalent deities: Sunna, Mani, Tîwaz, Woden, Thunor, Frigg and Saetere. Each of the rings of the Classical labyrinth is related to one of the planetary spheres, and hence to a day of the week.

This correspondence is still inherent in certain children's hopscotch pitches. it occurs also in medieval Christian tradition as 'the Throne of Majesty'. This representation of God's throne was shown with seven concentric part-circles of steps in front of it, leading down from Heaven to Earth. That this was related to the labyrinth pattern is shown by the arrangement at the church of San Michele in Pavia, Italy, where half of a circular pavement labyrinth showing Theseus and the Minotaur has been converted into a Throne of Majesty, complete with steps. These seven spheres appear in Dante's *Inferno* and in several Renaissance illustrations.

'The country whence none returned is divided into seven zones, like those of Dante's *Inferno*, upon the model of the seven planetary spheres,' wrote François Lenormant in his *Chaldean Magic*. 'This idea of the underworld is also found in the Egyptian mythology of the ritual of the dead – the deceased had to pass through fifteen pylons in his descent.' 'Pylons' here refers to ancient Egyptian ceremonial gateways. In the later Persian tale of Rustem, the Iranian Hercules, the *Shah-Nameh* of Firdausi, undertakes seven great labours in seven days. When he reaches a place called 'The Seven Mountains', he fights a demonic being 'within a deep and horrible recess'. Clearly this is yet another version of the myth in which the labyrinth is seen as a model of the universe.

The Fall of Jericho

In Finland, some labyrinths bear the name Jericho, which indicates that the biblical story must have some connection with the labyrinth mythos in general. If we examine the story of Joshua's siege of that city (Joshua 6:3-4), we can see that indeed it does contain all the legendary elements associated with the seven-circuit Classical labyrinth.

Before Joshua's attack, Rahab the prostitute had hidden in her house the two Jewish spies sent to reconnoitre the city. In this version of the labyrinth legend, there was a woman at the centre: Rahab, who was certainly not a virgin. The spies gave her a red thread which was hung from her window as a symbol that she and her kin should be spared in the general slaughter.

The traditional elements of the labyrinth legend are all present in the Jericho story: the seemingly impregnable walls, the woman inside the walls, the men who get in, the thread and finally the slaughter. The number seven, too, is vitally important in the Jericho myth: 'And ye shall compass the city all ye men of war, and go round about the city once. Thus shalt thou do six days. And seven priests shall bear before the ark seven trumpets of rams' horns: and the seventh day ye shall compass the city seven times, and the priests shall blow with the trumpets ...' Michael Ayrton pointed out the convention that a maze has seven turns or seven 'decision points' at which the intruder must decide whether to go onward or to abandon the quest for the centre. Joshua's sevenfold circuit of the walls, counter to the city's original foundation ritual would have had the effect magically of unwinding the maze defences, leaving the city open to attack and conquest.

Furthermore, after the city fell, the Israelites did not occupy the site, leaving it a deserted ruin but for Rahab and her family, who, like Ariadne, were abandoned after they had served the hero's purpose. The destruction of Jericho, accomplished by a sevenfold circuit, parallels the sevenfold 'lap of honour' circuit of the castle of Lanka made by Rama and Sita in the *Ramayana*.

A labyrinth of typical Indian design, illustrating yet another labyrinth myth, is carved on the Halebid Temple at Mysore. Dating from the period of the Hoysala dynasty, the same period as the construction of Chartres Cathedral (the twelfth and thirteenth centuries), it depicts a military array inside a simple unicursal labyrinth which ends with a reverse spiral. According to legend, this is a magical pattern arranged to keep out everyone but the intended victim. In the ancient saga known as the *Mahabharata*, Abhimanyu's death is engineered by means of this labyrinth. There the circular formation known as *Chakra-Vyūha* (the labyrinth) is set up by the agency of Drona, the warrior-magician, who says, 'Today I will slay a mighty charioteer, one of the foremost heroes of the Pandavas. Also, today I will form an array that is impenetrable to the very gods.' Once the labyrinth is made, the victim is lured into it. Although he can enter, it is impenetrable to his comrades, who are powerless to prevent his being slaughtered.

Patterns on the Ground

This magical impenetrability is a motif identical to that we know from European tradition. In India, as in Europe, the labyrinth design is used as a painted or chalked magical protection for the household, known as a *kolam*. (It is related directly to the threshold patterns of Britain.) These patterns invoke the power of the elephant god Ganesha, lord of obstacles, in his capacity as the preventer of entry of harm into the house. One of Ganesha's sigils is the swastika with dots between the arms. This lucky charm pattern may be seen painted on Hindu doorsteps in Britain today. Its geometrical connection with the labyrinth has been mentioned already. Another of his attributes is the axe, again related symbolically to the labyrinth.

In the Hindu tradition, the labyrinth design is known as *kota* which means 'the fort' or 'the city'. Traditionally it is drawn as the path of the maze rather than its walls. Writing in *An Account of the Primitive Tribes and Monuments of the Nilagiris* (1873), J.W. Breeks describes the labyrinths carved on stone walls in front of houses of the Indian Nilagiris. These patterns were intended to be followed by the finger and were of the Classical labyrinth pattern. In southern India, the labyrinth pattern has been noted in traditional body tattoos. Whilst stone labyrinths may last for centuries, a tattoo lasts only for the lifetime of its owner. Thus tattoo patterns have a tendency to last for only the generation which wishes to use them. (Unfortunately we have no knowledge whether the tattoos worn by the ancient Celts and Picts included protective labyrinth designs.) Another Indian usage of the Classical labyrinth is as a *yantra* used for concentration during childbirth, as mentioned above.

The word *kolam* has a number of related meanings, including line, current, snake, meander, watercourse, figure, ornament, mask, bird, display and the planet Saturn. The connection between this collection of seemingly disparate items is the principle of the continuously moving line upon which the concept of the labyrinth is built. It is applied to the threshold patterns used today in India and by people of Indian origin living in Britain. But it parallels directly traditional British usage. Making magically charged patterns on the ground, on thresholds and the floors of buildings is a folk tradition from all over the world.

1.11. Jericho as a moon-shaped labyrinth, after a twelfth-century manuscript painting from St Emmeram, Regensburg, Germany.

In Britain, the custom of making patterns from coloured chalks or sand was carried out in many places until World War II largely put an end to the practice. It continues as part of the May Day ceremonies at Knutsford in Cheshire. Until World War II, it was customary that on her wedding morning the bride would have the patterns drawn in sand upon her doorstep. In Scotland the doorstep patterns reproduced certain standard designs. The outline was rectangular, and at the centre was a motif such as the 'tree of life', an eight-petalled flower, interlaced ellipses or a star. Often surrounding this central motif was the 'tangled threid' pattern, done in red chalk. As ancient threshold-protective magic, it reflects the old Scottish adage, 'Rowan Tree and Red Threid, Gar the Witches tyne their speed', which in standard English is translated as, 'Rowan tree and red thread make the witches lose their speed.' The red thread of Ariadne and Rahab appears again as a key to entry. This pattern was known in England as 'continuous eights'. Where this was not used, the four corners were marked by quadrants or stylized plants. These patterns were chalked on the doorsteps on certain 'feast days' by the housewives. Formerly a similar custom was observed at Newmarket, where the racing stables were protected magically with patterns drawn in sand. Like the Scottish patterns, these used the continuous eights motif.

These patterns are the continuation in folk tradition of the ancient binding magic recorded in Norse sagas and ancient Welsh custom. Historically, the continuous eights pattern is encountered in Celtic and Norse art. In northern Europe it can be found as a border in medieval Irish manuscripts, Norwegian Viking period and later wood carvings, pagan era Swedish metal-work, on the memorial stones on the island of Gotland and Anglo-Saxon crosses and tomb slabs. Their magical function is an example of binding magic, well known in folk tradition even today. The tangled threads formed a protective border which was believed to bridge the material and non-material worlds, creating an entanglement that evil spirits could not penetrate.

Hopscotch

The name 'hopscotch' comes from the action of hopping over the scratch or 'scotch', the line which divides paving slabs. This prohibition against touching a dividing line is parelleled in maze-running or dancing, where the path must be followed without crossing the dividing-lines. For many years the hostelry known as 'The Fleece Inn' at Bretforton in Nottinghamshire, originally constructed in the fourteenth century, had the cracks between the flagstones of the floor whited 'to ward off witches'.

Just as the maze-treader symbolically threads the maze of life towards the 'goal', the child playing at hopscotch progresses with varying degrees of difficulty towards the 'goal'. Hopscotch games are known all over Europe, and some of them have an affinity with labyrinth patterns and labyrinth dances. British, German and Dutch hopscotch patterns have been investigated by a number of researchers,

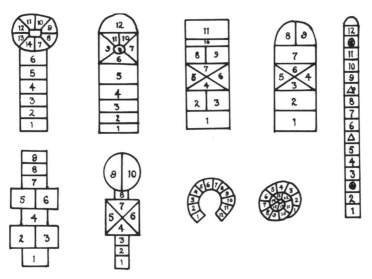

1.12. Traditional hopscotch patterns from Britain, the Netherlands and Germany.

who have recorded various types of 'dance', each with its own name and characteristic pattern: Paradise, Death's Head, Double Ladder, Hoppeby Bed, Pan Bed, Shoemaker's Game and Snail, for example. In her 1912 book *The Folk-Lore of Herefordshire*, Ellen Mary Leather recorded several variants of hopscotch then current in the shire. In Leominster, a very basic hopscotch pitch pattern was popular. It consisted of a simple long rectangle divided by a longitudinal line and thus into six compartments by two transverse lines. On this simple pattern the children would perform various versions of hopscotch. The simplest, known as Hops Bed, involved a single clockwise circuit of the pitch. More complex versions were Double Rounders, performing the circuit twice; Miss Bed, where numbers 2 and 5 were omitted from the hopping; Cross Keys, which produced an interlaced pattern; Postman's Knock, where the child would stamp after each hop, and Blind Man's Buff, done blindfold. The version known as Cross Keys created a pattern very similar to the Broom Dance, danced along and across the handle of a broom laid on the ground.

Many of the hopscotch patterns are simple ladders or grids, but some have a closer affinity with maze designs. The hopscotch pitch known in Cornwall as the Snail Creep and in France as La Merelle Colim Açon (Snail Merel, 'merel' being the name for a 'man' or playing piece in a merels game such as nine men's morris) is a spiral form. The Shoemaker's Game has a spiral form, which Frederick Hirsch (see Critchlow, Bibliog.) likened to certain prehistoric rock carvings in Sweden. But the name given to this labyrinth-like form links it firmly with the late-medieval shoemakers' turf mazes known from England and Pomerania. In some hopscotch games, the final 'goal' is called 'heaven', and that immediately before it, 'hell'.

It is thought that hopscotch patterns and games, which are now strictly the preserve of children, are the remnants of ancient adult ceremonies, whose precise forms and function are forgotten. There are a few hints to the earlier customs of hopscotch which relate them to traditional cosmology. Hirsch noted that children in Denmark call out 'One year old! I have a year!' when they have hopped successfully through the twelve 'beds' or 'fields' of their particular hopscotch pattern. It is possible that, as with the labyrinth, these twelve beds represent divisions of time. A Cornish example, recorded by R. Morton Nance, calls seven successive beds after the days of the week.

— 2 —

Ancient Turf Mazes

Although it is possible that the turf maze was derived from labyrinths made with pebbles or boulders, it is certainly a distinct type of maze in its own right. Basically, a turf maze is one in which the pathways are defined by banks of earth, upon which grass is growing. Obviously this allows for two possible basic types of maze.

The first type is where the maze has been cut from the greensward by the removal of turf in an appropriate pattern, leaving the remaining turf as the maze. The walker, dancer or runner makes his or her way to the centre of the maze by treading the original surface of the ground, delineated into pathways by the removal of the turf between them. The space where the turf is removed is kept free of plants by repeated scouring, leaving grassy 'baulks' to mark the pathway. Effectively, the top of the baulks of turf is walked in this type of maze. These baulks are on a level with the surrounding surface of the ground or, where repeated recuttings have taken place, are in a depression. Usually the pathway of baulks is unaltered turf, but there are at least two known examples, at Hilton and Comberton, where the pathway was composed of gravel. Whatever the surfacing of the pathway itself, the type with raised baulk pathways is taken by most labyrinth researchers as being the 'typical' turf maze, and it is represented by most of the surviving ancient examples.

The other basic type is where the pathway is defined by a groove between earthen banks. Like the gap between the path in the other type of maze, this pathway may be just bare earth, but examples are known where the gap was paved with gravel, as in some German mazes, or delineated with bricks, as at Saffron Walden in Essex.

Notwithstanding their large size, turf mazes are rather fragile monuments. They need to be kept in good order, their grass cut, their edges trimmed and their paths maintained. If this maintenance lapses for only a few years, the pattern of the pathways may be altered accidentally by the passage of feet, and vegetation may overgrow the maze, eventually destroying it. Although well over a hundred ancient turf mazes are known to have existed in Britain, only eight survive intact (described on pp.61–74), with two further overgrown and unmaintained sites which have not yet gone beyond reclamation. Little is recorded of their origin, and documentary material on many destroyed and even extant turf mazes is scant or non-existent in many cases. But some idea of their nature and function has been built up by comparative studies of their form, location and customary usages in different places.

The vast majority of known turf mazes are or were of unicursal form, with one path leading from the outside to the centre without deviation. Where multicursal mazes have existed, it is probable that these recorded designs were corrupt versions of mazes that originally were made unicursal. The patterns of most known turf mazes parallel the medieval Christian design and variants of it; a few are or were of the Classical form, whilst one at Pimperne was a strange winding pattern unlike any other.

In Britain, there is no general name for turf mazes. They have been called Mizmaze, Mazles, Shepherd's Race, Fairy Hill, Maiden's Bower, Julian's Bower and its derivatives, Troy Town, The City of Troy and The Walls of Troy. There appear to be no hard-and-fast rules for the names of mazes, other than the Troy names, which are applied only to mazes of the Classical labyrinth form and its close allies.

One of the earliest references to turf mazes can be found in William Shakespeare's *A Midsummer Night's Dream*, in which Titania, speaking of the supernaturally unseasonable summer weather, says:

> The nine men's morris is fill'd up with mud,
> And the quaint mazes in the wanton green
> For lack of tread are indistinguishable.

Many writers, taking the last two lines out of context, have given this as evidence for the decline of mazes in Shakespeare's day. The opposite is inferred, for Shakespeare's audience would have known of the 'quaint mazes' as commonplace.

Another intriguing reference can be found in a Welsh history book, *Drych y Prif Oesoedd*, published in 1740. This tells of the tradition in

Wales amongst shepherds of cutting turf labyrinths, known as *Caer-droia*, a word which has two parallel translations into English: 'The City of Troy' and 'The City of Turnings' (from the Welsh *Caer y troiau*). The custom was also described in 1815 in *Cambrian Popular Antiquities* by P. Roberts, who published a plan of the *Caerdroia* design. This is a version of the Classical labyrinth – the typical 'Troy Town' pattern with the entrance side 'squared off'. This same 'squared-off' pattern was also recorded in the 1920s as being a traditional seaside beach game in Scotland. It appears that both the Welsh and Scottish traditions were of making temporary rather than permanent patterns, to be used immediately for ritual or entertainment purposes and then left to degrade. A parallel which still continues today is the temporary hopscotch pitch chalked upon a pavement.

2.1. Horsemen, monkey and labyrinth from the Etruscan wine jug known as the Tragliatella Vase, sixth century BCE.

Maze-like patterns associated with sacred dance are known from various countries ranging from Britain, the Netherlands, Germany and Greece to India and the Pacific islands. Of these, the *Lusus Trojae* is the most connected with labyrinths. This 'Game of Troy', played by youths in ancient Roman times, is recorded by Virgil in the fifth book of the *Aeneid*, written 29–19 BCE. The seventh-century BCE Etruscan wine jug from Tragliatella, which shows mounted riders and a labyrinth with the word '*Truia*', appears to allude to the *Lusus Trojae*, which involved labyrinth-like manœuvres by a number of riders on horseback. Virgil compares the maze-like movements of the game to the labyrinth of Crete:

> As when in lofty Crete (so fame reports)
> The Labyrinth of old, in winding walls

A mazy way inclos'd, a thousand paths
Ambiguous and perplexed, by which the steps
Should by error intricate, untrac'd
Be still deluded.
(Trapp translation, 1718)

Jeff Saward's researches into the origin of the labyrinth design connect it with the *Geranos*, the Crane Dance, known still in Greece. In legend, this dance was performed by Theseus and his comrades after their flight from Crete. This connection goes back a long way, as it is shown on one of the Val Camonica rock-face labyrinth carvings which have been dated roughly to 1800–1300 BCE. The dance is said to mimic the mating display or dance of the crane, in which a pair of birds face up to one another with outstretched necks and then walk round each other in circles, frequently changing direction. This dance can be likened to the movements of dancers within a labyrinth.

Folk-tradition in several parts of Europe preserves the custom of dancing in or on a labyrinthine pattern. Until 1538 dances were performed on the pavement labyrinth in Auxerre Cathedral, France. In the last century a Cornish tradition of a labyrinthine folk-dance was recorded by W.G. Wade. Writing in *The Antiquary* in April 1881, Wade stated:

> The young people being all assembled in a large meadow, the village band strikes up a simple but lively air, and marches forward, followed by the whole assemblage, leading hand-in-hand (or more closely linked in the case of engaged couples), the whole keeping time to the tune with a lively step. The band or head of the serpent keeps marching in an ever-narrowing circle, whilst its train of dancing followers becomes coiled around it circle after circle. It is now that the most interesting part of the dance commences, for the band, taking a sharp turn about, begins to retrace the circle, still followed all before, and a number of young men with long, leafy branches in their hands as standards direct this counter-movement with almost military precision.

A similar dance-tradition existed in the Netherlands, at Ostmarsum. Here hundreds of people, holding hands, led by the town band, made a massive 'snake' which would spiral inwards and out again on the open spaces of the town, and then wend its way in and out of the houses. Another dance like this was performed annually at the turf maze at Kaufbeuren in Bavaria, southern Germany, where dancers held hands and proceeded in line through the labyrinth and out again. The intimate connection between the dance and the maze indicates that the maze may have originated as a permanent marking of a place where a sacred dance was customarily performed.

John Layard, who investigated the maze dances and rituals of Malekula in Melanesia, believed that 'ritual patterns' such as labyrinths were derived from sand-tracings that the magician or celebrant made in her or his ritual dances. Later these would have been stylized and fixed as ritual patterns in their own right. Perhaps this happened in Europe, too. Layard found that in Melanesia these patterns had two elements. Firstly they recorded the path danced by the celebrant, and secondly they were believed to be the actual body of the 'guardian ghost'. The framework, or never-ending line, represents the body of the ghost or spirit, and the interaction between this and the dancer achieves the consummation of whatever function the maze is intended to perform. In some way, the action of dancing the maze magically activates its inherent powers. The body of the ghost, as Layard called it, is given life.

Ancient Turf Labyrinths in England

There are only eight intact ancient turf mazes existing in England today. They are in or near Alkborough, Breamore, Dalby, Hilton, Saffron Walden, Somerton, Winchester and Wing. They are described below according to geographical groupings rather than in alphabetical order.

BREAMORE, HAMPSHIRE: MIZMAZE

The Mizmaze at Breamore is the most exceptional of all surviving English turf mazes. It is located inside a remote wood on the part of Breamore Down known as Mizmaze Hill – the Old Series Ordnance Survey Map of the 1820s calls it 'Mizaze Hill' (map grid reference SU 142203). This secluded place can be reached on foot by a track that leads from the Salisbury Road (A338) or through the grounds of the local manor, Breamore House. The maze itself it cut through the shallow turf into the chalk substratum, and its pathway, on top of the turf bank, is of the medieval Christian pattern. The whole maze is 25.5 metres (84 feet) in diameter, and at its centre is a circular mound 5.8 metres (19 feet) across.

In his 1913 book *The Ancient Earthworks of Cranborne Chase*, George Heywood Sumner published a drawing of the Mizmaze. 'Our turf-cut mazes are undoubtedly of medieval ecclesiastical origin,' he wrote. 'They are situated near a church or monastic settlement ... The Priory of St Michael's, Breamore, was founded for Austin Canons about 1129, and the Mizmaze may be connected with the priory.' Local lore asserts that the maze *was* constructed by the monks of nearby Breamore Priory. They were supposed to crawl the maze on their knees as a penance or as a substitute for a pilgrimage to Jerusalem. However, this theory, much reported in connection with medieval mazes, is not backed up by contemporary written material. Another piece of local wisdom concerning the Mizmaze states that a man can run from the maze to Gallows Hill and back (a round trip of over a mile) in the time it takes for another to run the maze.

ST CATHERINE'S HILL, WINCHESTER: MIZMAZE

The Winchester Mizmaze is the only surviving ancient turf labyrinth which is square in plan. It is located on St Catherine's Hill which rises above the village of Chilcombe to the south of the cathedral city of Winchester (map grid reference SU 484278). This is a holy hill which bears the traces of the ramparts of an Iron Age hill-fort, which was used from around 125 BCE until the Roman conquest. In medieval times a chapel, dedicated to the saint which gives the hill its name, stood inside these ramparts. Now its ruins are overgrown by a clump of beech trees. The chapel was founded around 1080 and destroyed during the dissolution of the monasteries in the 1530s.

The Mizmaze is located slightly to the north-east of the chapel site. It is roughly square in outline, though its paths conform to a nine-circuit version of the medieval pattern of unicursal labyrinths. It measures 86 feet (26 metres) by 90 feet (27.5 metres). The path is denoted by the hollow between the baulks, and not on top of them. As with the case of the Saffron Walden maze (see below), it has been suggested that this indicates that the labyrinth was cut from a plan by someone who did not know the 'right' way of making the pathways. But this is assuming that the 'correct' type of maze is one where the baulks are to be walked upon. If turf mazes were derived from stone or boulder labyrinths, one would expect to walk between the banks. The destroyed turf labyrinths at Pimperne and Sneinton, several in Germany and the former form of that at Hilton, had paths marked by grooves or gravel. Writing in 1915, J.P. Williams-Freeman noted that it was ' ... a sort of square edition of the Rockbourne maze, and, like it, is probably mediaeval and ecclesiastical'.

Apart from the labyrinth, St Catherine's Hill is an interesting place, being the 'holy hill' upon which generations of students from Winchester College have played. Paul Devereux has shown that it lies on a 'holy hill' alignment of sacred places which starts at Tidbury Ring to the north and runs through St Bartholomew's Church and the cathedral in Winchester, across the labyrinth, and then on to a bowl barrow tumulus further south (see *Lines on the Landscape* by Nigel Pennick and Paul Devereux).

Local tradition asserts that this Mizmaze was made by a schoolboy during a Whitsuntide detention in punishment for some misdemeanour. During this period, the student was exceptionally active, first composing the Wintonian tune '*Dolce Domum*', then cutting the

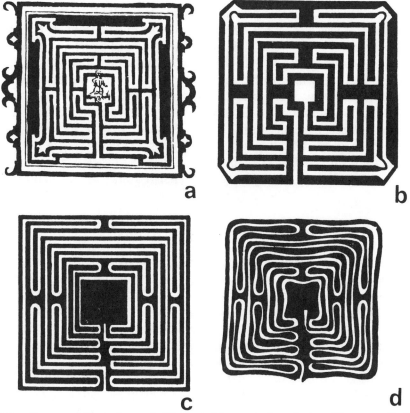

a **b**

c **d**

2.2. Square labyrinths. a) Herbal Maze designed by Thomas Hyll, 1579. b) Turf maze formerly at Clifton, Nottingham, pattern identical with Hyll's published design. c) Winchester Mizmaze after J. Nowell, 1710. d) Winchester Mizmaze, 1989.

labyrinth on top of St Catherine's Hill and finally drowning himself in the River Itchen which flows nearby!

As with most turf mazes, the dating of the Winchester labyrinth is difficult. The first known reference to it is in a plan by J. Nowell, which dates from 1710, but there is no suggestion that it was new then. Nowell's plan shows it with a much more rectilinear form than it has today, and considerably smaller than it is now – 70 feet (21 metres) along each side. The legend of the schoolboy does not help much either, for the musical composition '*Dolce Domum*' is dated at around 1690 but the story about the suicidal genius appears to have originated about a century later, when an 'old boy' of the college collected together some oral traditions. During the late eighteenth century the Winchester schoolboys used to 'toll the labyrinth' by running from the centre outwards, but this practice seems to have lost its appeal, for by the 1830s it was almost overgrown. However, it was recut in 1833 by the Warden of Winchester, following a plan owned by a 'lady residing in the neighbourhood'. It was then, probably, that the larger dimensions of the labyrinth originated and the curvilinear, rather than straight, pathways were made. There may well have been another, unrecorded alteration more recently, which made it rectangular, rather than square in form. In his famous *Memoir* of 1858, the Venerable Edward Trollope gave the dimensions as 86 feet (26 metres) along each side, and in 1899 the Revd George S. Tyack gave the same dimensions. It does not appear to have changed since the last century.

SOMERTON, OXFORDSHIRE: TROY TOWN

The maze at Somerton (map grid reference SP 519279) is unique among English turf labyrinths. Firstly it is enclosed inside the private grounds of a farm, the appropriately named Troy Farm, and secondly it is the only fifteen-ring Classical turf maze known in Britain. It is large, measuring 18.5 by 15.7 metres (60 feet 6 inches by 51 feet 6 inches). Unlike the other surviving English turf mazes, it is on private property, and not accessible to the public.

Troy Farm is believed to date from the mid-sixteenth century, but it stands beside the ancient trackway known as the Portway which is thought to be of Anglo-Saxon or perhaps earlier origin. During the eleventh century Somerton was among the property of Bishop Odo of Bayeux, a place which still possesses a labyrinth, although a pavement one in the cathedral chapter-house, William Matthews drew attention to the similarity between the Somerton Troy Town and the twelfth-century tiles of Toussaints (All Saints') Abbey, Châlons-sur-Marne, France, which was destroyed in 1544. The shape of the maze comes close to the form of some megalithic circles such as 'Long Meg and Her Daughters' in Cumbria and Merrivale in Devon. The archaeo-astronomical researcher Professor Alexander Thom classified this shape as 'Type B Flattened Circles', whose geometry, like that of the standard Classical labyrinth, can be made by using only a spade, five stakes in the ground and a rope. Jeff Saward suggested that the shape and pattern of this maze might indicate that it predates the designs which have a similarity to the medieval Christian labyrinth pattern. However, the nineteenth-century drawing by Herbert Hurst shows a rather broken-up design, perhaps reflecting a former neglected condition.

SAFFRON WALDEN, ESSEX: TOWN MAZE

The largest surviving ancient labyrinth in England is cut into the turf of the common about a quarter of a mile (400 metres) to the east of Saffron Walden town centre (map grid reference TL 543385), bordering Chater's Hill.

Known as 'the Town Maze', the labyrinth is constructed inside an earth bank and ditch which measures about 150 feet (46 metres) at its longest, and 110 feet (33.5 metres) wide. Across the bastions, it measures 132 feet (40.2 metres). Its design is unique, although it is related to the series of medieval labyrinth designs recorded from French cathedrals. Like them, it has the basic fourfold-cross division, but it is not the same as any known examples, having seventeen rings and consequently more turnings. Because of this, it has the longest pathway of any English labyrinth. Officially, the length of the pathway is given usually as the traditional one mile (rendered as 1,500 metres). At a reasonable pace, it takes between twelve and twenty-two minutes to walk the labyrinth. 'The design is most peculiar,' wrote George Tyack, 'being properly a circle, save that at four equal distances along the circumference, the pathway sweeps out into a horse-shoe projection.' Its design is unusual for a turf maze, having four corner protrusions, known as 'bastions', 'bellows' or 'ears'. As far as is known, of mazes large enough to walk through, only the obliterated maze at Sneinton had comparable structures. However, a drawing of a maze, preserved in a French manuscript at Trinity Hall, Cambridge (Ms. 12, Fol. 50, *c.* 1406) shows a rounded square with 'bastions' containing crosses. Also an interlaced Hiberno-Saxon-style knot in *The Book of Kells* has a close similarity to these 'bastions'. In recent years a maze based on the Saffron Walden design, but closer in form to the Trinity Hall manuscript diagram, has been made at Milton Keynes (see p. 169).

2.3. Mazes with corner 'bastions'. a) Robin Hood's Race, Sneinton, Nottingham. b) Town Maze on the common at Saffron Walden, Essex. c) Herbal labyrinth design by Thomas Hyll, 1579, a mirror image of Saffron Walden maze. d) Labyrinth design after a French manuscript of Boethius's *De Consolatione Philosophiae* at Trinity Hall, Cambridge, *c.* 1306.

The Walden 'bastions' have names related to the nearest large towns in the corresponding direction: Cambridge, Newmarket, Chelmsford and (Bishop's) Stortford (north-west, north-east, south-east and south-west respectively). At the centre is a mound 33 feet (10 metres) in diameter. During the nineteenth century, this was called 'Waterloo', after the celebrated battle. The pathway itself is marked by a depression in between the turf baulks, formerly a depression in the ground (as at Winchester and in several other known turf mazes). In 1911 the pathway was inlaid with 6,400 bricks which form the path. The whole maze is enclosed inside a bank and ditch, straight on three sides but curved at the northern (entrance) end, making an assembly-place, presumably for the runners. A document dating from the eighteenth century recorded that maze-running contests took place there: 'The Maze at Saffron Walden is the gathering place of the young men of the district, who have a system of rules connected with walking the maze, and wagers in gallons of beer are frequently won or lost. For a time it was used by the beaux and belles of the town, a young maiden standing in the centre, known as *Home*, while the boy tried to get to her in record time without stumbling.'

The earliest documentary reference to the maze comes from 1699, when it was mentioned in the Corporation Books of the town, from the accounts of the Guild of the Holy Trinity: '15s. 0d ... for cutting Ye maze at Ye end of Ye Common'. The Guild of the Holy Trinity was a trade organization which was formed around 1400, which may have had ceremonies, now unrecorded, at the maze. The Town Maze narrowly avoided being destroyed by enclosure in 1814, when the lord of the manor attempted to take over the common as his own property. Fortunately A.F. Gibson intervened and secured the site of the maze as part of the common, which it remains today. Like the mazes at Sneinton and Slupsk, and the surviving West German labyrinth at Hanover, the Walden maze had a tree at its centre. Unfortunately this ash tree was burned during Guy Fawkes' celebrations on 5 November 1823, and no replacement was planted. After that, the labyrinth was recut in 1828, 1841, 1859, 1887, 1911 and 1979. In 1979 3,000 damaged or disintegrated bricks in the pathway were replaced with new ones.

According to one legend, this labyrinth is a copy of a larger version which once existed close by. It is supposed to have been cut by a journeyman shoemaker, or alternatively by a wandering soldier. These origin stories need not be mutually exclusive, as during the seventeenth and eighteenth centuries paid-off ex-soldiers were allowed to pursue the craft of shoemaking as journeymen. Furthermore, the now-obliterated mazes at Kingsland, Shropshire and Boughton Green, Northamptonshire, were connected with shoemakers, that at

Kingsland being the property of the local guild. Another maze belonging to a shoemakers' guild existed at Stolp in Pomerania (since 1945, Slupsk, Poland), whilst elsewhere in Germany Swedish soldiers are reputed to have cut several turf mazes.

But at some time, presumably the Reformation, the Guild of the Holy Trinity was suppressed, and the use of the maze became more secularized. Today it remains as the finest surviving ancient turf maze in England.

HILTON, CAMBRIDGESHIRE (FORMERLY HUNTINGDONSHIRE): MAZE

The village green at Hilton, where the maze is located, is one of the most picturesque in eastern England (map grid reference TL 293663). It is reputed to have been laid out by Lancelot 'Capability' Brown, who lived at and is buried at nearby Fenstanton.

Unlike many turf labyrinths, that on the green at Hilton has no special name other than 'The Maze'. This example measures 16.7 metres (55 feet) in diameter. At its centre is a memorial – Sparrow's Monument – in the form of a square pillar surmounted by a stone ball which formerly held a sundial gnomon. William Sparrow is said to have cut the gyres in 1660, at the age of nineteen. It is thought that Sparrow actually recut an earlier maze, which had fallen into disuse and had become overgrown as the result of Cromwell's suppression of such 'relics of vile heathenism' as maypoles and mazes. The date, 1660, the year of the Restoration of King Charles II, adds to the likelihood of this.

The present form of the labyrinth dates from 1967, when it was recut by Philip Dickinson, the Huntingdonshire historian. This recutting was surrounded with controversy, for the original plan of the maze is not recorded. Documentary information on the Hilton maze indicates that formerly it was not a turf maze in the present meaning of the term. Also the plan has changed several times in the last 140 years. Whilst discussing the Pimperne maze, J. Hutchins, in his *The History and Antiquities of the County of Dorset* (1774), mentions Sneinton, near Nottingham, and Hilton: 'Another very curious example occurs on the village green in the parish of Hilton, Hunts., which instead of being composed of the usual banks of turf, has its intricate design laid in a neat paving of pebbles.' The 1854 *The History, Gazetteer and Directory of the County of Huntingdon* also states that the labyrinth was 'composed of small pebbles in the ground'. It appears that the pebbles were in the paths, which were, as now, on raised turf baulks. Some layers of pebbles between three and four inches (7.5–10 cm) thick were found in the turf cut away by Dickinson when he redesigned the labyrinth in 1967, but because the pebbles were in places which he believed had never been pathways, he called them the 'original pebble fillings of trenches'. Writing in 1967, W. Garnett believed that the pathway had been gravel laid on a flat surface and that trenches had not been cut between the paths until 1861. If this is the case, the Hilton labyrinth parallels directly such German Troy Towns as those still extant at Graitschen and Hanover. Garnett suggested that an excavation be undertaken over the whole maze, to recover the original plan from the buried pebble pathways, but this has never taken place.

The labyrinth was described by Albert Way in 1858 in an additional note to Edward Trollope's famous *Memoir*. Way believed that Sparrow ' ... doubtless copied the design of some older maze with which he was familiar, perhaps that in Lincs. above mentioned' – Way was referring to Julian's Bower at Alkborough. The maze has nine rings at the moment but appears to have been reduced from the eleven-ring medieval labyrinth form which has been reduced to allow the erection of the monument at its centre. Plans drawn during the last century and the early part of this (A. Way, 1858; J.S. Clarke, *c.* 1892; and the Revd Walker, 1908) show a corrupted version of a nine-ring unicursal labyrinth. According to the notes of the Huntingdon architect and antiquary Sidney Inskip Ladds, between 1861 and 1891 the grass was allowed to overgrow the maze, and cattle grazed upon it, using Sparrow's Monument as a rubbing-post. One of the Revd Walker's 1909 glass lantern-slides in the County Record Office at Cambridge is a plan that shows a pattern of pathways slightly different from those before or after. Walker's photograph of the maze *c.* 1908, shows a reasonably well-kept labyrinth, presumably the result of recutting in 1891 or 1899. When William Matthews visited Hilton in 1920, the pattern had changed again. Some paths had joined, whilst others had separated. This plan was published in Matthews' book *Mazes and Labyrinths* in 1922. Shortly afterwards, in 1926, it was scheduled as an ancient monument, and yet another plan was used in the official documents. A postcard issued by H. Coates of Wisbech in 1933 also shows the multiple-joining paths of the officials' diagram. This picture clearly shows the banking at the corners of the paths which enabled runners to make swift turns, which survived until recently.

In 1967 Philip Dickinson arranged a recutting which restored the

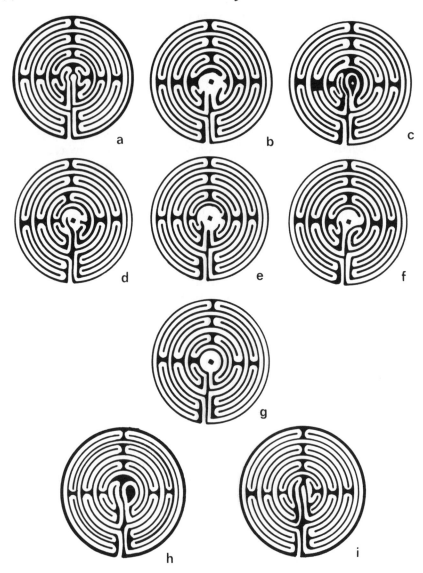

2.4. Historical variations in the pattern of turf mazes a–g, Hilton, Cambridgeshire; h–i, Wing, Leicestershire. a: Presumed original design of the Hilton maze, 1660–1729, medieval Christian pattern; b: pattern in 1858, after A. Way; c: 1892 after J.S. Clarke; d: 1908 after F.J. Walker; e: 1921 after W.H. Matthews; f: 1926 after Royal Commission on Historic Monuments; g: 1967 to date after recutting by P.J.M. Dickinson; h: design of Wing maze, *c.* 1850; i: present design of Wing maze to medieval Christian pattern.

labyrinth to a proper unicursal form. Dickinson held that Sparrow's original design (or recutting) was an eleven-ring unicursal labyrinth of the Alkborough-style design. He thought that, when Sparrow's Monument was erected, it obliterated the two central rings, and the maze was left in that condition from 1729 until the late nineteenth century, when it was recut badly. Finally Dickinson recut it to make it unicursal again, but with only nine rings. Not everyone agreed with this theory: in February 1967 correspondence in the *Hunts. Post* argued against Dickinson's recutting. The most recent recutting, in 1988, removed the banking which was a notable feature of the turns. At this time, too, the spaces between the banks were filled with bark chippings to suppress the growth of grass and weeds. Fig 2.4 shows the evolution of the 'design'.

A typescript by Dickinson in the Hunts Record Office at Huntingdon, dated 7 February 1973, notes that, as in other places, the maze had walking traditions. The entrant had to walk the whole length of the path without stumbling, turning back, falling into the ditch on either side of the path, or stopping. If the walk was marred by one of these failings, he or she would prove unlucky in marriage or would end up 'possessed by the Devil'.

The obelisk or pillar at the centre of the maze was erected in 1729 as a monument to William Sparrow, who had died on 25 August that year. Sparrow was reputed to have cut the maze in 1660, at the age of nineteen. In 1899 a Hilton resident removed the sundial from the maze and used it to top a brick gate pillar at nearby Grange Farm. Around 1928, according to one story, the stone ball was taken down and restored to the pedestal in the middle of the maze. But according to Philip Dickinson, writing in 1967, a larger ball was restored 'recently'. The sundial gnomon, which was missing from the original ball but was restored in 1928, fell out in 1982 and is now lost. Unfortunately, even if the gnomon were still there, the sundial is orientated 12 degrees away from a true meridional alignment and so is useless. The lettering on the pillar, which had been partially worn away by the cattle, was recut at the same time, incorrectly. Originally the inscription read: *'Sic Transit Gloria Mundi. Guilielmus Sparrow, Gen., natus ano. 1641. Ætatis sui 88 quando obiit, hos gyros formavit anno 1660'* – 'Thus passes the world's glory. William Sparrow, Gentleman, born 1641, died at the age of 88, formed these circuits in 1660.' Sparrow had lived at Park Farm, a seventeenth-century building near the maze which was demolished in 1945. During demolition, two seventeenth-century paintings of a woman dressed as a man were discovered behind wall panelling. These were portraits of Mary Frith, alias 'Moll Cutpurse', the highwaywoman who waged guerrilla war against Cromwell's supporters. She was a supporter of the Stuart cause who once held up and robbed General Fairfax. It is clear from these paintings that the Sparrow family were ardent Royalists, and the cutting of the maze to commemorate the Restoration in 1660 is a probability.

WING, LEICESTERSHIRE (FORMERLY RUTLAND): OLD MAZE

This maze is cut in the roadside turf on the southern side of the village recreation ground (map grid reference SK 895028), Its position is signposted for the convenience of visitors. It is well kept, enclosed by a white-painted wooden railing. In form, it is a circular eleven-ring medieval Christian design, 15 metres (50 feet) in diameter. During the last century, however, the maze had a slightly different design, the central area being composed of a loop which sent the runner back to the beginning without stopping and turning around. Such a central loop can be seen in illustrations of two lost mazes, those at Pimperne, Dorset, and one of the Sneinton, Nottingham diagrams. However, this loop was removed some time before 1901, for in that year Murray's *Hand Book for Northamptonshire and Rutland* refers to it as 'a maze cut into the grass on the roadside, similar to the one at Alkborough, in Lincolnshire', which is an eleven-ring medieval Christian design. Also nearby was once an earthen mound, 'a flat-topped, bowl-shaped tumulus', which was used by spectators of the maze-running. This is obliterated now.

ALKBOROUGH, HUMBERSIDE (FORMERLY LINCOLNSHIRE): JULIAN'S BOWER

Julian's Bower (map grid reference SE 880218) is one of the most celebrated turf mazes in England. It is an eleven-ring medieval Christian design which measures 13.25 metres (43 feet 6 inches) in diameter. It is located on high ground at the western side of the village, overlooking the confluence of the rivers Trent and Humber. The maze is easy to find, as, like that at Wing, it is signposted.

According to one origin legend, Julian's Bower was supposed to have been cut as a penance by a knight who was involved in the assassination of Thomas à Becket. He was told to go on a pilgrimage to

Jerusalem to expiate the crime, but as this was impossible, he had a labyrinth made instead. From about 1080 until 1220 there was a small monastic grange nearby, a subsidiary of the Benedictine abbey at Spalding. It has been suggested that this was the origin of the maze. But the earliest known documentary reference to the labyrinth is in Abraham de la Pryme's *Diary*, written between 1671 and 1704, where it is called 'Gillian's Bore'. It was, he wrote, 'nothing but [a] great labyrinth cut upon the ground with a hill cast up round about for the spectators to sitt round about on to behold the sport'. A contributor to *Notes and Queries* in 1866 writes of 'running in and out' the labyrinth at the beginning of the nineteenth century. May Eve games were played there 'under an indefinite persuasion of something unseen and unknown co-operating with them'.

In 1887, during restoration of the church, the maze pattern was inlaid in the floor as a record of its design for future reference. 'In the floor of the south porch of the church has been introduced a copy of the Julian Bower or Maze which exists on the hill at Alkborough. It has been cut in the stone and the grooves filled with cement,' reported the *Associated Architectural Societies Reports and Papers*. At that time the maze was maintained by the local squire, J. Goulton Constable, who was responsible for having the copy made in the church. Julian's Bower was recut last in 1987.

The name of this maze, 'Julian's Bower', has been associated with certain other turf mazes in England as well. It comes from the medieval legend of Julian the Hospitator, the patron saint of innkeepers. According to the story, Julian was a nobleman who was very fond of hunting. One day a fortune-teller warned him that he was destined to kill his father and mother, and shortly afterwards, through a mistake, he did accidentally kill them. To atone for his crime, he set up a hospice by a ford at which travellers could rest. This was the first Julian's Bower. There he remained for several years until the night he ferried a leper across the river. Because the leper appeared to be dying from the cold, Julian gave him his own bed to sleep in. At this act of selfless generosity, the leper miraculously turned into an angel and forgave him his sins.

The connection with labyrinths is not very clear, and their location sheds little light on the matter. Although the mazes at Saffron Walden and Hilton were near fords, they were never known as Julian's Bower. Neither was the labyrinth of Willie of the Boats at Rockcliffe Marsh, Cumbria (see below). The Alkborough Julian's Bower is nowhere near a ford, although it overlooks the confluence of two major rivers – the

Trent and Ouse. The traditional iconographical attributes of St Julian are a falcon, a stag and a sword, with river and boat in the background, and the boat may have some distant echo of the connection between labyrinths and seafarers in the Irish and Scandinavian traditions.

DALBY, YORKSHIRE: CITY OF TROY

This maze can be found beside the road from Dalby to Terrington, where it is identified by a low, white-painted railing on the roadside verge (map grid reference SE 626719). It is the only extant turf labyrinth in Yorkshire, and the only ancient seven-ring Classical design. Like the other Classical turf labyrinth at Somerton, the Dalby maze has a Troy name: 'The City of Troy'.

In former times there was a plan of the maze carved on a barn door at the nearby village of Skewsby. In 1860 it was used to guide a recutting of 'The City of Troy', but it exists no longer. Neither is the present site of the maze original: it is a recutting made in 1900 close by the original after horses and vehicles using the verge to avoid bad ruts in the road had made a mess of the original. At present the paths are banked to allow fast running of the maze, but local tradition warns against running it more than nine times, for that will bring bad luck.

Ancient Turf Mazes outside the British Isles

Although few survive today, a number of turf mazes are known to have existed in former Danish- and German-influenced areas. For example, Särestads hed, Asige parish, Halland, Sweden, once had a turf maze of eleven-ring classical design. According to a surviving plan, recorded by G. Brusewitz, the Särestads hed labyrinth was circular in form. It was located close to a prehistoric hill-fort, known as Kungsberget (King's Hill), and was destroyed around 1852 when the ground was ploughed. In Denmark proper, there was a pavement labyrinth in the market-place at Viborg.

There are more turf labyrinths recorded in Germany, and three survivors, one in western and two in the eastern zone of the country. But unlike the British Isles, where over a hundred sites of turf mazes are documented, there are only a few from Germany and former German territories. Unfortunately some have the scantiest of documentation, but the information that we have is valuable for the understanding of the British examples, to which they are related closely. For example, we know that people played in a *Wunderberg* in Querfurt in Thuringia in 1531, and wagers were laid on the running. Another Wunderberg, mentioned in C.C. Nauth's chronicle of 1721, existed at Rosswein in Saxony. This was said to have been cut by a dancing monk who was 'skilled in the art of witchcraft'. At Teicha, to the north of Halle, a labyrinth known as *Wunderberg* was mentioned in 1750. Like several others, this one was supposed to have been built in 1484 by a shepherd with his crook, which may refer to the mysterious object on the sixteenth-century labyrinth carving in the Augustinergasse, Zürich. Other turf mazes existed at Bergsheidungen an der Unstrut, Frankfurt an der Oder, Fürstenwalde and Calbe, by the River Saale, where the maze Wunderburg was called *Schlangenweg* (Snake's Path).

One of the best documented turf mazes in the German sphere of influence is the *Windelburg* (Coil City) or *Windelbahn* (Coil Track) at Slupsk, Poland (formerly Stolp, Pomerania, Germany). This was very large, 45 metres (150 feet) in diameter, and was cut in the turf on an earth platform next to the crossroads of the Aukerstrasse and Bütowerstrasse. This labyrinth was under the guardianship of the local shoemakers' guild, who celebrated at the monument every third year on the Tuesday after Whitsun.

Writing in 1784, Haken recounts that the journeymen of the shoemakers' trade guild organized the festival. Ceremonial officials were elected: a *Maigraf* (May Count) who had two assistants known as *Beistände*. These were accompanied by two *Oberschäffer* (stewards), as scribe and two 'fools' or clowns called 'Bruder Armel' and 'Bruder Halbsieben' (Brother Poor and Brother Tipsy). On the morning of the festival, the two clowns walked through Stolp with the apprentices, visiting houses and demanding largesse. In the afternoon, the guild, led by the masters, processed from their lodge to the maze. The clowns, carried in barrows propelled by the apprentices, came last. At the labyrinth, whose paths had been strewn beforehand with sand and fresh flowers, the *Maigraf* and his *Beistände* danced to the centre. There the *Maigraf* made a humorous oration. After hurrahs for the emperor, the town, the master and the women, the band struck up a tune, and the *Maigraf* danced out from the labyrinth. The dance was the '*Schwäbischen Pas*' or '*Kleibitzschritt*', which used the 'lapwing step'. This dance step, related obviously to the Mediterranean Crane Dance and to hopscotch, involves a forward leap followed by a stop, and then the dancer stands on one foot before proceeding. After this dance, the *Maigraf* was thanked by the oldest journeyman, and he was given a drink from the guild chalice. Next, the two *Schäffer* danced the maze, one from the centre, the other from the entrance. Where they met, they were given a drink by the oldest journeyman. If any of the dancers 'wrong-footed', they were jeered by the bystanders. After more speeches, the clowns or jesters had their say, telling traditional shoemakers' jokes. Then the whole assembly made a formal procession around the labyrinth. Finally the children were allowed to run the maze, collecting the flowers which had been strewn there previously. The official part of the ceremony over, the participants went to two temporary huts or 'bowers' in which they either danced or drank and smoked. The event ended at nine in the evening, with a procession back to town.

The connection of a shoemakers' guild with a turf maze is known also from England, both at Boughton Green, near Northampton, the shoemakers' town, and at Kingsland, near Shrewsbury, which was known as 'The Shoemakers' Race'. According to one local tale, a journeyman shoemaker is supposed to have cut the Saffron Walden maze.

In 1908 the last shoemakers' corporation festival was held at Stolp, after which the town museum bought the site, the costumes and other ceremonial paraphernalia from the guild.

The *Zauberkreis* (Magic Circle) at Eberswalde, Kreis Oberbarnim, Brandenburg, is said to have been built in 1609 by Christian Wachtmann, a schoolmaster, as a place of play for his pupils. It was cut in the grass of the hilltop known as Hausberg and measured about 20 metres (65 feet) across. It was reniform in shape (i.e. kidney-shaped). It was tidied up or recut by the school pupils every year on the Monday before Ascension Day, but its main ceremonial use seems to have been around Easter-time. Two children would enter the maze by each entrance and run or hop along it in opposite directions, passing one another on the way. Children who could get along the paths without making a mistake were rewarded with an egg.

According to local legend the Eberswalde maze was cut by a shepherd who had been condemned to death for some crime. One version of the story states that as a last request he asked to be allowed to view the valley from the Hausberg. Whilst there his crook dragged on the ground, making the labyrinth. An alternative version is that the judge promised that the condemned man would be pardoned if he could make a *Wunderkreis*. He did so and was freed. Whatever its origin, in 1758 Princess Amelie, sister of King Frederick the Great of Prussia, had the labyrinth refurbished for an Easter celebration. But this royal connection did not prevent the destruction of the labyrinth by excavations for gravel in 1786. Around 1850, under the influence of a popular gymnastic movement, a copy was built, with an oak tree at its centre. It had become disused and was almost unrecognizable when labyrinth-researcher Ernst Krause visited it around 1892. It is lost now.

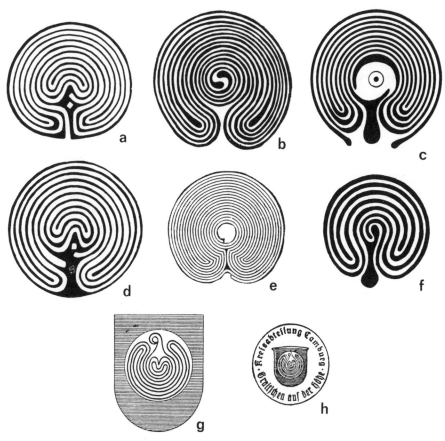

2.5. German turf maze patterns. a: Steigra, extant (after Jeff Saward); b: Kaufbeuren, destroyed 1942; c: Rad at the Eilenriede Forest, Hanover, extant; d: Graitschen, extant (after Jeff Saward); e: Shoemakers' maze, Slupsk; f: Dransfeld, destroyed 1957 (after Joachim Jünemann); g and h: Municipal crest and seal of Graitschen.

According to local lore, the labyrinth at Steigra, Kreis Querfurt, Thuringia, in the German Democratic Republic (DDR), is supposed to have been built by Swedish soldiers during the Thirty Years' War

(1618–48). It is called *Trojaburg* (Troy Town) officially but colloquially *Schwedenring* (Swedish Ring) or *Schwedengang* (Swede's Path). It is located between the villages of Querfurt and Freyburg. (Querfurt was formerly the site of another labyrinth, the *Wunderberg*.) Its design is an eleven-ring Classical pattern, measuring 12.2 metres by 10.8 metres (40 by 35 feet). Young people, having been confirmed recently in the church, would tend the maze on the third day of the Whitsuntide holiday. It was also reported in 1934 by Haye Hamkens that maintenance was carried out at Easter and during the annual 'beating of the bounds', which may have taken place at this time.

At Graitschen, Kreis Saalfeld, also in Thuringia, DDR, is another surviving turf maze. This labyrinth is located on top of a small mound, close to the church. It is called *Schwedenheib* (Swede's Cut) and measures 9.75 metres (32 feet) across. According to legend, like Steigra, it was cut during the Thirty Years' War by Swedish soldiers, and a Swedish officer is supposed to be buried under the labyrinth. It is a variation of the eleven-ring Classical labyrinth, with entrance and exit pathways. The pathway is between the turf baulks. The design of the labyrinth has changed slightly since 1926, when Franz Hennecke published a diagram showing an additional ring, which has disappeared now.

As with the English turf mazes, there has been an evolution and slight alteration in the designs of German labyrinths. The *Schwedenheib* was tended for many years by Curt Eisenschmidt, the last of a line of hereditary maze-guardians, who died in the early 1980s. Fortunately, after neglect caused by World War II and its aftermath, a restoration was carried out by the Junge Historiker youth organization. It is probable that the outer ring, which seems not to have been part of the original design, was removed at this time. The design of the labyrinth has been used for many years as the municipal seal and on the coat-of-arms, and this has not shown the outer ring.

Despite the 'Swedish' names of these two mazes, the Swedish labyrinth expert John Kraft believes that they are not of Swedish origin. Labyrinths in Sweden are invariably of stones, there being no known turf labyrinths.

The only surviving ancient turf labyrinth in the German Federal Republic is in the Eilenriede Forest near Hanover. This labyrinth, known as the *Rad* (Wheel), measuring 32 metres (105 feet) in diameter, is laid out in turf with gravel paths. It is surrounded by a low wall, and at its centre stands a fully grown linden tree. It is the only surviving ancient example of a maze with dual entrances, which enables a continuous stream of people to walk, dance or run it without conflicting with others coming out again. As in the other ancient giant labyrinth, the Town Maze at Saffron Walden, its entrance is to the north.

The early history of the *Rad* is obscure. The earliest reference known is from 1642, when Duke Frederick of Holstein and his entourage visited Duke Christian Ludwig at Hanover and visited the *Rad* during a shooting competition held in the duke's honour at the Eilenriede Forest. Seven years later Georg Schrader, a Hanover schoolmaster, made a speech in praise of the city which mentioned the *Rad*. In it, he spoke of courting couples who would run the maze: one would begin at the centre, whilst the other started at the entrance. The labyrinth's plan has altered somewhat over the years, most notably in the removal of a central S-shape to accommodate a linden tree. The city magistrate was responsible for the labyrinth's upkeep, and it was refurbished or recut each Whitsun by the muncipal gardeners.

Like the Eberswalde labyrinth, the Hanover *Rad* is of the 'Baltic' type, with two entrances. In the nineteenth century this pattern was adopted by an athletics' movement as a useful exercise track. In the first half of the nineteenth century Friedrich Ludwig Jahn, 'the father of German gymnastics', introduced labyrinths to his repertoire of athletic devices. In his attempt to improve the general level of physical fitness, in 1816 he built a replica of the Eberswalde labyrinth at Hasenheide in Berlin. In 1828 another was made at Munich. Two others were constructed at Berlin in 1841 and 1844. H.F. Massmann's book of 1844 illustrated several possible designs, some of which are shown here. Around 1850 a new labyrinth was made at Eberswalde itself. Another 'gymnastic' turf maze, known as the *Wunderkreis*, was built in 1846–7 at Kaufbeuren, Bavaria, to the south-east of Munich. This labyrinth had a design similar to that of Hanover and Eberswalde. It survived until 1942, when a barracks was built upon it. Kaufbeuren was famous for the children's skipping festival held there, which was reputed to have been founded by the Swedish King Gustavus Adolphus during the Thirty Years' War.

The last German maze to be destroyed was the *Trujaburg* at the highest point of the Dransberge, a hill near Dransfeld in Kreis Göttingen. This two-entrance maze, which in legend had been made by a shepherd's croomstick (i.e. crozier), was obliterated by basalt-quarrying works as late as 1957. It was next to a 'dancing place'. Writing in 1878, Wilhelm Lotze reports that on Ascension Day 1614 there was a procession up the hill with a ceremony at the labyrinth.

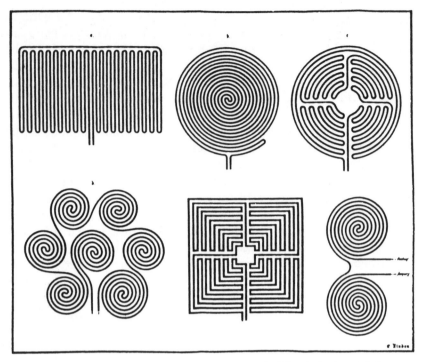

2.6. Exercise labyrinths from H.F. Massmann's *Wunderkreise und Irrgärten*, 1844.

Renovation and recutting of the labyrinth took place each Ascension Day. Lotze records the diameter of the maze as 73 paces (estimated by Joachim Jünemann as 17.43 metres, 57 feet), made up of fifteen *Schlangenwegen* (Snake-Paths).

Lost Turf Mazes in Britain

Although there are eight surviving ancient turf mazes in Britain, they are only a small percentage of those which are known to have existed formerly. The sites of well over one hundred turf mazes are known now, with further evidence available in likely place-names and oblique references for a substantial number of others. At the present level of knowledge, it is possible to suggest that there could well have been over 200 ancient turf mazes in Britain – though, of course, they would not all have existed at the same time. Of these, many have disappeared through neglect, changing social patterns, enclosure of common land or other forms of development. A few have survived into quite recent

1   The ancient stone labyrinth at Ulmekärr, Sweden. Labyrinths like
this, laid on turf, may have been the origin of turf mazes

2   The Hollywood Stone, in the National Museum of Ireland, Dublin.
This seven-circuit Classical labyrinth pattern stone is believed to be
connected with the early Celtic Church

3 The enigmatic seven-circuit Classical labyrinth carvings on valley-side rock face at Rocky Valley, Tintagel, Cornwall. The accompanying plaque credits them to the Bronze Age, but this is unlikely

4 The unique eleven-circuit Classical labyrinth in a carved stone on the wall of a building in the Augustinergasse in Zurich, Switzerland. This monument was restored in 1987, when the original colours, red and green, were reinstated. It is the only surviving example in Europe of a labyrinth on a secular building

5   A Classical labyrinth and accompanying Celtic rose.
Seventeenth-century chalked graffiti in the abandoned firestone mine
at Chaldon, Surrey

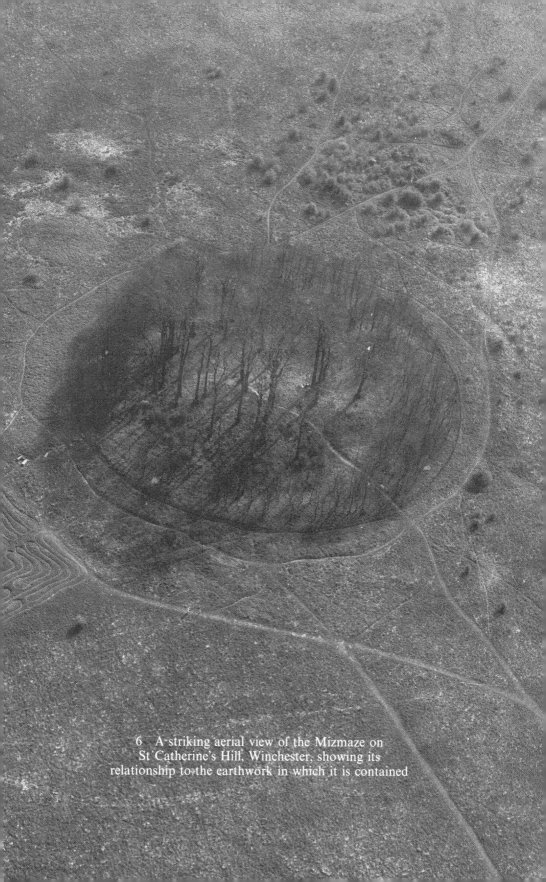

6   A striking aerial view of the Mizmaze on
St Catherine's Hill, Winchester, showing its
relationship to the earthwork in which it is contained

8   The roadside maze known as 'The Walls of Troy' near Dalby, Yorkshire, is the only surviving seven-circuit Classical labyrinth cut into the turf. This is a 1900 recutting of an older maze which existed on the roadside nearby

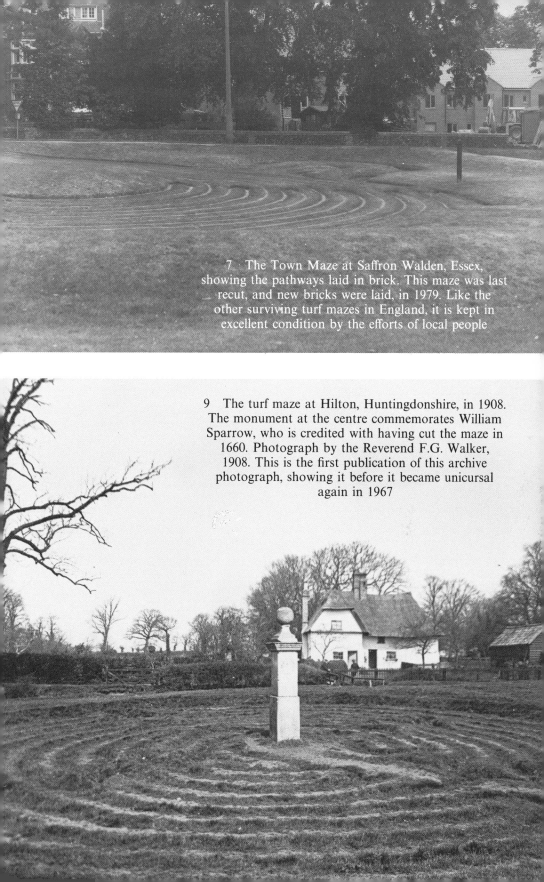

7 The Town Maze at Saffron Walden, Essex, showing the pathways laid in brick. This maze was last recut, and new bricks were laid, in 1979. Like the other surviving turf mazes in England, it is kept in excellent condition by the efforts of local people

9 The turf maze at Hilton, Huntingdonshire, in 1908. The monument at the centre commemorates William Sparrow, who is credited with having cut the maze in 1660. Photograph by the Reverend F.G. Walker, 1908. This is the first publication of this archive photograph, showing it before it became unicursal again in 1967

10   The broken-down remains of the turf maze at Comberton, Cambridgeshire, 1900. This is the only known photograph of the maze before the final recutting of 1909, when the medieval Christian design was adopted in imitation of the Alkborough maze. It was buried under tarmac in 1928

11   The oldest known photograph taken in Nottingham is of the copy of the original Sneinton labyrinth, 1870. Although not of good quality, this is of great historic importance, being the only extant photograph of a Nottingham maze. It shows us that, as with the prototype, a tree was planted at the centre and also at other strategic positions. This is the first publication of this archive photograph

times, only to succumb to these continuing pressures, whilst at the time of writing two actually remain, overgrown and capable of restoration. In recent years, one ancient lost maze has been recut, close to its original site but unfortunately not to the original design.

Several of these lost ancient mazes are well documented, with published descriptions and surviving plans, whilst of others we know scarcely more than their erstwhile location. Although information is sparse, there are several examples known where mazes existed quite close to one another, which appear to be related in some way. Perhaps there was a local tradition in these districts, or the related labyrinths may have been the work of specific village maze-makers whose craft was exercised in places close to their home villages. Another possibility is that these groupings are artefacts resulting from the nature of the documentation. Much of this information comes from the individual antiquaries and historians of former years, whose 'spread' across the country was almost random. Consequently the data-base may be equally random, leading to apparent clusters. This is an area in which research has been co-ordinated by the Caerdroia Project, of which the author has been a contributing member since the outset. Although the majority of sites must have been recorded by now, work is still continuing. The most notable and best-recorded mazes are described below, in a county-by-county way.

DORSET

Pimperne, close to Blandford, Dorset, once possessed a labyrinth unlike any other recorded. The antiquarian Stukeley noted the maze and speculated that it was one of the 'Julian Bowers', like that at Alkborough, which he ascribed to Roman workmanship. The major record of the maze at Pimperne – 'a remarkable piece of antiquity' – is in *The History and Antiquities of the County of Dorset*, written in 1774 by John Hutchins. Following Stukeley, Hutchins noted that such mazes were found frequently at Roman towns and were 'very common in Lincolnshire'. From Hutchins comes the plan, drawn by J. Bastard in 1758, which shows it as an irregular unicursal turf labyrinth of unusual form, being roughly triangular, though with turnings comparable with the typical medieval design. The maze was cut in the turf of Maze Field and, according to John Aubrey, ' ... was much used by the young people on Holydaies and by Ye School-boies'. According to Edward Trollope, it ' ... covered nearly an acre of ground ... It was formed of small ridges, about a foot high.'

Unfortunately it was destroyed by ploughing in 1730.

Another famous Dorset maze was at Leigh, near Yetminster (map grid reference ST 620082), known, like several others in the south-west, as 'The Miz-Maze'. It existed formerly within a hexagonal bank which still stands on private land. This bank once had a protective wall of stones around it, but this has been removed for a considerable time. The Miz-Maze which was cut in the turf inside the bank was 20 metres (65 feet) across, and circular.

Before it was allowed to become overgrown in the latter part of the nineteenth century, it was the location for village assemblies, where, according to Hutchins, ' ... it was the custom for the young men of the village to scour out the trenches and pare the banks once in six or seven years, and the day appointed for the purpose was passed in rustic merriment and festivity.'

The Leigh maze is of particular interest because it is still capable of restoration. It is a scheduled site, and it is to be hoped that one day it can be restored to its former glory.

Elsewhere in the county, at Puddletown (map grid reference SY 738940), was a Troy Town which was still visible in the early part of the twentieth century, but its plan is unrecorded.

WILTSHIRE

There were formerly turf mazes at Mizmaze Hill, just to the north of Salisbury, and at West Ashton. Andrew and Davy's map of Wiltshire, published in 1773, shows the Salisbury hill as 'Mismass Hill', whilst the 1820s One Inch series of the Ordnance Survey has it as 'Mizmaze Hill'. (The same map shows the Breamore maze as 'Mizmaze Hill'.) These maps were of too small a scale to record its design, which appears to be lost.

An ancient earthwork on Wick Down Hill, near Downtown, was described by Sir Richard Colt Hoare in his *Ancient Wilts*, as a maze, which had 'the appearance of a low barrow surrounded by circles within circles'. There is no other record of this maze.

HAMPSHIRE

According to J.P. Williams-Freeman; a maze once existed on Rockbourne Knoll, near Fordingbridge, Hampshire. It was circular and may have had the same path-plan as that on St Catherine's Hill, Winchester. It appears to have existed as late as 1915. Williams-

Freeman states that it was medieval and ecclesiastical in origin. But the nature of this maze demonstrates the problems one encounters in attempting to locate lost sites, for in his book *Mazes and Labyrinths* William Matthews appears to have thought this was another name for the maze commonly called Breamore, described above. However, on old maps the Breamore maze is shown as within Breamore Down, with Rockbourne Down being to its west and quite separate. If this is an authentic maze site, it would make a cluster of three in the locality, along with that at Breamore and Salisbury.

Elsewhere in the county, there is another 'Miz-Maze' place-name, near Wherwell Priory, which indicates another former maze site.

SURREY

In Surrey, the only site for which there is any real evidence is at Hillbury, near Farnham, recorded in the writings of some early antiquaries including H.L. Long. This was called 'Troy Town'. St Martha's Hill, near Guildford, another reputed site, was the venue for the young people of Guildford to hold Good Friday celebrations in former days. Putney Heath, now in Greater London, is another Surrey maze site about which little is known.

KENT

The vestiges of a Troy Town were visible in 1893 near Walmer, and there is a reputed site of a maze at Rochester, where undulations in the ground of the park known as 'The Vines' may be the site. But the Kent County Record Office has no details of either.

GREATER LONDON

No turf labyrinths exist now in London, or have for many years. The best documented maze was on the Tothill Fields, close to Westminster Abbey (map grid reference TQ 298795). Known just as 'The Maze', it is referred to in several documents, including a play by John Cooke, dating from 1614, entitled *Tu Quoque: or The Citie Gallant*. In it, one character, Staines, is challenged another, Spendall, to a duel:

Staines: 'I accept it; the meeting-place?'
Spendall: 'Beyond the Maze in Tuttle.'

Fifty-eight years after Cooke's play was written, the maze was recut by William Brewer at the cost of £2. It is noted by John Aubrey, who in his *Remaines of Gentilisme and Judaisme* (1686–7) remarked, 'There is a maze at this day in Tuthill Fields, Westminster, and much frequented in summer-time in fair afternoons.' It is not known when the Tothill Fields maze was destroyed. There is no extant plan known.

Another area known as 'The Maze' existed in Southwark, bearing the street names Maze Pond, Maze Lane and Maze Street. According to Owen Manning and William Bray in their *History of Surrey* (1814), the area comprised the former grounds belonging to the abbot of Battle Abbey, which were 'spacious gardens with walls and a maze'. This was known as 'The Manor of the Maze'. In 1422 the place was referred to as the 'Maeze in Southwark', belonging then to Sir John Bucestre. 'At Southwarke was a Maze which is converted into buildings bearing that name,' remarked Aubrey. In Volume III of her *Lives of the Queens of England* (1851), Agnes Stickland states that this site marked the place of Princess Mary Tudor's residence. Aggas's map of London shows a garden with a spiral in it in Southwark, which may have been a maze of some sort, but this is not on the site of the area later known as 'The Maze'.

Maze Hill at Greenwich derives its name from a turf maze which existed on Blackheath near the entrance of Morden College. A further turf maze was reputed to have existed close to the present Hampton Court hedge maze (map grid reference TQ 161687), whilst another was on Putney Heath. Strangely for an area known for its many eminent diarists and antiquaries, not one design has come down to us.

BEDFORDSHIRE

The golf course at Heath, near Leighton Buzzard in Bedfordshire, contains the last remnants of 'The Shepherd's Maze', which was last in reasonable condition around 1870. A plan of 1927 exists, showing what appears to be a quarter of a round maze or the corner of a square one (map grid reference SP 921277).

OXFORDSHIRE

At Temple Cowley, 3.2 km (2 miles) south-east of Oxford, was a labyrinth known as 'Tarry Town'. It existed on a piece of land once belonging to the Knights Templar and had a very basic four-circuit design, measuring 5.2 metres (16 feet 6 inches) in diameter. It was destroyed by enclosure of the land in 1852. There was a rhyme

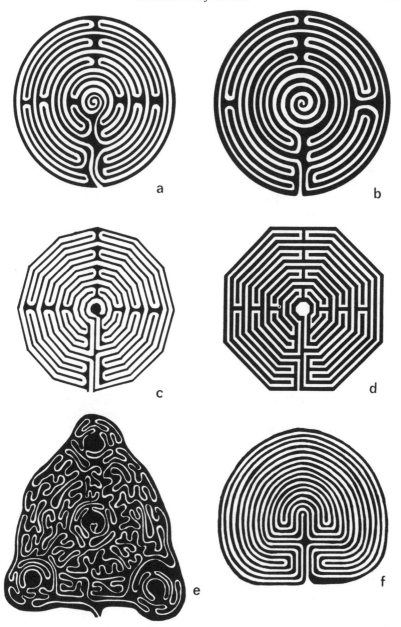

2.7. Variant forms of English labyrinths: a: Ripon (destroyed); b: Boughton Green (destroyed 1917); c: Marfleet, Holderness (destroyed); d: Kingsland, Shrewsbury (reconstruction after Jonathan Mullard, destroyed); e: Pimperne (destroyed); f: Somerton (extant).

associated with the maze, recited by people who walked it:

> So my boy, you wish to marry,
> 'Twere better far for you to tarry.
> Each one's load's enough to carry,
> And it's doubled when you marry.

A copy of this maze was cut at some time 800 metres (½ mile) to the north-east of the first one, on Bullingdon Green. A plan of this maze, photographed from a blackboard drawing in chalk, exists as a slide prepared in 1908 by the Revd F.G. Walker. This one was obliterated at the same time as the Temple Cowley maze. A second copy was made around 1854, 400 metres (¼ mile) south of the Temple Cowley maze. For some reason, this was soon obliterated through lack of maintenance. There are buildings on the sites of these mazes now.

Another Oxfordshire maze is reputed to have existed near the church on Tadmarton Heath. Its only known record was from a manuscript by the Revd T. Leman, quoted in a county history of 1861.

GLOUCESTERSHIRE

Near Chipping Campden in the Cotswold Hills, upon Dover's Hill, was a turf labyrinth. This hill (map grid reference SO 140398) was named after Captain Robert Dover, founder in 1604 of the 'Cotswold Olympick Games'. This version of the Olympic Games included horse-racing, cudgel-fighting and shin-kicking as well as the more customary Olympic pursuits such as javelin-throwing, running, fencing and wrestling. The labyrinth was an integral part of the sports and pastimes, but whether it predated the Cotswold Olympick Games is not known. The games were suppressed for sectarian reasons during Cromwell's reign, but they were restored at the time of the monarchy's reinstatement. After that, they continued until 1852, when they were suppressed by Act of Parliament, which was passed expressly to stop the drunkenness and violence which perennially accompanied the sports. With the suppression of the games, the maze fell into disrepair and soon disappeared.

SHROPSHIRE

'The Shoemakers' Race' at Kingsland, Shrewsbury, is one of the most interesting of the documented but lost mazes of Britain (map grid reference SJ 485118). It is known to have been owned and maintained by the Patriotic Company of Shoemakers, exactly the same tradition that existed at Stolp (Słupsk), Pomerania. It seems to have dated from 1598, when 'the trades began to go to Kingsland', to avoid clashes with religious fundamentalists who had begun to interfere with the Shrewsbury Show in the town itself. At Kingsland the various trade guilds and unions built 'arbours' in which they conducted their ceremonies and made merry. The shoemakers' guild arbour had an entrance depicting the patron saints, Crispin and Crispianus, which is preserved now in the local park, Shrewsbury Quarry. Next to the arbour of the shoemakers' guild was a maze known as 'the Shoemakers' Race'. Records of this shoemakers' trade guild, which date back to 1637, recall several recuttings of the maze, and prosecutions of those caught vandalizing it and its arbour. In 1673, for example, the maze was enclosed, and in 1645, 1676 and 1677 it was repaired.

Unfortunately, the Shrewsbury Patriotic Company appears to have left no plan of the maze. Its enclosure was octagonal, and so it is likely that the maze was, too. In *Shropshire Folklore*, Charlotte Burne records that at the centre of the labyrinth was a face cut in the turf, 'the Giant's Head'. On reaching the centre, it was customary for the maze-runner to jump, landing with one heel on each eye. (It is surprising that these were not footprints, as known from the Polish church labyrinth at Właclawec, rather than eyes.)

Although the precise details are not recorded, the shoemakers' festivities were held on the first Tuesday after Whitsun, the same day as those at Stolp. The maze was destroyed in 1796, when the Patriotic Company sold the land so that a windmill could be built there. The details were recorded by John Tarbuck, a Shrewsbury shoemaker and diarist, known as 'The Shrewsbury Pepys'. The whereabouts of this important document 'recording the occurrence of local events of more than ordinary importance' is unknown, but fortunately a transcript of some of it still exists.

'It must have been extremely old,' wrote Tarbuck (see Mullard, Bibliog.) 'and I have never met with anything of the like in all my travels. It was a labyrinth of walks that contained a measured mile in the diameter of a few yards. These walks were thrown into a regular confusion, so that before you ran halfway, it was ten to one but you lost your route and became more and more perplexed. It never wanted repair, the boys taking care of that by regular use; it was much admired by curious strangers.'

Subsequently, in 1861, when the pageant of the Shrewsbury Show was suppressed, the mill was demolished. The site is now part of a school playing-field.

Another Salopian maze, at Nesscliffe, was still visible in 1897, but it is lost now.

HEREFORDSHIRE

A maze is said to have existed on the summit of Herefordshire Beacon (map grid reference SO 760399), inside an Iron Age hill-fort. This site is similar to the known 'Miz-Maze' at Winchester and the destroyed site north of Salisbury.

NORTHAMPTONSHIRE

Boughton, near Northampton, was the site of a well-known maze which was cut on the fair green outside the village (map grid reference SP 763653). The maze existed not far from the original parish church, which was built by the abbot of St Wandregesile in Normandy. It was dedicated to St John the Baptist, whose holy day is 24 June, once Midsummer's Day. Next to the church was a holy well or spring, described in Whellan's *Directory* of 1849: 'St John's Spring, which rises from the east bank of the church yard, formerly furnished the element for the holy rite of baptism, but now supplies the water for culinary purposes at the fair.' It was the custom in many places for the local children and youth to assemble at holy wells on the eve of the festival of St John the Baptist. As part of the St John's Eve festivities, wrestling, football and other rural sports were enjoyed at these wells. At Boughton Green, as at the Cotswold Olympick Games, the fun of the fair included maze-running.

The Boughton Green maze was of a design related to the medieval Christian pattern but with a spiral centre. It measured 11.25 metres (37 feet) in diameter. Known as 'The Shepherd's Ring' or 'Shepherd's Race', it was 'trod' ceremonially at the three-day Midsummer Fair, which dated from a charter granted by King Edward III in 1353. Murray's *Hand-Book for Northamptonshire and Rutland* (1901) states: '¾ m. from the village is the Green, where a considerable fair is held here at midsummer, which formerly attracted all the neighbouring farmers and gentry.' G.N. Wetton's *Guide-Book to Northampton* (1849) tells of the maze's being in a neglected state. But later writers refer to its being in use, and it is probable that it was recut in the mid-nineteenth century. Sadly, for some inexplicable reason, in 1917 during World War I, soldiers being trained in warfare on the Western Front dug practice trenches straight through the maze. It was never restored.

CAMBRIDGESHIRE

A former turf maze known as 'The Mazles' existed at Comberton, 8 km (5 miles) west of Cambridge (map grid reference TL 382563). The Mazles was an important part of the village's Easter Fair, being recut every third year at Easter-tide. The recutting crew were given a 'feast' for their trouble. It was located close to a crossroads and in 1846 was enclosed in the playground of the village school, just outside the front door. The foundation deeds of the school stipulated that the maze should be kept and maintained, which it was for a number of years. This land was formerly the village green, which was immediately adjacent to land owned by Barron Britton, who married Martha Sparrow of Hilton in 1654. She is thought to have been the sister of William, to whom is ascribed the creation of the Hilton labyrinth in 1660. Because of this connection, it has been suggested that the Mazles was cut some time after 1660 as a copy of the Hilton maze.

A plan prepared in 1897 by the Cambridge pamphleteer and columnist 'Urbs Camboritum' (W.R. Brown) shows 'the almost worn-out traces of a large circular maze, or turf-cut labyrinth'. It shows a very irregular, entranceless pattern, with a spiral at the centre something like those at Ripon and Asenby (see below). It had a diameter of 15 metres (50 feet). The plan given in 1959 by H.C. Hughes to the Cambridge Antiquarian Society and now in the Cambridgeshire Collection at the Central Library, Cambridge, is also of Brown's design. It is a copy of a plan made for the Cambridgeshire Rural Community Council in February 1929. Unfortunately this much-reproduced 'plan' was never intended to be an accurate reconstruction. In 1897 Brown admitted that 'Its grassy balks have all disappeared, and so scant are the vestiges of the intervening paths, that it is now very difficult to map out their serpentine course. Our illustration may serve, however, to shew the probable plan of what the maze was like in the days of its prime.' Clearly it was little more than conjectural but having reached print was taken as authentic.

The text with the 1959 'plan', taken from a paper by the Yorkshire Architectural Society, reads: 'The Comberton maze is almost identical

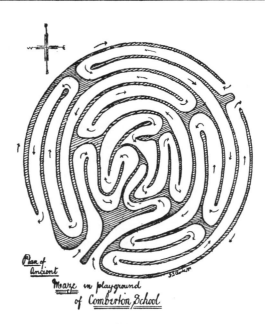

COMBERTON MAZE.

It is now some time since Comberton became noted for the curious old Maze so deeply cut in the turf of the village green. In the days of its prime, when its serpentine paths were well and carefully kept, it naturally excited much attention, and attracted many visitors to the village. Though its grassy embankments are so worn down that it is almost a hopeless task to trace out its devices, yet it has not outlived its fame; it still ranks as a local curiosity of considerable note. The illustration at the head of this article is an attempt to map out its windings which, we need scarcely say, are still a puzzle to many. The Maze is now enclosed in the playground of the village school, and many of the lads affect to know the "Old paths," and pleased enough they are to show off their ability in tracing them. As this is so near to Cambridge, and there is not another like it in the county, it is fairly entitled to be better known than it is. It is within an hour and a half's walk from the Backs of the Colleges by way of Newnham and Barton; the return by Coton or Madingley might extend and diversify the route. For those of our readers who are cyclists, we may mention that there is a similar piece of ingenuity cut in the turf of the village green at Hilton, near St. Ives—it is in a capital state of preservation and well worthy of a visit—and at Saffron Walden in Essex there is a still more remarkable labyrinth, very ancient, and well kept. The details of these objects of interest are worth puzzling over and working out. There are many others in various parts of the country.

2.8. The Comberton Maze by J.S. Clarke, from *The Cambridge Express*, 1892.

with that of Wing. The path is of gravel, two feet wide, its windings are separated from each other by little trenches, nine inches wide ... the outer margin is on a level with the surrounding ground, but the area of the maze itself gradually sinks towards the centre.' The gravel pathway links it to its nearest neighbour, that at Hilton, which had the same mode of construction. However, a plan drawn by J.S. Clarke five years before that of W.R. Brown and published in the *Cambridge Express* ('An Artist's Rambles in Cambridgeshire, 12 December 1892) can in no way be interpreted as the same diagram. 'In the days of its prime, when its serpentine paths were well and carefully kept,' wrote Clarke, 'it naturally excited much attention, and attracted many visitors to the village. Though its grassy embankments are so worn down that it is almost a hopeless task to trace out its devices, yet it has not outlived its fame; it still ranks as a local curiosity of considerable note.' The photograph reproduced here as Plate 10 shows the state of the maze *c.* 1900.

On the urging of the maze enthusiast the Revd F.G. Walker, a new Mazles was cut in 1909 by members of the Cambridge Antiquarian Society. In a lecture given on Monday 8 February 1909, Walker stated that the maze at Comberton was 'almost like Wing' and that it was 'in the process of restoration'. When recut, the Mazles was made to the medieval Christian labyrinth design, copied from that at Wing. During the restoration Walker stated that the maze 'would once more exist as it was originally made'. As reconstructed, it was circular, with a diameter of 14.5 metres (47 feet 6 inches). The average height of the bank, upon which people walked, above the intervening hollow, was 10 cm (4 inches). The path was 251.5 metres long (275 yards), and the centre was marked by a wooden peg. This maze was cut on a new site, close to the old one but away from the entrance. A fence was erected around it, and it was kept in pristine condition by schoolboys who were paid to do the job. Despite this encouraging recutting, the new Mazles was destroyed in July–August 1928 when the school was extended and the playground surfaced with tarmac. For some inexplicable reason, a plan of the maze that used to hang behind the schoolroom door was burned at this time, along with other records, presumably to extirpate the deeds which stipulated the upkeep of the Mazles. It is said that for some years afterwards the 'ghost' outline of the maze could be seen on the tarmac when there was a heavy frost.

It is interesting to speculate whether this maze was the Cambridge 'bastion' referred to in the Saffron Walden maze, for there seems also to have been a maze at Bishop's Stortford, Hertfordshire, named as one of the other 'bastions' at Walden. This was at Maze Green, but no details are recorded.

NOTTINGHAMSHIRE

Nottinghamshire once had three turf labyrinths, as noted in the

Records of the Borough of Nottingham. On 14 July 1732 Mr Chamberlain Burden paid 12 shillings to Mr Samuel Newton for 'Cleareing of the Three Mazes'. Which three mazes they meant was not recorded, but it is possible that two of them were at Sneinton and Clifton.

Robin Hood's Race at Sneinton, otherwise called 'The Shepherd's Race', is an exceptionally well documented turf labyrinth. It was cut on common land 'about half a quarter of a mile east of St Anne's Well' at a site with the modern map grid reference SK 592421. According to the Nottinghamshire chronicler Dr C. Deering, whose *History of Nottingham* was published in 1751, ' ... there is a kind of labyrinth cut out of a flat turf, which the people call *Shepherd's Race*: this seems to be a name of no old standing, probably occasion'd by its being observed that those who look after the sheep on this common often run it for an airing ...' A local legend accounted for the names by asserting that the labyrinth had been cut by a shepherd who used to tend a flock there in the time of Robin Hood. In the eighteenth century artefacts which were supposed to have belonged to Robin Hood were exhibited there for tourists to see. John Throsby's drawing of the relics and maze, dating from around 1790, shows 'part of Robin Hood's Chair', his reputed grave slab and his alleged cap, along with a diagram of a labyrinth. The labyrinth's design is, however, a square one, that of Clifton, nothing like other representations of the maze at St Anne's Well. However, Throsby noted that, 'I perceived a number of the initials of names cut in the turf about the Shepherd's Race, done by those, I am told, who have run it; and I also saw two or three humble imitations of this celebrated race cut, on a small scale, out of the turf near it ...' Perhaps one of these was a copy of the square Clifton maze close by.

This labyrinth was unlike the majority of ancient turf ones, having a different mode of marking the pathways: ' ... there are no banks raised, but circular trenches cut into the turf, and those so narrow that persons cannot run in them, but must run on top of the turf,' explained Deering. The path, however, was delineated by a trench in the turf. The method of marking a pathway between the baulks, instead of on top of them, is known from two surviving ancient labyrinths, those at Saffron Walden and Winchester. Several modern examples use this method, which has the disadvantage of being altered accidentally by becoming overgrown more easily than the other type of turf maze. The corruption of the design, and the alteration of the pathways, as apparent from various surviving plans, may well have come from this difficulty. At Saffron Walden bricks were laid in the grooves to overcome this problem. Wear and tear of the labyrinth can cause hitherto unconnected paths to join.

These alterations over the years can be seen from surviving plans of the Sneinton labyrinth. Dr Deering's papers, kept at Bromley House Library in Nottingham, contain a plan of the labyrinth, dating from the 1740s. It differs from other, later plans of the labyrinth, such as those published by J. Hutchins. J. Wigley, Bishop E. Trollope and W.H. Matthews. Deering's plan shows the entrance pathway going almost directly to the centre, from which two alternative pathways emerge, leading to the rest of the gyres. Each of the bastions contains a cross, joined to the pathways. Although he did not refer to earlier accounts, Deering used these crosses as evidence for dating the labyrinth. He wrote that it was ' ... more ancient than the Reformation, as is evident from the four cross-crosslets in the centres of the four lesser rounds ...' In his 1774 *History of Dorset*, John Hutchins reproduced a plan of the two Nottingham labyrinths (Clifton and Sneinton) as a comparison with his plan of that at Pimperne. This engraving is dated 1758 and has a design different from that recorded by Deering. Hutchins' design lacks the crosses in the corner bastions and is also truly unicursal, having the goal quite close to the entrance, though not at the centre. Perhaps Hutchins had access to a plan of the labyrinth as it was before Deering's time, as it appeared with the Pimperne maze, destroyed in 1730.

The Sneinton labyrinth was recut in 1778. This is recorded in Bailey's *Annals of Nottinghamshire*: 'A number of gentlemen, during the summer of this year, entered into a subscription to restore the labyrinth ... The lapse of years had so far erased the paths, that the form of its course had become almost obliterated.' At this recutting, the pathways appear to have been changed yet again. But unfortunately it was destroyed by the enclosure of the common and its subsequent ploughing on 27 February 1797, a much-regretted event. In his *History of Nottingham*, John Blackner wrote: 'This spot, so long sacred to rural amusements, on enclosing the Lordship of Sneinton, was ploughed up ... here the youth of Nottingham were wont to give facility to the circulation of their blood, strength to their limbs, and elasticity to their joints; but callous-hearted avarice has robbed them of the spot.' In March 1797, a month after the ploughing, J. Wigley, a local publisher, issued a pamphlet which he sold for 'sixpence plain, eightpence coloured'. The cover engraving depicted the final arrangement of the paths and recorded its length as 535 yards (489

THE MIRROR.   297

Shepherd's, or Robin Hood's Race.

SHEPHERD'S, or Robin Hood's Race, was a curious labyrinth or maze, cut in the ground, on Snenton Common, about a mile from Nottingham, and within a quarter of a mile of Robin Hood's, or St. Ann's Well, of which we shall give an account in our next. This maze, of which the above is a correct engraving, though only occupying a piece of ground about eighteen yards square, is, owing to its intricate windings, five hundred and thirty-five yards in length; at the four angles were oval projections intersecting the four cardinal points.

Dr. Deering, in his " History of Nottingham," printed in 1751, gives an interesting account of Shepherd's Race; we differ, however, with him in considering the cross croslet at the corners as a proof that it was made before the Reformation, it being more probably a compliment to some person who might bear the cross croslet fitchée in his arms. The following is the description of this maze by Dr. Deering :—

" Shepherd's Race is made somewhat in imitation of those of the ancient *Greeks* and *Romans*, who made such intricate courses for their youth to run in, to acquire agility of body. Dr. Stukeley, in his Itinerary, speaks of one of Roman origin still in being, at Aukborough, in the county of Lincoln, called *Julian's Bower*, which comes pretty near ours ; he says it is a kind of circular work made of banks of earth, in the fashion of a maze or labyrinth, and that the boys to this day divert themselves with running in it one after the other ; that which I mentioned differs from the Doctor's, in that it pretends to no Roman origin, and yet is more ancient than the Reformation, as is evident from the cross crosslets in the centres of the four lesser rounds ; and in that there are no banks raised, but circular trenches cut into the turf, and those so narrow that persons cannot run in them, but must run on the top of the turf. Nobody can at this time give any account when it was first made, nor by whom ; neither is it known whose business it is to keep it in repair ; but might I offer my conjecture,

2.9. The Sneinton turf maze, from *The Mirror*.

metres) and its diameter at around 100 feet (30.5 metres). As with the Saffron Walden Maze, local lore stated that the labyrinthine pathway measured a mile! However, Hutchins stated that it was 18 yards (16.5 metres) across, Bishop Trollope 17 yards (15.5 metres), and J. Potter Briscoe 21 yards (19 metres). Perhaps the recuttings, as in so many other cases, were not on the same site, and variations occurred. Also, one of the copies mentioned by Throsby may have been taken as the original. Throsby quotes Deering as mentioning the projections, which were 'facing the cardinal points', whilst the plan by J. Wigley shows the entrance to the west, and hence the projections ('ears' or 'bastions'), towards the intercardinal directions. Yet another variant design appeared in the 1789 edition of Camden's *Britannia*, where it is described as unicursal. It is probable that the editors were using J. Hutchins' plan.

Nothing is known of the true origin of the Sneinton labyrinth, but the heraldic crosses, known as 'cross-crosslets fitchy', have been taken as indicating a medieval age for the maze. But generally speculation has centred around its proximity to the holy well, a connection also important at Boughton Green. Unlike the Boughton Green well, which was sacred to St John the Baptist, the Sneinton well was dedicated latterly to St Anne. Near the Sneinton well and labyrinth was St Anne's Chapel, built in 1409. Because of this, Deering speculated: 'I should think this open maze was made by some of the priests belonging to St Anne's Chapel, who, being confined so far as not to venture out of sight or hearing, contrived this to give themselves a breathing for want of other exercise.' St Anne's Well was the most celebrated medicinal spring in the county, being recorded as far back as the thirteenth century, at which time it may have been called 'the Owswell'. By the fifteenth century, the Robin Hood legend had become attached to it, as it was known as 'Robin Hood's Well'.

According to Charles Deering, the fifteenth-century chapel to St Anne was built by a religious order from Nottingham, probably the Cluniacs from Lenton Priory. After the dissolution of the monastery, the spring was taken over by the corporation of Nottingham and became a pleasure resort. The labyrinth, spring and 'Robin Hood's relics' were the main attractions. After its destruction in 1797, the labyrinth was remembered with affection by those who had run on it as children. 'Many and many a time I have run it with great delight,' wrote Mrs Dunne in her *Recollections*, 'It was a great shame to destroy it. From this labyrinth you went down a steep hill called Blue Bell Hill (which in its season was covered with flowers) to a small house of entertainment called St Anne's Well. Here was a bath of intensely cold water: here the gentlemen of the town frequently went to bathe.'

John Throsby's record of the supposed or pretended relics of Robin Hood which had been shown at St Anne's Well indicates that in his day the place was a major local tourist attraction. Even when the common was ploughed up for agriculture, the recreational nature of the area was not destroyed. In the mid-1820s a tea-garden was opened next to St Anne's Well at a former public house which had lost its licence. In the garden, the proprietor constructed a copy of Robin Hood's Race, though smaller than the original. White's 1832 *Directory of Nottinghamshire* stated: 'On the green in the garden, a maze or labyrinth has been cut, as a miniature resemblance of the Shepherd's Race, which occupied an elevated spot on the opposite side of the valley.' Like the original, the paths were cut in the turf. A photograph, taken around 1870, shows a tree growing at the centre, and others between the banks of the bastions. With this maze, the tradition associated with the original labyrinth was continued by children. In his *History of Nottingham* (1840), James Orange records that, 'No sight is more pretty or engaging than to behold six or eight young girls and boys running at the same moment the varying and seemingly interminable windings of the Shepherd's race.' This one existed until around 1870.

Another tea-garden, at the top of Blue Bell Hill, overlooking the valley of St Anne's Well, also had a labyrinth. In the 1830s this was known as Poynter's Tea Garden, after the proprietors. This, too, was a copy of Robin Hood's Race but was made from Beeston gravel paths demarcated by hedges of box. The proprietors owned a 'partly-clipped poodle dog', which periodically was sent to run round the maze for the entertainment of visitors. Having accomplished this feat successfully, the dog was applauded by the spectators and rewarded with a halfpenny, which it carried into the tea-house and exchanged for a biscuit!

The other Nottingham labyrinth for which there is some documentary evidence was that at Clifton, 6.5 km (4 miles) south of the city. This maze was cut to a square design identical to that in Didymus Mountaine's (Thomas Hyll's) gardening book *The Gardener's Labyrinth* (1579). It seems to have been destroyed around 1800, and its location is uncertain, though it could have been in the grounds of Clifton Hall, where a modern turf labyrinth, cut in 1981, exists today. Unfortunately this new maze does not reproduce the earlier form.

The third Nottingham maze was sited at The Meadows at the

modern grid reference SK 579388, near an old wooden bridge over a canal. It was obliterated at some time during the nineteenth century, but even though it was in a town in which antiquarian interest in mazes was great, no plan has yet come to light.

LINCOLNSHIRE

In addition to the still-extant Julian's Bower at Alkborough, the county of Lincolnshire before the 1974 boundary changes once held other labyrinths. Abraham de la Pryme's account of Alkborough also tells of a similar maze 9.5 km (6 miles) south-east of Alkborough, at Appleby. It appears to have been of similar design to that at Alkborough, although little is recorded. It was destroyed in the latter part of the eighteenth century.

Two other 'Julian's Bowers' are known certainly to have existed in Lincolnshire. Near Louth was Gelyan Bower, known to have existed in 1544, for a payment is recorded in connection with it: 'To nych mason for making at gelyan bower a new crosse, iij s.' The cross at the centre of the maze is part of the traditional symbolism which expresses the cosmos in terms of the stable cosmic axis at the centre of the whirling heavens, symbolized by the gyres of the labyrinth. (This symbolism is also preserved by Sparrow's Monument at the centre of the Hilton maze.) A public house in Mercer Row, Louth, formerly kept a large dolerite boulder which, according to tradition, had stood at the centre of the labyrinth, presumably before a cross was erected there. It was known as 'the Blue Stone', the classic name for such *omphaloi*. The fourth Lincolnshire Julian's Bower was at Horncastle, though little is known about it. Even its precise location is uncertain.

Lincolnshire seems to have been an important centre for mazes; in the dialect of the shire, the word 'gillimber' means a labyrinth or any puzzle.

YORKSHIRE

Between the villages of Paul and Marfleet, in the Holderness district of what was once Yorkshire and is now North Humberside, was a twelve-sided maze called 'The Walls of Troy'. Its plan was recorded by 'C.R. Jun.', a correspondent to *The Repository of Arts* in 1815, but its exact location is not known. It measured 12 metres (40 feet) in diameter. Its paths measured '13 or 14 inches broad' (33–36 cm), and the depressions between the paths were six inches (15 cm) deep. Its pattern was the standard medieval design, like Alkborough's, on the opposite bank of the River Humber, but modified to a dodecagonal shape. The centre had an additional loop rather than the expanded goal of some similar mazes. According to C.R. Jun., 'Particulars respecting the time of its construction, or the purport thereof, I am unable to discover; though I remember, about five years since, on observing it attentively, a passing countryman voluntarily gave me to understand, that he himself had planned and finished it; but not at that time paying regard to his veracity, I did not question him.'

Near Asenby, behind the Shoulder of Mutton public house, was one of Yorkshire's most famed mazes, Fairy Hill (map grid reference SE 396572). The site is a curving earthwork joined to a mound upon which are the neglected remains of a turf labyrinth, 15.5 metres (51 feet) in diameter. The mound itself was once a castle motte, upon which at some time the labyrinth was cut. The maze, which had a pathway 307 metres (1,008 feet) in length, was kept in a state of good repair until the latter part of the nineteenth century, since when it has deteriorated. The design was of the typical medieval-type pattern, with a spiral at the centre. People would run the maze and at the centre touch an ear to the ground 'to hear the fairies singing'. In his *Earthwork of England*, published in 1908, A. Hadrian Allcroft made the melancholy remark on this maze: 'It is marvellous that the memory of such things, once prominent features of rural life, can die out so rapidly as it does.'

Another maze with the same spiral-centred design existed formerly at Ripon. This one was half a mile from the town on a triangular plot of land by the roadside (map grid reference SE 312720). Unfortunately the plot of land was enclosed in 1827, and consequently the maze was obliterated. Strangely Walbran, Ripon's historian, does not mention the maze, but its design was recorded by the antiquary John Tuting Senior (1785–1865), who drew a plan of the labyrinth. Executed in pale blue and pink paint, the diagram was kept at Wakeman's House Museum. It was circular, having the same spiral-centred plan as that at Asenby, measuring about 18 metres (60 feet) across, with a pathway 372 metres (407 yards) long.

Another lost maze once existed near Whitby by the village of Egton. This was a roadside labyrinth like the surviving examples at Dalby, Saffron Walden and Wing. It was still visible in 1872. Also near Whitby, at Goathland, was July Park, also called St Julian's, where a labyrinth once existed.

CUMBRIA

On the south shore of the Solway Firth between the villages of Burgh and Rockcliffe, in the county now called Cumbria, were formerly at least three turf labyrinths. Writing in *Notes and Queries* (Series ii, Volume V, p. 211), Captain William Henry Mounsey wrote: 'On the extensive grassy plains of Burgh and Rockcliffe marshes contiguous to the Solway Sands in Cumberland, the herdsmen at the present day are in the habit of cutting labyrinthine figures, which they also call *The Walls of Troy*.' But in 1883 R.S. Ferguson stated that the practice had died out: 'Nor does any tradition now remain of any turf-mazes on Burgh marshes. The field reeve knows of none, nor can he that finds the herds even recollect even hearing of them.'

The best-known Cumbrian maze, called 'The Walls of Troy' was still visible in 1883, when R.S. Ferguson, aided by W. Nanson, was able to trace out the paths and record its pattern. When they visited it, it had not been recut for ten years, and subsequently it faded out and is lost now. It was located on Rockcliffe Marsh. Its final form was a spiralling 'Baltic'-type labyrinth, measuring 7.9 metres by 7.3 metres (26 by 24 feet) The paths were 23 cm (9 inches) wide and the gaps between them 20 cm (8 inches). According to local lore, it was made by Robert Edgar in about 1800, a local sailor subsequently lost at sea, supposedly as a copy of the mazes mentioned below. But this also appears to connect the labyrinth-making with sailors' wind-raising traditions, as in the Baltic. Another story, reported by Ferguson, ascribed the mazes to foreign sailors.

Nearer Burgh by about a mile were two other mazes. They were cut at a place called Greenbed, where a man known as 'Willie of the Boats' could be found to guide people across the trackless marshland before a road was built in 1816. One was a copy of the other, made around 1815, when the first was recorded as being overgrown. The newer of the two was supposed to have been made in 1815 by a Christopher Graham, then sixteen years of age. He was a son of a herdsman of the marsh, and an apprentice seaman who was 'afterwards drowned in foreign parts'. The mazes disappeared in the latter part of the nineteenth century. The Willie of the Boats maze 'was more or less in evidence about six years ago [1877],' wrote R.S. Ferguson in 1883, 'but the vast number of cattle that constantly resort to the gates at "Willie of the Boats" have poached it out of existence, and its precise site cannot be ascertained.'

SCOTLAND AND IRELAND

Although it was a Scottish custom to make temporary labyrinths on beaches, there are only two examples of turf mazes known from Scotland, both destroyed. These are a site at Aberdeen, known as 'The Walls of Troy', and another at Stewartfield, where traces were visible in the last century.

Ireland, too, has few sites. Two known as 'Walls of Troy' existed in County Londonderry, but their exact location is not recorded. As may be inferred by their name, both were of the Classical labyrinth pattern.

British Turf Maze Design

Overwhelmingly, the basic design of recorded and extant turf mazes is the medieval Christian pattern. Of extant mazes, those at Alkborough, Wing and Breamore have a perfect version of this design. The central 'goal' at Breamore is larger than at Wing or Alkborough, but apart from this they are identical in form. The pattern also exists in a square

2.10. This simple labyrinth design once existed at Temple Cowley, Oxford, now built upon (after F.J. Walker).

form at St Catherine's Hill, Winchester. At Hilton, the erection of Sparrow's Monument at the centre appears to have obliterated the inner ring of a medieval Christian design, which was rationalized into a unicursal pattern once more only by modification in 1967. Saffron Walden's Town Maze is an expanded version of the medieval Christian design, with added 'bastions' or 'ears'. This has been created by adding more circuits, but the basic principle of the medieval design was retained.

The last two of our eight survivors are variations of the Classical labyrinth. At Dalby, there is the basic seven-circuit pattern, and at Somerton is the expanded, eleven-ring design. Both have a Troy name, which is not applied to any mazes of the medieval Christian pattern.

Of the lost mazes, few are recorded in sufficient detail. It is possible that the maze at Leigh in Dorset was a medieval Christian pattern. Another is known to have existed in a dodecagonal form at Marfleet, Holderness. The Mazles at Comberton was recut in 1909 to the medieval Christian pattern, but it is by no means certain that this was the original design. The Sneinton labyrinths, which went through several phases, also appear to have been derivations of this design. Those at Asenby, Ripon and Boughton Green were likewise derived from the medieval Christian pattern but modified with a spiral at the centre. The lost 'Walls of Troy' on Rockcliffe Marsh in Cumbria were

2.11. The Walls of Troy, Rockcliffe Marsh, Cumbria, a pattern resembling that of many Scandinavian stone labyrinths.

modified spirals or corrupt Classical labyrinths. Finally the Troy Towns at Temple Cowley near Oxford were of a four-circuit design unlike any others recorded in Britain but, like the Rockcliffe Marsh examples, related to the Classical labyrinth. The traditional *Caerdroia* pattern of the Welsh shepherds is always shown as a Classical labyrinth.

It has been suggested that the earliest maze designs were made according to the Classical labyrinth pattern and that the medieval Christian design was introduced by the Church. This theory suggests that it replaced the earlier pattern gradually, or by a deliberate recutting of the earlier mazes to obliterate their supposed pagan nature. However, from the above we can see that the Classical pattern has survived into modern times, twenty-five per cent of extant ancient mazes adhering to this design. Because of the construction of mazes of the medieval Christian design in churches in the thirteenth century, it has been thought that this dates at least some of the British turf mazes. Also the sunken surfaces of some of them have been cited as evidence of continuous recutting, with consequent removal of spoil, since the thirteenth century. But this is only speculation. it is not possible to date a maze on other than the most basic stylistic grounds, such as that it could not date from a period before the introduction of a certain design. For example, at the present time all sorts of mazes are being constructed. A Classical design turn maze was cut at Rosehill Quarry in Swansea in 1986, two years after a modified medieval Christian design maze was made in a park at Warrington, Lancashire.

Recuttings of historic turf mazes are documented poorly, if at all, and there is no way of telling how many full-scale recuttings have taken place at any site. Certain mazes, such as that at Saffron Walden, have some documentation, but nowhere does this go back beyond the end of the seventeenth century. At a number of places, too, it is clear that copies of earlier mazes have been made to replace those which have, for various reasons, become worn out or obliterated. This is reputed to have happened at Saffron Walden and at a number of German sites. The several mazes which existed successively at Sneinton and Temple Cowley are a good example of this. New mazes, cut close to older, destroyed ones, were made at Dalby in 1900 and at Comberton in 1909. Furthermore, it is possible for a maze to be restored, or a new one made at the site, after a lapse of many years. For example, a new turf maze was cut by Ray Lee at Clifton Hall, Nottingham, in 1981 close to the site of a lost labyrinth which appears to have been destroyed around 1800. All these possibilities make the dating of any but the best-documented turf mazes a hazardous task.

3

Pavement and Church Labyrinths

I give you the end of a golden string,
  Only wind it into a ball,
It will lead you in at Heaven's Gate,
  Built in Jerusalem's wall.

William Blake

Mosaics and Labyrinths

The use of mosaic pavements in Europe is believed to be derived from an early technique of flooring perhaps dating back to late first millennium BCE. In his book *The Technique of Mosaic*. Arthur Goodwin explains this origin in the ancient use of pebbles as a means of making a durable pavement in earth-floored houses. This method involved pressing pebbles into the damp mud floor of the house. When the mud had dried out, the pebbles were held firm by the dried earth, making a significant improvement on a mud floor. Pebbles laid as a floor in decorative or magical patterns were thus the origin of mosaic.

Formerly such floors existed in traditional buildings all over Europe, and there are even a few surviving in use today. Occasionally, instead of pebbles, the flooring was composed of bones, which gave it an added magical function. But whether pebbles or bones were used, many of them were arranged in significant patterns. Only one is recorded which had a labyrinthine form, but this is of great interest. It is one of the few labyrinths known from Ireland and is the only recorded example of a labyrinth floor in the vernacular architecture of the British Isles. But unfortunately, although it still exists, it is no longer accessible. It is in an eighteenth-century farmhouse, in which river-smoothed pebbles were used to lay the floor of a kitchen.

The farmhouse, Bridgetown House, stands to the south of the village of Castletownroche, County Cork, in the Irish Republic (map grid reference R 691001). It was constructed in 1782, and the floor with its labyrinth was laid out by a local paviour, Joseph Knott, using the technique of *opus vermiculatum*. The outline of the maze was made by pebbles laid end-to-end, and the infill was of pebbles laid in a different, contrasting pattern. The Bridgetown House maze was too small to walk, measuring 1.63 by 1.37 metres (5 feet 4 inches by 4 feet 6 inches). Its design was a seven-circuit Classical labyrinth with right-hand entrance.

By the 1960s, the floor had begun to deteriorate and subside, and so the owners decided to pave it over. But before doing so they approached the authorities of the National Museum of Antiquities in Dublin, asking whether they would like to take up the floor for preservation and display. There was no response, and the owners, faced with a rapidly sinking floor, were forced to cover it up. Fortunately they first photographed the labyrinth, and then covered it with a polyethylene sheet and sand before pouring concrete over it to make a new floor. But it is hoped that it will be possible to recover it at some time in the future and that it will be put on display at a notable relic of folk tradition in vernacular architecture.

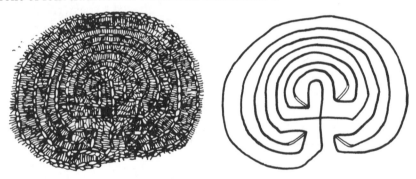

3.1. Left: The pebble mosaic floor of the Castletownroche farmhouse (after Jeff Saward). Right: The labyrinth design to the Classical pattern.

Roman Labyrinths

Mosaic labyrinths and pavement labyrinths are inextricably linked, merging one into the other. The earliest known examples are from the Roman period, when mosaic paving was the most popular means of flooring official buildings and the homes of the wealthy. Strictly

Roman labyrinths are dated from around 100 BCE until the fall of the Western Empire in the early fifth century. They exist all over the former empire, in Europe and North Africa.

There are relatively few known examples, but there must have been many thousands. For example, at Pompeii, a relatively small town, four were discovered. Four others are excavated at Conimbriga, near Coimbra, in Portugal. The most comprehensive study and catalogue of these Roman labyrinths is in the work of Wiktor Daszewski (1977), who lists fifty-four examples. The earlier Roman labyrinths are all classified as 'simple labyrinths' by Daszewski, who uses a classification system which has been criticized by some other labyrinth workers.

The typical Roman labyrinth is unicursal and composed of four meander patterns arranged in a cross. These meanders range from the simplest double meander to more complex repetitions. The principle, however, is the same. One enters at a certain point and traverses the whole quarter before passing on to the next quarter. This is traversed in turn and so on until, after the final, fourth quarter is walked, the centre is reached. This quartered pattern is the typical Roman town layout, derived from the Etruscan Discipline, a pre-Roman system of geomancy. Of the simple labyrinths, there are four types, the simple meander, the complex meander, serpentine and the spiral type. The meander type comprises most of the known Roman labyrinths.

The two-coil meander labyrinth pattern can be derived directly from the Classical labyrinth pattern. It is as though a Classical labyrinth has been 'opened out' to form a quarter of the new labyrinth. Four of these sectors are then linked together to make the whole new pattern. The complex meander pattern is a development of this, where the coils are turned in on themselves, increasing the number of turns in each quadrant. The serpentine form involves a simple back-and-forth movement in each sector, whilst the spiral type makes each quadrant into an in-and-out spiral. In all these cases, there is a fourfold division of the maze in either a circular or square format.

A few known labyrinths vary from this overall design, having a threefold or eightfold division. About a dozen circular labyrinths are known, too. The earliest known Roman labyrinth, at Selinunt, Sicily, dated at 125–100 BCE, was circular. The most common shape is square, but whatever the shape, at the centre of many Roman labyrinths there is sometimes a flower or a mosaic of the Minotaur legend. Sometimes the labyrinth is surrounded by a mosaic depicting a city wall, alluding perhaps to the Trojan story. The Classical labyrinth design was not, however, a popular one with the Roman mosaicists. There are only three examples known, one of which is an interesting variant form. The two 'perfect' Classical labyrinths are at Conimbraga (Coimbra) in Portugal. One is rectangular and the other circular in shape. The only other example, the variant form, which is square, was found at Saint-Côme-et-Maruéjols, in the south of France. Most of these labyrinths are relatively small and, being made of mosaic, have pathways too narrow to walk properly. Because of this, they were just decorative, were held to be magically protective or were objects of contemplation. Later Roman labyrinths, such as that from Kato Paphos, Cyprus, which dates from around the year 350, vary from the typical Roman pattern and show a tendency towards the later-formalized medieval Christian design. These labyrinths include the Byzantine one at the church of San Vitale in Ravenna, which is a transitional form. These later pavement labyrinths are dealt with below.

In Britain, at present there are five recorded Roman labyrinths, though this must be a tiny fraction of those that existed once or remain yet to be unearthed. Their design and symbolism are identical to the others in the empire. Like the later labyrinth designs, this emphasizes the place of British labyrinths in the mainstream of European tradition from the earliest times. Although there are only five true Roman labyrinths in Britain, two of them are known from one place – Cirencester in Gloucestershire, the Roman city of Corinium. In 1968 a fragment of labyrinth was unearthed in the garden of a house in The Avenue. Unfortunately it was only a small fragment, and although it can be seen to have been a labyrinth, its exact form is uncertain. The second fragmentary labyrinth was found in the remains of a corridor on the north side of a Roman building excavated in 1972 in Beeches Road. It is believed originally to have measured 2 metres (6 feet 6 inches) square and was laid in grey and white tesserae. It is a two-coil meander pattern, the predominant Roman labyrinth design. It varies from the majority of known examples in the rebated corners, which give each pathway a zigzag effect. After excavation and record, both of these labyrinths were reburied.

A Roman labyrinth that can be seen today in Britain is at the City Hall, Kingston-upon-Hull, Humberside. It was excavated in 1904 from Roman remains under Crosstrod Field, at Harpham in East Yorkshire, and measures 3.35 metres (11 feet) across. It is a square three-coil, meander-type maze. As with the Beeches Road labyrinth from Cirencester, the paths take an anti-clockwise route to the centre, at which there is a stylized flower. The Harpham labyrinth is dated to the early fourth century, as inferred by an uncirculated coin of the year 304 which was found as a foundation sacrifice beneath a mosaic in an adjoining room.

3.2. Roman mosaic labyrinth from Harpham.

At Caerleon in Gwent, a second–third-century Roman pavement was excavated in 1865 from the remains of the headquarters of the legionary fortress. It was found at the north-east corner of the churchyard (map grid reference ST 339907) and measured originally about 2.4 metres (8 feet) across. Like the Harpham maze, it was of a triple-coil meander pattern, but unlike it, its entrance and direction of passage were clockwise, the only known example of this from Britain. The labyrinth pattern itself is made of blue and white tesserae, and it is surrounded by a vine-scroll border. It is now on show in the Caerleon Museum.

In 1870 another triple-coil meander-type labyrinth was excavated at Manor Field at Oldcotes in Nottinghamshire (map grid reference SK 586887). This measured 2.9 metres (9 feet 6 inches) square and was bordered with grey and red triangles. At the centre was a square containing a mosaic depicting the legend of Theseus and the Minotaur. Unfortunately this labyrinth was not brought out and displayed in a museum but was buried again. One must hope that it will be re-excavated again some day and put on display.

The final known Romano-British example is rather anomalous, for it is questionable whether it is a labyrinth at all. It is a fourth-century mosaic excavated in 1964 at Fullerton in Hampshire (map grid reference SU 374401), which has an involuted square spiral pattern. It has been suggested that this may be the work of an inexperienced mosaicist, who attempted, and failed, to re-create a proper labyrinth pattern. Strangely, it resembles somewhat an odd and undated spiral pavement pattern in the floor of the church at Thornton in Leicestershire (q.v.).

The Etruscan Discipline and the Christian Labyrinth

The simplest Classical labyrinth pattern has a cross form implicit in it, from which the outer form is developed. As the earliest form, the Classical labyrinth probably predates formalized systems of geomancy, by which towns and the surrounding countryside were laid out according to a cosmologically determined scheme. The Etruscan Discipline (a system first practised in Etruria, northern Italy) later served as the pattern for the layout of towns and colonies in the Roman Empire and its successors.

The Etruscan Discipline first involved locating an appropriate central point by a subtle combination of divination techniques with reading the topography and its symbolic interpretation. At this central point, the *omphalos* or *umbilicus* (literally 'the navel of the world'), the augur would sit, facing towards the south, where he would divide the visible horizon into the natural fourfold division inherent in the structure of the human body. Thus the area in front of the augur was designated *pars antica* – the forward part. This was divided into left and right sections, with the left to the east as *templum anticum sinistrum* and the right to the west as *templum anticum dextrum* (the forward left and right quarter respectively). Likewise behind the augur the north-east quarter was designated *templum posticum sinistrum* and the north-west as *templum posticum dextrum* (the rear left and right quarter). The visible world from the centre to the horizon was thereby divided into four quarters. The two lines dividing the quarters, crossing at the *umbilicus*, were known as the *cardo*, which ran in a meridional (north-south) direction, and the *decumanus*, which ran equinoctially (east-west). The surface of the Earth, and implicitly the vault of heaven too, is thereby quartered by the Etruscan Discipline.

This technique of symbolic surveying produced the standard layout for Roman towns, which can be seen still in Britain at places such as Colchester and Chichester, and in a later, derived form at towns such as Dunstable and Royston. Christian medieval maps, such as the Hereford *Mappa Mundi*, are stylized in this way. This geomantically inspired layout is implicit in medieval labyrinths, which are based upon the circle and the cross, with a representation of the 'city at the centre of the world', whether Nineveh, Babylon, Troy, Jericho or Jerusalem as the central 'goal' of the labyrinth.

Jewish esoteric cosmology stated that the rock in Jerusalem upon which Solomon's Temple had stood was of utmost sanctity. It was held that in some miraculous way this stone was eighteen miles (29 km) closer to Heaven than any other place on Earth. In Talmudic tradition it was 'The Pot-lid of Hell', a stone which sealed the entrance to Earth from the underworld. It is equivalent to the stone known as the *lapis manalis* which sealed the shaft dug at the *umbilicus* during the foundation ceremonies of the Etruscan Discipline. In later times this was often a millstone, such as that found in 1742 sealing the ancient shaft at the crossroads in the centre of Royston, Hertfordshire. In Jerusalem the temple rock is now inside the Islamic mosque known as the Dome of the Rock.

In medieval times Jerusalem, the Holy City, was depicted by Christian artists as a quartered circle, with the Church of the Holy Sepulchre, built over the reputed site of the tomb of Christ, at its centre. This central point, transferred away from the Jewish holy centre, was known as the *compas*, taken, in flat-earth cosmology, as the centre of the world. It marked the rock-cut shaft in which Christ was buried, sealed with a circular stone of *lapis manalis* type. Here the *mundus* of Etruscan geomancy was the tomb, through which, according to *The Gospel of Nicodemus*, Christ entered the underworld in order to free the captive souls of the righteous. This 'Harrowing of Hell' is associated mythologically with the entry of Theseus into the labyrinth to slay the Minotaur. It can be speculated that this transference took place by way of Mithraism, in which Mithras, identified with the Christ by way of his identical birth dates and legends, slew the demonic bull of the underworld in a cavern. The appearance of the pagan legend of Theseus in the centre of medieval Christian labyrinths, such as that at Chartres, may have been intended as an allegory of salvation in this way.

As images of the stable Earth and the whirling heavens, millstones laid in the pathway as a magically protective device can still be encountered in British vernacular architecture. One can be seen in the high street of Tintagel, Cornwall, outside the Old Post Office. In the early part of this century, the custom was taken up from Surrey folk tradition by Gertrude Jekyll and Edwin Lutyens in many of their notable garden designs, in which real millstones, or paving laid to imitate millstones, were used at key points in pathways. At Munstead Wood, Gertrude Jekyll's house, the steps leading to the workshop were treated in this way.

Church Labyrinths

The earliest known church maze was in the Roman basilica at El Asnam in Algeria (known as Castellum Tingitanum by the Romans and as Orléansville by the French colonial powers), latterly in Algiers Cathedral. Dating from the year 324 CE, it was of the Roman type, square, measuring 2.5 metres (8 feet 2 inches) along each side. The whole labyrinth is followed by an anti-clockwise progression. The entrance pathway is followed by a wavy 'thread' for a short way, and there is a literary labyrinth or acrostic at the centre square, composed of thirteen-by-thirteen characters. This word-pattern was based on the letters of the words *Sancta Eclesia* (Holy Church). But the numerology of the square of thirteen is rather curious, as in Western demonology this number, 169, is more traditionally associated with the Devil! Perhaps this numerological interpretation had a different meaning in Roman times.

Several Italian churches of the first millennium are known to have had, or still retain, labyrinths. The most celebrated of these is the Byzantine church of San Vitale at Ravenna, dating from the year 530 CE, the period of the reconquest of Italy from the barbarians by the Eastern Empire. The dominance of Greek theology from Constantinople is evident in the magnificent mosaics of San Vitale. The labyrinth is small, measuring 3.6 metres (12 feet) across, laid as part of the rich Byzantine mosaic floor of the church. The pathway is denoted by triangles which to the modern eye look like 'arrows' pointing the way. However, it is not clear whether Byzantine people used such a

3.3. Otfrid-pattern labyrinth, transitional between the Classical and the medieval Christian patterns (after Otfrid von Weissenburg).

symbol to denote direction. There seems to be little evidence of mosaics in Italian churches again until the eleventh century, when renewed contact with Constantinople led to the construction of new pavement labyrinths. The Ravenna pattern is a forerunner of the more complex unicursal labyrinth pattern known as the medieval Christian labyrinth design, of which the Chartres maze is the best-known example.

The Ravenna labyrinth is circular and unlike the typical Roman fourfold meander pattern, such as that used at El Asnam, but it is not without precedent. Some late imperial examples showed tendencies towards the pattern now associated with the medieval period. For example, a fourth-century mosaic labyrinth from Kato Paphos in Cyprus, known as 'The House of Theseus', is intermediate between the typical Roman type and the later, wholly Christian labyrinth. Unlike the typical Roman labyrinth, some of the paths cross the quarters, though in an irregular manner. The pathway is shown as a 'twined rope' pattern, which may allude to Ariadne's 'clew'.

After the disintegration of the Western Empire, pavement labyrinths were made no longer, but it was a fertile time for labyrinth development. Labyrinths continued to be drawn in manuscripts, and at this time both the Otfrid type and the medieval Christian labyrinth came into being.

The Otfrid type is a modified version of the Classical labyrinth, named from Otfrid von Weissenburg (*c*. 790–875), a priest who taught at the monastery of Weissenburg in Alsace, France. It is a form unknown in pavement labyrinths. The medieval Christian labyrinth was, however, destined to have a much wider currency, being the pattern for the famous labyrinth at Chartres and its many subsequent copies.

In his *Memoir* of 1858, Bishop Edward Trollope remarked: 'But perhaps the most surprising fact connected with the mythological labyrinth is its acceptance by Christians, and its adaptation by the Church to a higher significance than it originally bore.' He noted that the labyrinth with a Minotaur at the centre was used as an ornament on one of the specific ceremonial state robes of the Christian emperors before the ninth century. Labyrinths are known from manuscripts of the tenth and eleventh centuries, before the earliest-known labyrinth carvings in churches, which survive from the twelfth century in Italy at Pavia, Piacenza and Lucca.

The Symbolism and Uses of the Christian Labyrinth

More than any other labyrinth design, the Christian one is concerned with the believer's journey or pilgrimage from perdition to salvation. Of course, in all religions and none the journey is a well-worn allegory for life. From ancient mythology to the 'Yellow Brick Road' of *The Wizard of Oz*, the perils and adventures of the journey have symbolized the vicissitudes of existence. Within this general allegory appears the concept of the cosmic journey, such as the quest for the Holy Grail. Often this aspect has been translated into reality in the form of pilgrimage.

3.4. The medieval pattern of the world, derived from the Etruscan Discipline.

Clearly the unicursal labyrinth has always been recognized as a kind of pilgrimage, with its twists and turns first bringing the pilgrim close to the 'goal' and then taking him or her away before finally the centre is reached. An inscription at the church of San Pavino at Piacenza in Italy, *c.* 900 CE, states:

> The labyrinth represents the world we live in,
> Broad at the entrance, but narrow at the exit.
> So that he who is held captive by the joys of this world
> And weighed down with his vices,
> Can regain the doctrine of life only with difficulty.

This pattern is shown perfectly in the medieval Christian labyrinth, which may have been worked out by French mathematicians as early as the ninth century. Sometimes this design is known as 'the Chartres pattern'. It is unicursal in form, being arranged in such a way that, if its paths are analysed by being 'opened out', it creates an arrangement

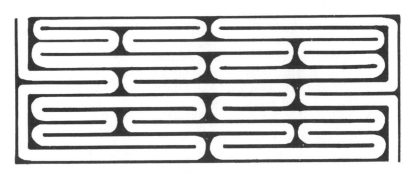

3.5. Above: The medieval Christian labyrinth. Below: The labyrinth 'straightened out', showing the inherent symmetrical pattern.

of paths with a sequential symmetry. There are thirty-five separate paths in all, with twenty-eight points at which the walker turns back. On entering the labyrinth, the walker makes seventeen moves. The eighteenth is effectively a linking move to the final seventeen which will bring the walker to the centre. The second group of seventeen moves is effectively a mirror-image of the first seventeen. Walking in to the centre, and then out again, one makes seventy moves, which parallels the Biblical 'threescore years and ten' of human life.

The modern maze-maker Adrian Fisher has analysed the Christian labyrinth in depth. He has shown that the point at which the pilgrim is turned away from the innermost ring signifies physical death. Until then, the walker has been getting closer and closer to the centre, the 'goal' of salvation. But he or she cannot get to the centre without first experiencing death. Having reached this innermost ring, the pilgrim is forced outwards again. In the Chartres labyrinth, this motion is by way of three semicircular counter-clockwise moves, which symbolize the three days between the Crucifixion and the Resurrection. The pilgrim is brought outwards again to the path adjacent to the entrance path. Fisher suggests that after this point the path begins to symbolize eternal life, moving on larger radii which permit faster movement. Although it is represented on the outer turns of the labyrinth, eternal life is experienced in the certainty that the centre is, in reality, close at hand. The points of Paradise and Judgement are passed through in this section. Pilgrims treading the Christian labyrinth should somehow experience the sequential processes through which they will have to pass to reach the Holy City. In the medieval Christian labyrinth pattern, the labyrinthine motifs of life and death have been modified to accommodate the beliefs of the faith.

The pattern of the labyrinth is related also to the ancient Greek *chorus*. In pagan times, this was a body of dancers who performed in the *orchestra*, which was 'a levelled ground strewn with sand, hence called "konistra" or "place of dust",' according to R. Maisch in his *Greek Antiquity*. Furthermore, 'Originally it was circular, and long kept this form.' The dancers of the *chorus* danced around an altar or an image of a deity at the centre of the *orchestra*. Writing in *The Attic Theatre* (1898), A.E. Haigh noted that, 'Lines were sometimes marked on the floor of the *orchestra* to assist the chorus in their evolutions.' Clearly this is yet another example of the dance's being marked out by lines as an aid to its correct performance.

Perhaps the tradition of the church labyrinth is derived ultimately from pagan Greek practice, transmitted by way of the rituals of the

Byzantine Church. This is a plausible route, for the revival of Roman-style mosaics in the West in medieval times was due to Desiderius, abbot of the Benedictine monastery on the holy mountain of Monte Cassino, Italy. Desiderius had been sent as papal legate to Constantinople, and on his return to Monte Cassino in 1066 he reintroduced Byzantine architectural techniques to the West. There he established a school of mosaic work under the direction of Greek masters.

From Monte Cassino, the knowledge and use of mosaic pavement work were spread and developed into various distinct forms. Mosaics in which glass or enamel was employed were known as 'Cosmati work' after the Greek family Cosmas, the chief exponents of the style during the thirteenth century. The alchemically symbolic pavement at Westminster Abbey, laid in 1269, is of Cosmati work. Another form, *Opus Alexandrinum* whose invention was attributed to the Emperor Severus (222–35 CE), was made in Italy exclusively of porphyry and serpentine, but in northern Europe coloured marbles, usually red, dark green, white, yellow and black, were substituted for the rarer stones. A third type of paving revived at this time was *Opus Sectile*, otherwise called *Opus Sartulatum*, which was composed of large slabs of coloured marble. The best ancient example of this work is in the Pantheon in Rome, built on the orders of the Emperor Hadrian around the year 115 CE. It was this type of paving which was most suited to labyrinth construction. Much of the early medieval development of mosaic pavements which led to the church labyrinths took place in Italy. The earliest surviving labyrinth pavement, in the chapel of San Zeno in the church of Santa Prassede in Rome, was made of marble slabs. The pavement of Santa Maria in Trastevere, also in Rome, was laid out on the orders of Pope Innocent II (1130–43) and contains a labyrinth, much altered. A small labyrinth also exists at the church of Santa Maria in Aquiro, likewise in Rome. It is laid out in porphyry and yellow and green marble.

The tomb of William, Count of Flanders, who died in 1109, also had a significant influence on later church pavement design. He was buried in the abbey of St Bertin in Saint-Omer, and the associated mosaic included the signs of the zodiac. Executed in the second half of the twelfth century, the pavement used engraved stones or dalles, their hollows filled with coloured cement. Saint-Omer appears to have been a major centre of the manufacture of these dalles, as they appear in the zodiacal surrounds of the *Opus Alexandrinum* pavement at Canterbury Cathedral. N.E. Toke noted that the dalles at Saint-Omer and Canterbury are of commensurable size, using a modified 'Roman foot' of 295 mm (11.61 inches). Emmanuel Wallet, in his work on the abbey of St Bertin, noticed that the pavement stones there used the old 'Saint-Omer foot' of 270 mm (10.63 inches). This is thought to suggest that the dalles were made at Saint-Omer by Italian workmen using their own craftsmen's measure. Like the Canterbury pavement, the St Bertin pavement had dalles bearing the signs of the zodiac and the labours of the seasons.

3.6. Continental church labyrinths: a: San Vitale, Ravenna, Italy, sixth century (extant); b: Chartres, France, *c.* 1220 (extant); c: Sens, France, (destroyed 1769); d: Bayeux (extant).

The best-known labyrinths were laid in cathedral pavements, mainly in France. The possibility that these French labyrinths were derived from Italian models cannot be discounted. France is at the crossroads of two seemingly parallel traditions: the Mediterranean labyrinth (as represented in pagan form by that at Kato Paphos and in Christian guise by San Vitale at Ravenna) and the Germanic-Norse-Celtic tradition from the north of Europe.

A perfect example of the microcosmic symbolism which they contained is the octagonal labyrinth in the cathedral of Notre Dame at Amiens, known as 'The House of Daedalus', after the Cretan myth. It was constructed in 1288, according to an inscription which was inlaid around the octagonal stone at its centre. This was a grey marble slab, inlaid with copper plates, similar to the monumental brasses familiar in English churches. It consisted of a central cross, orientated towards the cardinal directions through alternate vertices of the octagon. Four human figures occupied the spaces between the angles of the cross. These were effigies of Bishop Evrard de Fouilloy and his three master masons, Robert de Luzarches, Thomas de Cormont and Regnault de Cormont, the latter two being father and son.

At the points of the cross were the spiritual guardians of the four directions – the archangels Gabriel, Uriel, Michael and Raphael, Jewish archangels whose names superseded the pagan divinities invoked in the Etruscan Discipline. According to the Belgian researcher Paul de Saint-Hilaire, this cross indicates the orientation of the cathedral towards the winter solstice. In his work of allegorical alchemy *Le Mystère des Cathédrales*, Fulcanelli interpreted the central stone as emblematic of the rising sun, here, at midwinter. In medieval times the main relic of Amiens Cathedral was a piece of skull, reputed to be that of St John the Baptist (another was kept at the Grand Mosque in Damascus!). The Baptist's holy day is the old Midsummer Day, and if the church was oriented towards midwinter sunrise, it would be oriented automatically to midsummer sunset as well.

The labyrinthine pathway is of the medieval Christian design, though it is laid out as a black pathway on a white background. It was one of the largest pavement labyrinths, measuring 13.2 metres (43 feet 4 inches) in diameter. It appears to have been the model upon which the octagonal labyrinths at Arras (destroyed in the French Revolution) and Saint-Quentin were copied. This labyrinth at Amiens was destroyed between 1825 and 1828. Writing in *The Bible of Amiens*, John Ruskin noted that the labyrinth 'was removed to make the old pavement more polite'. Fortunately it was reinstated in 1894. The octagonal pavement at St Quentin's basilica in the town of Saint-Quentin was laid out in 1495 after the fashion of that at Amiens.

This labyrinth measures 11.6 metres (35 feet 4 inches) across, with a black pathway divided by black 'walls'. It is known as the *Lieue de Jérusalem* (the League of Jerusalem). At the centre is a black octagon.

The labyrinth at Reims was an octagon with four 'bastions', something like a rectilinear version of the Saffron Walden turf maze. Laid down in 1240, it measured 10.6 metres (35 feet) across. At the centre was an effigy of Aubri de Humbert, who laid the cathedral's foundation-stone in 1211, whilst the four master masons who oversaw the work were commemorated inside the four bastions. The figures were ascribed as follows: to the right of the entrance, the Master Bernard de Soissons, master mason for thirty-five years, tracing a circle with his compass; opposite, the image of Gaucher de Reims, master for eight years; the other two bastions were filled by the masters Jean de Loup and Jean d'Orbais. According to J.B.F. Géruzez, the Reims labyrinth was an emblem of the interior of Solomon's Temple at Jerusalem. The pathway was of dark stones – blue according to W.H. Matthews, and to Saint-Hilaire, black and white. In 1779 Canon Jacquemart, annoyed by children who enjoyed themselves on the labyrinth during services, had it destroyed. He paid 1,000 *livres* to obliterate the masons' sacred monument. Where he got the money from is unrecorded. Like most cathedral labyrinths, that at Reims was located in the western part of the nave, with the entrance to the west.

Another medieval version of this 'bastioned octagon' design was found in 1954 on a stone in the parish church at Genainville, Seine-et-Oise, France. Another slightly different version was used later by G.A. Boekler in his *Architectura Curiosa* of 1664. Finally it appears to have influenced Sir Gilbert Scott in designing his maze of 1870 for Ely Cathedral.

The labyrinth at the Cathedral of Notre-Dame at Chartres is undoubtedly the world's most famous pavement labyrinth, being used as the typical image of the labyrinth in many media. This dates from the thirteenth century, between 1240 and 1260, the date at which the church was completed. It appears that it was traditional to lay the labyrinth pavement upon the completion of the work, as at Amiens and Reims. 'The Chartres labyrinth is absolutely the same in design as one on the door jamb at Lucca,' wrote W.R. Lethaby, 'with this difference, that the former, thirty feet across, is ornamented at the centre, and the latter is but a scratched line. This one in turn is exactly like that on the Hereford Map of the World, and that one also in the sketch book of Vilars de Honecourt, with the only exception that this last is reversed. These four, then severally in Italy, France and England, are absolutely related – in form and proportion, number of walls and planning of their revolutions, they are all transcripts of one another or a common original.' This pattern is commonly called the 'medieval Christian labyrinth' and has served as the model for many others, including the existing turf mazes at Alkborough, Breamore and Wing. The frequently reproduced engraving of the labyrinth from Gailhabaud's *L'Architecture de Vme au XVIIe siècle* (1858) is incorrect, for it shows far too few scallops around the perimeter. There are in fact 113.

The pathway at Chartres is delineated by white stones, separated by black dividers. This pathway formerly bore verses taken from the 51st Psalm, which allude to Jerusalem's walls. Verses 18 and 19 read: 'Do good in thy good pleasure unto Zion; build thou the walls of Jerusalem. Then shalt thou be pleased with the sacrifices of righteousness, with burnt offerings and whole burnt offerings: then shall they offer bullocks upon thine altar.' This is another instance of the Roman 'walls of the city' motif and also, allegorically, of the bull (Minotaur) connection. At the centre of the Chartres labyrinth was a stone showing the traditional Roman motif of Theseus and the Minotaur, the whole labyrinth measuring 12.87 metres (42 feet 2 inches) across.

The name of the labyrinth, *La Lieue* (The League), is an allegorical measure, like the customary 'mile' of British turf mazes. Its actual length is about 137 metres (450 feet), whilst the 'league' used in medieval times in the Eure-et-Loire district was something nearer 2,088 metres (6,850 feet). To walk the maze properly and in the correct pious frame of mind was equated with a pilgrimage to Jerusalem. In addition, if the layout of the church is taken to denote the crucified Christ, various parts of the church relate to his body. This was the standard church symbolism of the medieval period. The position of the feet in this correspondence is that place traditionally reserved for pavement labyrinths. This 'foot connection' existed in the cathedral labyrinth at Właclawec in Poland and in the turf 'Shoemaker's Races' at Shrewsbury and Słupsk. The labyrinths in the French cathedrals of Reims and Chartres (among others) were located with regard to the underlying sacred geometry of the buildings.

Like many virgin-centred cathedrals in this region, Chartres had a 'Black Madonna', as did Guingamp, another place with a pavement labyrinth. These images, known from France to Poland, are believed to be a Christian continuation of pagan worship of the Great Mother

3.7. The St Bertin type of labyrinth. The square design is from St Bertin's Abbey (extant) and Notre-Dame Cathedral (destroyed) at Saint-Omer. A similar labyrinth, dating from 1445, was in the church of St Euverte at Orléans. A maze of this design was laid in 1985 in the parish church at Batheaston in the county of Avon. The smaller labyrinth (1533) is near the chapel's entrance in the City Hall at Ghent, Belgium.

Goddess at the same site. The mazes at Amiens, Arras, Bayeux, Chartres, Reims and Saint-Omer were all in churches or cathedrals dedicated to Our Lady. The centre of the labyrinth at Guingamp has the words '*Ave Maria*' inlaid in black-letter characters. At some time in their history, the Amiens, Chartres, Guingamp, Ravenna, Reims, Saint-Quentin and Ghent labyrinths have all had a special stone, the 'goal' of the pilgrimage, at their centre. In Christian tradition, the 'goal' of the pilgrimage to Jerusalem was the rock upon which the Holy Sepulchre church was built, the same stone into which, it was believed, the tomb of Christ was hewn.

A labyrinth of the 'Chartres design' with an extra central circle exists in the chapter-house of the cathedral at Bayeux, Calvados. This one is small, measuring 3.78 metres (12 feet 5 inches) across. It is composed of circles of tiles ornamented with shields, gryphons and fleurs-de-lys, separated by bands of black tiles. The use of such heraldic ornament in the medieval cathedrals of France and England was widespread, some of the tiles coming from the same workshops. This is not surprising, as it should be remembered that during the genesis of medieval pavement labyrinths, France and England were nominally the same kingdom, with considerable interchange of craftsmen, techniques and information. The rightly famed ornamental tiles at Great Malvern Priory, Hailes Abbey and Titchfield in Hampshire, are fine examples of this art. It is surprising that in England there is no evidence for any medieval church labyrinths, for very complex mosaics exist at Canterbury, Westminster Abbey and Salisbury, where the octagonal motifs could well form a labyrinth like that at Amiens. Excavations during the 1970s and eighties of complex mosaics at Warden Abbey in Bedfordshire and at Norton Priory in Cheshire offer the possibility that a future excavation may reveal a full-scale church labyrinth somewhere in Britain.

The nearest thing found so far is a curious spiral pavement 'maze' in the floor of the parish church of St Peter's at Thornton in Leicestershire. It was located at the west end of the church in front of the entrance to the tower. It was not a Christian labyrinth design, however, but a simple spiral form, composed of fifteen stone slabs which became progressively smaller from the outside towards the centre, where it was finished with bricks. When a new floor was laid in 1975, the vicar contacted the archaeology department of Leicester University, which conducted an excavation amid accusations of sacrilege. Before it was dug up, Paul Devereux and his colleagues, who were conducting a study of Leicestershire's geology, unusual

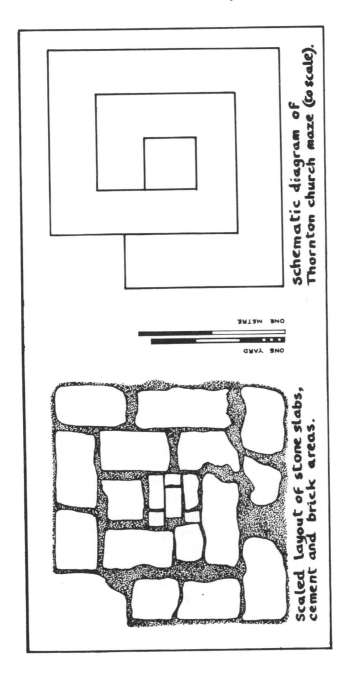

Schematic diagram of Thornton church maze (to scale).

ONE METRE

ONE YARD

Scaled layout of stone slabs, cement and brick areas.

3.8. Plan of the spiral pavement 'maze' at Thornton, Leicestershire.

phenomena, traditions and antiquities, examined it and produced an accurate scale drawing. The maze measured approximately 1 metre 62 cm (5 feet 4 inches) along each side. Various suggestions were put forward to account for this feature, which appears to be unique in British church architecture. Most prosaically, it was explained as a font-base or just an inept piece of floor-patching. But Paul Devereux discovered that there was more to it than that. Local people knew of it as a maze, and there is also the Scandinavian link between St Peter and the labyrinth. Clearly the Thornton maze is one of the most enigmatic floor patterns in an English church.

Like its Roman forebear, the medieval Christian labyrinth design was not always large enough to walk upon. The design exists in a small form at Mirepoix, where it encompasses nine floor tiles, each of which measures 23 cm (8 inches) across. It was laid around 1530 in the bishop's private chapel. The whole labyrinth pattern is encompassed in the nine tiles. The square tile at the centre contains a representation of the Minotaur. Guingamp, Côtes-du-Nord, has a nineteenth-century labyrinth in a side chapel of the basilica of Notre-Dame-de-Bonsecours. It is a copy of that at Chartres but measures only 5.5 metres (16 feet 9 inches) across. The path is laid out in black tiles with red walls, and at the centre are three fleurs-de-lys and the text '*Ave Maria*' in neo-Gothic lettering. Another nineteenth-century labyrinth was built in the church of Notre-Dame-de-la-Treille at Lille. Laid out in the 1850s, it was octagonal, a copy of those at Amiens and Saint-Quentin.

A curious group of rectangular and square pavement labyrinths is based on the former labyrinth at the abbey of St Bertin in Saint-Omer, Pas-de-Calais. This measured around 14.6 metres (44 feet 6 inches); the date of its construction is unrecorded. At Saint-Omer there is a connection between megalithic monuments and a legendary maze-founder. There the tomb of St Erkembode (also called St Archembault), abbot of St Bertin's, who, died in 737 CE, is a monolithic stone believed to be megalithic in origin. St Erkembode is also held to be connected with the cathedral at Sens, which also sported a labyrinth. The date given at Sens, however, is 968 CE, so it may have been another monk with the same name. Even so, this is an interesting 'coincidence'. The influence of Saint-Omer may reflect its former importance as a place for the manufacture of dalles.

The square labyrinth in Notre-Dame Cathedral in Saint-Omer is a sixteenth-century copy of the original. Known as '*Le Chemin à Jérusalem*' ('The Path to Jerusalem'), it has a white marble pathway divided by black marble 'walls' and, like the St Bertin labyrinth, is laid out on a grid of forty-nine by forty-nine squares. Because it is square, it bears a superficial resemblance to Roman labyrinths. However, on closer inspection it can be seen that it does not follow the Roman pattern at all but is derived from the medieval Christian pattern. A new feature is the obvious incorporation of the Christian cross in the design. The St Bertin design has been copied several times. One early copy was at the church of St Euverte in Orléans, whilst another, made in the 1980s, exists in England at Batheaston. The City Hall at Ghent, Belgium, has another version of this pattern, derived from the St Bertin design. This is a reduced version in which certain elements, such as the cross, are retained, but the number of turns is reduced, and a fylfot pattern is introduced. This design is unknown elsewhere. Built in 1533, the Ghent labyrinth is located near the entrance of the municipal chapel, 'the place of tribunals, and is said to have been used for penitential purposes.

Other French cathedrals possessed labyrinths of varying design, but many are lost. That at Auxerre was destroyed about 1690, and its design is not recorded. However, this labyrinth was associated with *pelota*, a ball-game played by the clergy, with accompanying music and dance, on the labyrinth itself. A cathedral decree of 1396 records that the rules of this game stipulated that the ball was to be supplied by a newly ordained priest. On the afternoon of Easter Sunday the ball was presented to the dean. It had to be sufficiently large so that a player had to use both hands to hold the ball. Holding the ball under one arm, with his free hand the dean took the hand of the nearest priest, who linked with the others in the same way, forming a chain. Then, accompanied by the organ, the hymn '*Victimi Paschali Laudes*' was sung. The 'snake' of priests would wend its way around the labyrinth with the *tripudio*, the three-step dance. As the procession proceeded, the dean would throw the ball to one of the dancers, who would throw it back to him. This would continue, with different priests catching and throwing the ball until the ceremony ended. After the dance, a feast was held in company with the local noblemen. Finally, after the feast, at which appropriate biblical texts were read, the participants attended Evensong. This unusual ritual was performed annually until 1558, when it was suppressed. Clearly the symbolism and timing of this sacred labyrinth dance and ball-game were emblematical of the death and resurrection of Christ. The hymn, sung during the dance on the labyrinth, was about Christ's victory over death, and his entry into and exit from Hell. It is probable that the ball represented the sun, a symbol in its own right and in medieval

Christendom symbolic of Christ as *Sol Resurrectionis* (the Sun of Resurrection). A folk tradition, formerly current in Britain, Switzerland and Scandinavia, told of the sun's 'dancing' on Easter morning. In former times people would wait for sunrise on Easter morning in the hope of observing this phenomenon. The movement of the ball around the labyrinth echoed this belief and symbolized the sun's daily movement in and out of the underworld.

Poitiers is another French cathedral which possessed a pavement labyrinth once. Although its design survives as a schematic wall-painting, the date of its obliteration is unrecorded. Also it is possible that at Poitiers it was not in the cathedral at all but in the church of St Radegonde. The magnificent example at Sens, Yonne, which measured 9 metres (30 feet) across, was formed from incised lines into which molten lead had been poured. Its design, with a large central circle, was reminiscent of the Breamore turf maze and possibly that which existed at Leigh in Dorset. It was obliterated in 1768 or 1769. The labyrinth at Arras, Pas de Calais, a copy of that at Amiens, was destroyed at the Revolution. Another existed at St Stephen's Abbey in Caen. Measuring about 3 metres (10 feet) in diameter, it was destroyed in 1802.

Outside France, a labyrinth of unknown design existed formerly at the church of St Severin in Cologne. It had an image of a knight in combat with a devil-like horned figure, a twelfth-century version of Theseus and the Minotaur. It was destroyed in 1840. There were no more church labyrinths in Germany until a new one was laid in 1977 at the foot of a staircase in Cologne Cathedral. It is a small octagonal design, 1.4 metres (4 feet 6 inches) in diameter, too small to walk, with a pathway of white marble and 'walls' of black basalt. There are no recorded medieval church pavement labyrinths in the British Isles, although there is a roof-boss in the church of St Mary Redcliffe in Bristol, dating from the fifteenth century, which is of the medieval Christian design. It can be found over the north aisle. Another ecclesiastical labyrinth carving exists at the church of St Lawrence, Rathmore, County Meath, Ireland (map grid reference N 753670). Like the Bristol example, it is a medieval Christian design, measuring 35 cm (14 inches) across. It was dug up in 1931. In 1866, the Rev C.R. Conybeare laid a circular Christian brick labyrinth in his new church at Itchen Stoke, Hants. It is still in existence.

Occasionally Canterbury has been mentioned as having had a pavement labyrinth, for example in *The Architectural Dictionary* of 1867, W.R. Lethaby's *Architecture, Mysticism and Myth* and William

3.9. Sir Gilbert Scott's labyrinth of 1870 in the pavement under the west tower of Ely Cathedral, Cambridgeshire.

Matthews' *Mazes and Labyrinths*. But Colin Dudley, the cathedral's historian states categorically: 'There is no record of any kind of maze in the Cathedral, nor in the precincts.' It appears that a Tudor hedge maze that existed once at the royal lodge which was once St Augustine's Abbey, about 200 metres (220 yards) to the east of the cathedral, has been confusedly ascribed to the cathedral's pavement.

But there is one cathedral in Britain which does have a labyrinth. In 1870 Sir Gilbert Scott laid one in Ely Cathedral (map grid reference TL 541803), during restoration of the fabric. The design that he chose was a new unicursal one, however, based on no known medieval ecclesiastical labyrinth. It was laid in white stone with 'walls' in black and is based upon a square with 'bastions'. It is small, measuring 6 metres (20 feet) across. It is located in the west end, almost in the customary position of labyrinths in French cathedrals. Its existence can be attributed to the mid-nineteenth-century revival in ecclesiastical mysticism. It was constructed shortly after the British architects Clutton and Burges won first prize in the competition for the labyrinth-containing church of Notre-Dame-de-la-Treille at Lille

3.10. The 1875 maze in the parish church at Bourn, Cambridgeshire. This is an altered version of the Hampton Court puzzle maze.

in France. Its symbolic location in the church was expressed by W.R. Lethaby in his 1892 book *Architecture, Mysticism and Myth*: 'Left behind in the west end of the church was the labyrinth of the lower world, but the holy place, raised seven steps, was heaven itself.' A copy of this maze was laid in 1981 in the cathedral at Pietermaritzburg in the Republic of South Africa. The choice of this design appears to have been influenced by the fact that Scott's maze was the only one in a Protestant cathedral.

Around the same time as Scott's labyrinth foray, in 1875–8, the floor was lowered and a labyrinth was laid in red and black tiles in the parish church of St Helena and St Mary at Bourn in the same county of Cambridgeshire (map grid reference TL 325563). It is located beneath the west tower, as is that at Ely, but its design is not unicursal, being a squared-up copy of the seventeenth-century puzzle maze at Hampton Court. In 1912 the font was moved from its original site and re-erected on top of the maze, thus destroying the pattern.

A fourth Victorian church maze was laid in 1897, when the church at Alkborough, Lincolnshire (map grid reference SE 882219), was

12 The turf maze formerly at Kaufbeuren, Bavaria, Germany, during
a dance festival in 1937. This maze was destroyed by the military in
1942 for the erection of a barracks on the site

13 The Rad turf maze at the Eilenriede Forest, Hanover, 1940.
This is the only ancient turf maze still extant in the Federal Republic
of Germany

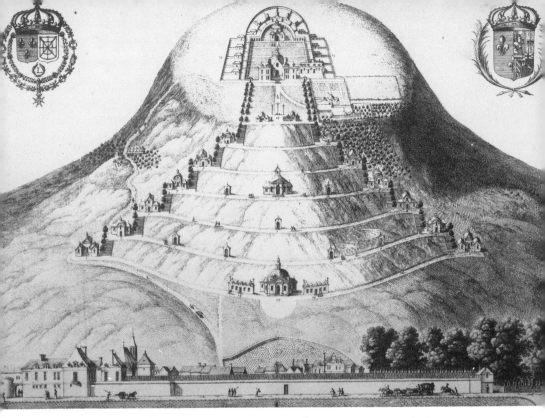

14 Mont Valérian, near Paris. Seventeenth-century engraving showing terraced pathway with chapels dedicated to the Stations of the Cross. After the Revolution, this Calvary Mount was converted into a military fortress, which was destroyed by the Prussian Army in 1871

15 The medieval spiral pavement 'maze' in the church at Thornton, Leicestershire, before alterations to the church

16 The traditional labyrinth dance being performed at Ostmarsum, in the Netherlands, in 1939. The dancers, holding hands, coil inwards and outwards in a manner identical to the Cornish labyrinthine 'snake dance'

17 Temporary brick-walled maze of double-meander Roman design constructed by Nigel Pennick at Art in Action, Waterperry House, Oxfordshire, 1987

18 Aerial view of Hever
Castle, Kent, showing the hedge
maze, planted in 1905 and still
flourishing

19   Stone labyrinth constructed on the shore at Camp, County Kerry, Ireland, August 1988. This design, built by an international team, used the 'Baltic-German' maze design with two entrances and a spiral centre

20   The largest turf maze in the world, at Willen, Milton Keynes, with an oak tree planted at the centre. This is close to a 'pagoda of peace', although labyrinths are not part of the Buddhist tradition, being connected in the popular mind with Christian monasticism

21   The first permanent stone labyrinth in North America. Laid out
by Nigel Pennick in California in 1986

22   London's only urban labyrinth – the pavement maze at
Warren Street

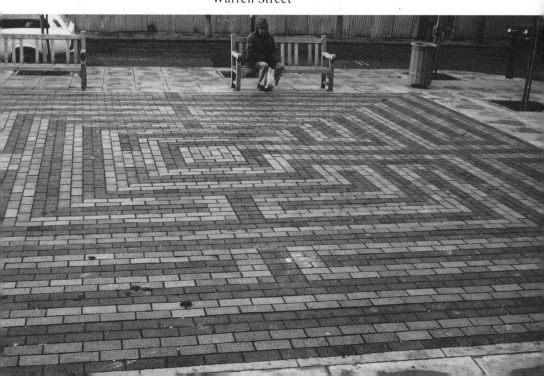

23 The memorial to the sculptor and maze-maker Michael Ayrton
over his grave in the churchyard at Hadstock, Essex. The bronze
plaque it bears is a model of the walkable brick-walled maze he
constructed in the late 1960s at Arkville in New York State, USA

restored at the behest of J. Goulton-Constable, the lord of the manor. He arranged that a design should be cut in the flagstones of the church porch and inlaid with cement as a record of the design of the nearby Julian's Bower. This church also has the design reproduced in stained glass in a window over the altar, and in less permanent form in embroidered 'kneeler' cushions. Goulton-Constable's tombstone in the village cemetery is in the form of a Celtic cross with a labyrinth at the centre. It dates from 1922. Another labyrinth tombstone can be seen in the churchyard at Hadstock in Essex (map grid reference TL 559448), where the sculptor, author and maze-maker Michael Ayrton (1921–75) is buried. On the stone is a bronze model of the maze that Ayrton made at Arkville in the United States.

A pavement maze based on the medieval Christian labyrinth design can be walked in a playground at Warren Street in central London (map grid reference TQ 293821). Designed by John Burrell, it uses the central seven rings of the Christian labyrinth design, modified to make it a puzzle maze laid out as a square in red and black brick pavers.

The most recent British ecclesiastical pavement labyrinth at the time of writing is at Batheaston, near Bath (map grid reference ST 777679). There, in 1985, a modern church labyrinth was laid by the Revd Paul Lucas. It is located in the south aisle and is another example of the St Bertin type. It is made of local stone and measures 5 metres (16 feet 6 inches) square.

Other Ecclesiastical Labyrinths in the British Isles

Labyrinthine architectural features on churches are much rarer than one might imagine. In the British Isles there is little documentation of carved labyrinths, and it is possible that many have been lost without record.

However, there is one important survivor of the medieval period, and this is not in one of the great cathedrals but in the church of St Mary Redcliffe at Bristol (map grid reference ST 611729). This parish church contains a fifteenth-century roof-boss in the form of a gilded medieval Christian-pattern labyrinth. The boss measures 20 cm (8 inches) across and is the only known labyrinth roof clave in a medieval church. Although Merton College, Oxford, is said to possess a medieval roof boss that shows a rabbit or hare running around a labyrinth, enquiries have proved fruitless. The whole matter of labyrinths in Oxford is complex, but it appears that only the turf mazes at Temple Cowley and the former block hedge maze at Trinity College have solid documentary evidence.

The Watts Memorial Chapel stands in the village graveyards at Compton in Surrey, 3 km (2 miles) south of Guildford (map grid reference SU 956474). This is a most remarkable building, in the 'Arts and Crafts' style, planned as a Greek cross, clad with symbolic ornament. It was designed by Mary Watts as a memorial to her late husband, the painter George Frederick Watts, and shows the symbolic influence of the Arts and Crafts architecture mystic William Lethaby. It was erected in 1896, five years after Lethaby's influential *Architecture, Mysticism and Myth* was published. His idea was that architecture should be a synthesis of the fine arts and crafts that express eternal philosophical and psychological principles in symbolic form. The Watts Memorial Chapel is based on that principle. Internally, the chapel is decorated in a lavish cladding of gesso, carved and painted with angels and exuberant interlacing patterns of Celtic inspiration. The altar is most notable, for three angels support a labyrinth whose design is an eleven-circuit form similar to, but not the same as, the medieval Christian pattern. Beneath the altar labyrinth is the text 'He shall dwell with them.' Externally, the overhanging upper parts of four quarter 'apses' are clad in terracotta panels bearing angels surrounded by Celtic and Art Nouveau interlace patterns. Each of these upper portions is supported by three corbels in the form of angels, with wings folded above and below. Each angel holds a circular 'shield', four of which are incised with a unicursal labyrinth. Externally, the labyrinth design is the seven-circuit pattern of the pavement labyrinth at San Vitale, Ravenna, as reproduced on p. 151 of Lethaby's *Architecture, Mysticism and Myth* (see fig. 4.8).

The church of St Regnus at Burt, County Donegal, Ireland (map grid reference C 365212), is another very unusual building. Built in the mid-1960s and consecrated in 1967, it is a circular building 31 metres (103 feet) in diameter, with walls 4.5 metres (13 feet) thick, the curious dimensions being derived from the nearby hill-fort of the Grianan of Aileach. The church doors all have metal handles bearing the Classical labyrinth design, the 'walls' being broken to create a Christian cross from the pattern. Externally, there are a number of panels, one of which has an unbroken Classical labyrinth.

Because the labyrinth can take many forms, each of these forms has been utilized as a means for expressing some aspect of religious symbolism. In this vein, Wyck Rissington in Gloucestershire had one

3.11. Plan of the now-destroyed hedge maze at Wyck Rissington, built after a dream vision by Canon Cheales.

of the most unusual hedge mazes ever constructed in Britain. In 1950 Canon Harry Cheales had a dream in which he was commanded to create a maze in what was then a tangled, overgrown thicket in the rectory garden. The dream was a classic revelation of its kind. 'It was as though a blank screen appeared before me,' he said in 1969, when recounting the labyrinth's genesis, 'and a pattern of white light was traced on it like toothpaste from a tube. As soon as it was light, I went outside in my pyjamas and, in fact, I found the traces of a pathway through the thicket exactly as the dream had foretold.'

Five years of work went into the perfection of the maze, which involved planting boundary hedges of yew, privet and willow. Finally the path was about 700 metres (765 yards) long, a chaotic, winding design unlike any of the traditionally well-planned puzzle mazes. However, unlike most puzzle mazes, it was full of Christian symbolism.

It was based on the 'Mystery of the Rosary', containing the fifteen 'Mysteries' of the Gospels. 'Our life is a journey,' explained Cheales (see Stares, Bibliog.). 'The feet and yards of the path through the maze are the months and years of our time. The junctions are the decisions we have to face and the wrong turnings represent the mistakes we make. The centre symbolizes Heaven.'

Canon Cheales held an annual ceremonial walk, on St Laurence's Day, the day of the tutelary saint of his church. Pilgrims were encouraged to enter the maze in a spirit of reverence, as a form of open-air worship. At the place representing death was a notice requesting those who did not believe in the after-life to take a certain path; if they did, they found themselves outside the maze and missed the goal. Regrettably, upon his retirement the maze was destroyed by his successor. However, the design is not lost, for a memorial to Canon Cheales designed by Adrian Fisher, in Wyck Rissington parish church, records the labyrinthine plan in mosaic.

Another maze, built some years later, was also the result of a dream experienced by a Church of England clergyman. In his enthronement sermon, on 25 March 1980, the then new Archbishop of Canterbury, Dr Robert Runcie, said: 'The trouble is, to get to the centre [of the maze]. It is easy to get lost. I had a dream of a maze. There were some people close to the centre, but they could not find a way through. They had taken a wrong turn right at the very beginning and would have to return to the start if they were to make any further progress. Just outside the maze, others were standing. They were further away from the heart of the maze, but they would be there sooner than the party that fretted and fumed inside. I long to be able to speak, while archbishop, with men and women who stand outside the Christian Church. I would say to them: "You can teach us so much if together we could look for the secret of the maze-like muddle in which the world finds itself." '

As at Wyck Rissington, a maze came into physical being as a result of the archbishop's dream. Lady Brunner suggested making the maze on her estate at Grey's Court at Henley, Oxfordshire (map grid reference SU 725834), and the maze-makers .at Minotaur Designs were commissioned to design and construct it. The design is based on Christian symbolism, as the Crown of Thorns laid out in bricks in a cruciform design. It is a seven-circuit design, a reduced version of the medieval Christian pattern. The seven rings of the maze symbolize the legendary seven days of the Creation. At the centre the turfed area measures nine times the width of the turf between the pathways. This signifies the nine hours of Christ's passion. At the centre there are two crosses, a simple cross of Bath stone within a Byzantine cross of blue Westmorland stone. They denote the hoped-for reconciliation between the Churches of the East and West, Orthodox, Catholic and Protestant, an important aspect of the archbishop's beliefs. At the centre of the two crosses, one placed within the other, stands a pillar surmounted by an armillary sphere sundial, reminiscent in some ways of the Hilton turf maze. Also near the centre, where the path makes its final turn, is a lozenge-shaped inscription which records the labyrinth's dedication: 'This maze was dedicated by Robert Runcie, Archbishop of Canterbury, 24th October, 1981.'

The path of the maze brings the walker within sight of the goal, which in Christian terms is salvation, but she or he cannot immediately reach it. As in the medieval French cathedral labyrinths, the place where the path turns away from the centre is death, and from there the path winds outwards again to the perimeter. Then, as with the traditional designs, it comes back again to the centre. The maze combines both the traditional unicursal pattern and a puzzle dimension. If the true path is followed, it is unicursal, with one single, tortuous way to the centre. In following this, one crosses over the diamond-shaped thorns, tracing the Path of Life. This pathway is around 400 metres (440 yards) long, contained in a relatively large labyrinth measuring 26 metres (85 feet) in diameter. But there are also cross-overs as short-cuts, making it materially different from traditional church labyrinths, which are strictly unicursal.

This idea of making short-cuts was adopted later at Milton Keynes in the Willen Bowl labyrinth, which also has a religious connection, but with the Buddhist faith and not with the Christian. Seemingly the labyrinth continues as a universal figure of faith to this day.

4

The Origin and Development of Puzzle Hedge Mazes

Of course the varieties in the mere design of mazes would be
infinite; their resemblance is the striking fact, so that, considered
merely as a device or pattern, the tradition is one for the two
thousand years from the Greek coin of Gnossus to Botticelli's
print in the Renaissance, and we wonder how it passed from place
to place. There are no false paths, not a single *cul-de-sac*, but
simply the longest involved path, from the entrance to the eye;
you follow far enough, and necessarily reach the centre. When the
root of the tradition was broken away from at the Renaissance, all
this was altered, and mazes became inventions, every one
different from the others – spiders' webs of enticing false paths.'

William R. Lethaby, *Architecture, Mysticism and Myth*

The Devotional Labyrinth

As has been shown above, the 'medieval Christian' labyrinth design,
was derived from earlier Roman labyrinth designs. It seems that in
Christian terms this new form was intended to symbolize the city of
Jerusalem, the object of pilgrimage. Originally drawn small or carved
on walls, as at Lucca, the Christian labyrinth came into its own when
it was laid as a pavement inside a church. These are said to have been
used by the devout, who held crawling round them on their knees to
be the spiritual equivalent of a pilgrimage to Jerusalem. This idea was
promoted in 1858 by Edward Trollope, later suffragan bishop of
Nottingham. However, this attractive theory is no more than that, for
there is no contemporary documentation of pilgrims traversing
labyrinths whilst kneeling.

Writing in *Ecclesiastical Curiosities* in 1899, George S. Tyack stated that, 'Easy substitutes for the more exacting devotion were found in many ways. The introduction of the custom of following the Stations of the Cross is ascribed to this cause, the devout following in imagination of the footsteps of the Saviour in His last sufferings, being accounted equivalent to visiting the holy places; and somewhat similarly, the maze, or labyrinth, is said to have been pressed into the service of religion ... being reckoned as a simple substitute for a longer pilgrimage.'

Whether or not they were substitutes for pilgrimage, these labyrinths proliferated during the thirteenth century in French cathedrals (e.g. Chartres, 1220; Reims, 1240; Amiens, 1288). Around that time the design reached England, where it was applied to new or recut turf mazes. As mentioned in Chapter 2, many turf labyrinths were constructed at sacred sites where observances may have taken place on the appropriate saints' days. Among these were St Anne's Well at Sneinton, near Nottingham, where a holy well, chapel and subterranean rock-cut hermitage accompanied the labyrinth, known as 'Robin Hood's Race'. In Northamptonshire; at Boughton Green, a turf labyrinth accompanied a chapel dedicated to St John, and at Winchester the labyrinth chapel was dedicated to St Catherine.

Basing his ideas on *Meditations on the Life of Christ*, by the Italian Franciscan monk, St Bonaventure, the Dominican mystic Heinrich Suso (*c.* 1295–1365) re-created a 'way of the cross' in his meditations in the manner now known as 'pathworking' or 'guided imagery'. In this meditational technique, one visits in spirit each of the 'Stations of the Cross' in turn, experiencing Christ's torture for oneself. Because politically it was becoming increasingly difficult for pilgrims to visit Jerusalem to walk the path of the real Stations of the Cross, someone came up with the brilliant alternative that the stations could be re-created physically in European holy places. The progressive pathway of the unicursal labyrinth was the conceptual model which this followed. When visiting Jerusalem, pilgrims stopped to pray at the places said to be the actual stations. Representations of the original seven stations were placed inside the church, to be visited in turn by the devout. (Later, in 1731, these seven were increased to fourteen.) But the mere following of a pathway inside a church was rather effete for those with a taste for the more robust aspects of Christian asceticism, so it was not long before a Franciscan monk, Bernardino Caimi (died 1499), thought up the idea of displaying the stations outdoors, along a pathway up a holy mountain, making the pilgrims

Vtinam dirigantur viæ meæ ad custodiendas iustificationes tuas! Psal. 119.

17.

4.1. Engraving by Boetius von Bolswart for Hermann Hugo's *Der christliche Seele im Labyrinth der Welt.*

exert themselves to reach them. This may be a development of the sacred pathways or 'holy hill alignments' to chapels or labyrinths on top of sacred peaks. (For further details, see Pennick and Devereux, *Lines on the Landscape*.) Accordingly Caimi fashioned the first Cavalry Mountain, in the foothills of the Alps at Varallo, northern Italy. The idea soon caught the imagination of the devout, and other Calvary Mountains were instituted, for example at Orta (1583) and Varese (1604). One of the largest was made in France at Mont Valérien in 1633 by a religious order established with the express function of managing these new holy mountain shrines. Mont Valérien had fifteen chapels dedicated to the Passion, linked by a pathway whose only method of ascent was back-and-forth and ever upward, very similar to a straightened-out unicursal labyrinth (fig. 3.5).

The motif of pilgrimage as an ascent appears in other Catholic Counter-Reformation works of the period, especially *The Ascent of Mount Carmel* by St John of the Cross (1542–91). In true labyrinthine fashion, *The Ascent of Mount Carmel* begins by picturing a man setting out from a known land by night by way of a path he cannot understand towards a goal he cannot see. At that time the standard Christian unicursal labyrinth was still a symbol of salvation or damnation. This is best illustrated by an engraving by Boetius van Bolswart (1580–1634) in the Jesuit Hermann Hugo's *Die christliche Seele im Labyrinth der Welt* (*The Christian Soul in the Labyrinth of the World*), written as an illustration of Psalm 119. It shows pilgrims walking on top of the walls of what appears to be a hedge maze. One hapless soul has fallen between the walls, whilst another, standing at the centre, holds a cord, the other end of which is held by an angel standing on top of a tower upon which a beacon fire is burning. The pilgrim who has gained the centre of the labyrinth has also gained salvation, linked to God's messenger by the ubiquitous labyrinth motif of the thread.

Non-Devotional Garden Mazes

A secularization of this sacred theme may be accounted as one of the origins of the garden labyrinth, and thus of the puzzle maze. Some of the earliest features in Renaissance gardens were small artificial hills or 'mounts' upon which 'rustic' temples were erected. The antiquary John Leland, writing in 1540 of Wressel Castle, near Howden in Yorkshire, described these patterns: 'The gardens within the mote, and the orchards were mounts *opere topiaro*, written about with degrees like the turnings in cokill shelles, to come to the top without payn.' This seems to imply that some sort of topiary work bordered the paths. Access to these features was often by a spiral path, and the whole ensemble was related geometrically to the garden, which was laid out in 'knots'.

First recorded as early as 1494, the knot garden or 'flower knot' consisted of a small rectangular bed upon which a pattern was outlined in box, rosemary, thrift or some other low-habit plant. Usually the patterns were geometrical, and the spaces between them were filled with coloured gravels, minerals or even coal dust. These gravel fillings are equivalent to the pathways of a maze. The use of the work 'knot' appears significant here. The *Oxford English Dictionary* has many alternative definitions of the word, but in connection with the 'garden knot' the maze is mentioned. According to John Harvey, writing in *The Medieval Garden* (1981), by 1494 'a knot in a garden, called a mase' was a commonplace thing.

As early as the fourteenth century, the garden laid out on the orders of the French King Charles V (1364–80) at the Hôtel Saint-Pol in the upper Rue Saint-Antoine contained a labyrinth designed by Phillipart Persant, the royal gardener. But an important influence on maze construction at this period appears to have been through one of the main architectural works of the Renaissance, Alberti's *De Re Ædificatoria* (*On Building*), dating from 1452, which urged the restoration of the villa and garden of Roman antiquity. For the garden, it recommended symmetrical planting of trees and shrubs in geometrical forms related to the geometry of the villa itself. Alberti's gardens were to contain pergolas, groves and labyrinths. In fifteenth- and early sixteenth-century France, knot gardens and garden labyrinths outlined by low shrubs were fashionable. French shrub labyrinths of this period were known as *Dédales*, after Daedalus, mythical builder of the labyrinth of Crete. *Dédales* existed in the gardens of the Hôtel de Saint-Pol in Paris and in the park of Louise of Savoy in 1513.

An important feature of *Dédales* and knot gardens was the dwarf box plant. This had been used in Roman times to border gardens, and its use was revived in the Renaissance. In his *Paradisus*, John Parkinson, herbalist to Queen Elizabeth I and King James I, wrote of box that it ' ... serveth very well to set out any knot or border out any beds, for besides that it is ever greene, it being reasonable thick set, will easily be cut and formed into any fashion one will ...'

At this period flower-bed labyrinths became fashionable, and authors started to publish books showing their designs. The Italian architect Serlio published a number of maze plans for use in formal gardens in his book *Libri Cinque d'Architettura* (1537). In England, Thomas Hyll wrote an important work titled *A Most Briefe and Pleasaunt Treatyse Teachynge How to Dress, Sowe and Set a Garden.* Published in 1563, this book contains two 'herbal labyrinths' whose designs are versions of the medieval church and turf labyrinth pattern. The 1579 edition of his book emphasizes the herbal nature of the labyrinth, which he describes as ' ... proper adornments upon pleasure to a Garden'. A square maze published by Hyll is identical in design to a turf maze cut at Clifton, Nottingham. This plan was used later in a book by William Lawson, *A New Orchard and Garden* (1623), where it is shown with a tree at the centre.

In 1583 Jan Vredeman De Vries published *Hortorum Viridariorumque Formae* at Antwerp. The book contained plans for gardens, nine of which were in the form of labyrinths. These had pathways divided by flower-beds or shrub 'walls'. Around this time, the gardens of the Villa d'Este at Tivoli had four rectangular labyrinths, walled with shrubs, probably of dwarf box. Similar flower labyrinths are mentioned in Adam Islip's 1602 work *The Orchard and the Garden.* Curiously, a derivation of one of his maze designs, incorporating a circular part within a square one, exists as a stone labyrinth at Pahaluoto in Finland. Circular labyrinths of a similar form were popular at that time. They feature in illustrations of the period, such as a spring landscape by Lucas von Valkenborch (*c.* 1540–1625) and etchings by Hans Vol (1543–93). A painting of Edward, Lord Russell (1551–72), now in Woburn Abbey, shows the aristocrat with an inset picture of a simple gravel-pathed puzzle maze with the subject standing at its centre. A motto in Latin, *'Fata Viam Invenient'* ('Fate will find a way'), is written below the inset picture of the labyrinth. This dated labyrinth pattern is a perfect example of the transition between turf and gravel/flower labyrinths and later puzzle mazes. In 1983 a replica of this maze was constructed by Denys Tweddell and his assistants at Chenies Manor in Buckinghamshire, the reputed site of the original in the painting. Its pattern is based on a double-involute spiral, measuring 16 metres (50 feet) in diameter, clearly a modification of a sacred unicursal pattern.

It is most likely that many labyrinth designs, even those of turf mazes on village greens, were copied from pattern books, in the form of either manuscripts or printed volumes. For example, the design of the Clifton maze in Nottinghamshire was identical with the 'second

herbal maze' of Thomas Hyll. It may have been copied from the
second edition of his book *A Most Brief and Pleasant Treatyse
Teachynge How to Dress, Sowe and Set a Garden*, called *The Garderner's
Labyrinth*, published in 1579 under his *nom de plume* Didymus
Mountaine.

Another intriguing connection between built mazes and pattern-
books is in the surviving work of Thomas Trevelyon, reproduced in
The Embroidery Patterns of Thomas Trevelyon (Walpole Society, 1966).
Not much is known about him. He was born around 1548 and was a
Protestant writing-master of Cornish descent who lived near
Blackfriars in London. He drew at least two massive volumes of
designs. The first, done in 1608, is a manuscript 'commonplace book'
of embroidery patterns, consisting of 290 folios measuring 42.5 cm by
28 cm (16¾ inches by 11 inches), containing also such niceties as the
occupations of the months and a gazetteer of *Thomas Brentnor's
Almanach*. A larger document, consisting of 1034 pages, dated 12
September 1616, is also extant. A section titled 'The Greene Dragon
for Ioyners and Gardeners' includes the text ' ... here followeth some
thinges for Ioyners [joiners], and Gardeners, as Knots, and Buildyngs,
and Morysies and Termes, with many other thinges to serve their use
very well'. Amongst these is a labyrinth. Trevelyon is thought to have
copied many Continental engravings, as his work parallels several
well-known cuts of the period, and also that people went to Trevelyon
for all sorts of designs, including gardening, hence the 'knots' and
'morysies' (labyrinths). As at the present time the books of Trevelyon
appear to be unique, it is difficult to know how many such copyists
existed, making books available for tradespeople to consult when they
needed a design. But like the medieval architectural design book of
Villard de Honnecourt, it does point to the possibility that there were
books of labyrinth design around at the time. This period is only a few
years before the supposed dates of the first cutting of turf labyrinths
such as that at Hilton, and the first record of several others.

In 1613 Gervase Markham, in his book *The English Husbandman*,
asserted that knots were ' ... at this day of most use amongst the
vulgar though least respected with great ones, who for the most part
are given pover to novelties. You shall understand that Knots and
Mazes were the first that were received into admiration.' The fashion
was common enough for it to be condemned by none less than Francis
Bacon. In his essay 'Of Gardens', which gave instructions for devising
a green garden of four acres, he wrote: 'As for making knots or
figures, with divers coloured earths, that they may lie under the

windowes of the house ... they be but toyes: you may see as good sights, many times, in tarts.' This scathing attack of 1625 confirms that, in the puritanical view, garden ornament was frowned upon and the symbolic element of such patterns was not appreciated.

Bacon's viewpoint was, however, outside the mainstream of thought. Guillaume de Salluste de Bartas, who died in 1590, for example, saw things differently. In his paean to technology, *La Premier Semaine, ou la Création*, translated into English by Joshua Sylvester (1563–1618), Salluste de Bartas refers to the Garden of Eden as the formalized garden of the aristocrat:

> Musing, anon, through crooked walks he wanders,
> Round-winding rings, and intricate meanders,
> False guiding paths, doubtful beguiling strays,
> And right-wrong errors of an endless Maze:
> Not simply hedged with a simple border,
> Of Rosemary, cut-out with curious order,
> In Satyrs, Centaurs, Whales and Half-Men Horses,
> And thousand other counterfaited courses.

In Salluste de Bartas's time, the knot and floral maze, successor to the turf labyrinth, was on its way out of fashion. Condemned by Bacon and his generation, it was to succumb to the hedge maze, as prefigured by de Bartas's 'endless maze'. The unicursal form, perfectly fitted for religious observance or for ornamentation, was nothing short of boring when applied to the garden for the entertainment of bored aristocrats. William Lawson, in *A New Orchard and Garden*, published in 1618, referred to this aspect: 'Mazes well framed to a man's height, may perhaps take your friend wandering in gathering of berries till he cannot recover himself without your help.' By this time it seems that the only maze worth consideration by the garden-designer was the puzzle maze.

By 1663 this division was formalized. In that year the scientist and diarist John Evelyn published his *Plan for a Royal Garden*. This work was broken down in heading form, all that remains of most of it. Only one of these sections was actually finished: 'Acetaria, a Discourse on Sallets'. The unpublished sections VII and VIII would have been very interesting to us today, for they were: 'VII: Of Knots, Trayle Work, Parterres, Compartiments, Borders, Banks and Embossments. VIII: Of Groves, Labyrinths, Dedals, Cabinets, Cradles, Close Walks, Galleries, Pavilions, Porticos, Lanterns, and other Relievos of Topiary and Hortulian Architecture.' In Evelyn's reckoning, knots were divorced from labyrinths and 'Dedals', which by now were categorized among the trees and groves. During the Civil War and subsequent Commonwealth, Evelyn had been in exile on the Continent, and his ideas must have been influenced by what he saw there during his extensive travels. Exactly parallel with this was the suppression by Cromwell of many indigenous folk customs in England, during which time many turf labyrinths must have declined and vanished. The transition from knot garden and turf labyrinth to fully hedged puzzle maze appears to have been gradual, with a realization that, if the low box hedges were made higher, a structure would be produced in which it would be possible to get lost.

The French Renaissance garden at Gaillon, the *Château* of Georges, Cardinal d'Amboise, planted around 1510, contained square and circular unicursal labyrinths. The circular one had corner 'bastions', a variation known from some pavement labyrinths. In Italy, the Villa d'Este at Tivoli had gardens laid out in the 1540s, which contained at least four square labyrinths. These gardens were designed by the humanist antiquarian Pirro Ligorio for Ippolito d'Este, Cardinal of Ferrara, as a symbolic celebration of Hercules and Hippolytus. The illustrations available do not appear to be good enough to show whether Ligorio's labyrinths were unicursal or not. But it was a most celebrated garden, visited by many famous people of the period. An engraving of it appeared in France in 1573, and it was described by Pighius in his book *Hercules Prodicius* in 1587. François Schott's influential guide-book to Italy of 1600 included the gardens of the Villa d'Este.

The influence of the gardens of the Italian Renaissance, especially that at the Villa d'Este, was apparent in England in several late Tudor gardens. The influence has reasserted itself in modern times in the shape of an Italianate maze built in 1989 at Capel Manor at Waltham Cross to the north of London. But unfortunately the formal gardens of England of the sixteenth and seventeenth centuries, many of which contained mazes, have been utterly extirpated; not one remains intact. It is a sad fact that in England there is no garden, and hence no garden maze, that dates from before the Civil War.

King Henry VIII's famous Nonsuch Palace was erected on the site of the village of Cuddington, at the foot of the North Downs between Ewell and Cheam, whose population was evicted so that the village could be demolished to make way for the king's folly. The palace was erected between 1538 and 1547, an attempt to outstrip the French King Francis I's ostentatious palaces, especially Fontainbleau. The

4.2. Garden maze design. Left: Theobalds, Hertfordshire, *c.* 1560. Right: Design by André Mollet, *c.* 1641.

gardens included a puzzle maze to the west of the house. 'You will enter a tortuous path and fall into the hazardous wiles of the labyrinth,' wrote Anthony Watson. Thomas Platter, writing in 1599, stated that the maze's hedges were so high that one could not see through them. It is unusual for a hedge maze of that early period. It is possible that the maze was planted in imitation of those at Gaillon but was of a puzzle rather than a unicursal design.

At this period various kinds of mazes were part of the normal repertoire of the gardener. When Queen Elizabeth I was entertained by Lord Burghley at Theobalds in May 1591, a speech given in her honour by a gardener described a garden being constructed at Pymms, 6.5 km (4 miles) away:

> The moles destroyed and the plot levelled, I cast it into four quarters. In the first I framed a maze, not of hyssop and thyme, but that which maketh itself wither with wondering; all the Virtues, all the Graces, all the Muses winding and wreathing about your majesty, each contending to be chief, all contented to be cherished; all this not of potherbs, but of flowers, and flowers fairest and sweetest; for in so heavenly a maze, which astonished all earthly thought's promise, the Virtues were done in roses, flowers fit for the twelve Virtues, who have in themselves, as we gardeners have observed, above an hundred; the Graces of pansies partly-colours, but in one stalk, never asunder, yet diversely beautified; the muses of nine several flowers, being of sundry natures, yet all sweet, all sovereign.

This speech was written by George Peele, a metaphysical poet.

The gardens of Theobalds itself contained a famous maze, laid out around 1560, which had as its goal a statue of the goddess Venus. This feature of the maze was described by J. Neumayr in *Des Durchlauchtigen*, published at Leipzig in 1613: ' ... you come to a small round hill built of earth with a labyrinth around. It is called the Venusberg.' The surviving plan shows it as unicursal, of the form of one of Thomas Hyll's published labyrinths. This is the square one, with the design identical with the turf maze at Clifton. It is also the same design as a French one in the gardens of the palace of the archbishop of Rouen at Gaillon, with a minor access modification. John Evelyn records that the house and its gardens were 'demolish'd by the rebels' on 15 April 1643.

The Hortus Palatinus at Heidelberg was laid out by Salomon de Caus between 1613 and 1619. This had a simple hedge maze, made of concentric circles, at whose centre was an obelisk. It may have been derived from a square version which had existed at Jerusalem, as shown in a pictorial map of the Holy City published in 1588. Outside the city walls, in the Hortus Regius (Royal Garden) there was a primitive hedge maze composed of concentric squares with staggered entrances.

A maze of similar form to that at Heidelberg existed in the garden at Wilton, near Salisbury in Wiltshire, which was created by William Herbert, third Earl of Pembroke. It was visited in 1623 by John Taylor, 'The Water Poet', who described the circular maze thus: 'Moreover, he hath made his Walks most rarely round and spaceous, one Walk without Another (as the Rinds of an Onion are greatest Without, and less towards the Centre), and withal the Hedges betwixt each Walk are so thickly Set one cannot see through from one Walk who walks in the Other; that, in conclusion, the Work seems endless; and I think that in England it is not to be followed, or in haste will be followed.' (John Taylor, *A New Discovery by Sea, with a Wherry from London to Salisbury*, London, 1623.)

King Charles I bought Wimbledon House from the Cecils in 1639 as a present for his wife, Henrietta Maria. Its gardens were redesigned by André Mollet. They included a maze which may have been octagonal with integral corner 'bastions' as one of Mollet's published labyrinths shows. An account of the grounds, published in *Surrey Archaeological Collections* in 1871, shows that when it was expropriated by the Parliamentarians in 1649, the maze was composed of young trees: 'On the south syde of the saiyd turfed tarras they are planted one great maze, and one wilderness, which being severed with one gravelled alley, in or near the midle of the sayd turfed tarras, sets forth the maze to lie towards the east, and the wilderness towards the west; the maze consists of young trees, wood and sprayes of a good growth and height, cutt out into severall meanders circles semicyrcles wynding and intricate turnings the walkes or intervalls whereof are all grass plotts; this maze as it is now ordered, adds very much to the worth of the upper level.' The whole assemblage, 'late Parcell of the Possession of Henrietta Maria, the Relict and late Queene of Charles Stuart, late King of England', was valued by Cromwell's surveyor at £90. It is not clear whether this maze was destroyed at that time. A labyrinth existed at Wimbledon in the eighteenth century, and this has been taken as evidence of the survival of Mollet's maze beyond the Commonwealth period. However, it is no longer in existence.

An important octagonal hedged puzzle maze of this period still exists, in perfect condition, in the Herrenhausen Gardens in Hanover, Germany. Measuring 23 metres (75 feet) in diameter, it was laid out between 1666 and 1674. The maze was rebuilt in 1936–7 and refurbished in the 1970s, when the gardens, which are a brilliant example of the formal palace gardens of the late seventeenth century, were returned once more to their original splendour.

By the end of the seventeenth century, the hedge maze was the preferred form of labyrinth. Numerous examples of hedge mazes, existing and projected, are illustrated in the literature of the period. The fashion of the period was described by the French author Louis Liger of Auxerre in his book *Le Jardinier Solitaire*: 'A labyrinth is a Place cut into several Windings ... The most valuable Labyrinths are always those that wind most, as that of Versailles, the contrivance of which has been wonderfully lik'd by all that have seen it. The Palisades, of which Labyrinths ought to be compos'd, should be ten, or twelve, or fifteen foot high; some there are that are no higher than one can lean on, but those are not the finest. The Walls of a labyrinth ought to be kept roll'd, and the Horn-beams in them shear'd, in the shape of Half-moons.' Liger's work was translated into English and published with other material by F. Gentil in 1706 as *The Solitary Gardiner* by G. London and H. Wise.

The puzzle maze in the grounds of Hampton Court Palace (map grid reference TQ 161687) is the oldest surviving hedge maze in Britain. Certainly it is the most famous one. Although it may have originated in Elizabethan times, the present maze dates from a replanting in 1690. Its trapezoidal shape is unusual, being defined by the symmetrical layout of baroque paths in the 'Wilderness', the area in which the maze is located. The longest side of the maze measures 68 metres (222 feet). It covers about a quarter of an acre of ground. At first the hedge was planted in hornbeam, but later repairs were made with other species, including whitethorn, privet, holly, sycamore and yew.

The Hampton Court design has been the inspiration for a number of copies; however, usually these have been rectangular in outline, rather than the curious trapezoidal shape of the prototype. It has been imitated at least a dozen times in Britain, including those at Tatton Park, Knutsford, Cheshire, at a hotel near Tunbridge Wells, in some seaside 'pleasure beaches' in Lancashire and in a park at Sutton Coldfield. There are also copies and variants of the Hampton Court maze design in Australia and the United States. A nineteenth-century pavement maze in the parish church of St Helena at Bourn, Cambridgeshire, laid out in red and black tiles, is a rectangular copy of this design. Even the earliest 'behaviourist' experiments on laboratory rats in mazes used the Hampton Court design!

Being the most famous and long-lived puzzle maze in Britain, the Hampton Court maze has figured in literature. Daniel Defoe wrote of it in his *Tour Through Great Britain* as a 'labyrinth'. It is also the location of a famous comic incident in Jerome K. Jerome's *Three Men in a Boat*, in which Harris, rashly claiming knowledge of the maze, offers to conduct a party around it. 'It's absurd to call it a maze,' claims Harris, 'You keep on taking the first turning to the right. We'll just walk round for ten minutes and then go and get some lunch.' Of course, they are fated to remain in the maze for a considerably longer period!

4.3. Plan of the oldest surviving hedge maze in Britain – the famous maze at Hampton Court.

The Hampton Court Maze is still a great attraction: over half a million people a year visit it to suffer Harris's fate. The formula is to turn left on entering the maze, then right, right again, left, left, left and left. Then the visitor will be at the centre. To leave the maze without getting lost, one must first turn right, then right three more times, left at the next two turnings, and then one reaches the exit.

The Hampton Court 'Wilderness' once contained another maze, 'the Plan-de-Troy' which is shown (inaccurately) in J. Roque's engraving of 1736. Sometimes this is called 'the Hampton Court Little Maze'. Unlike the extant maze, this was made from tall espaliers, but it was demolished many years ago and replaced by a rockery. There was also a turf labyrinth somewhere in the vicinity, but details are not available. Hampton Court remains as the last ancient hedge maze in the area now covered by Greater London.

Kip's engraving after Knyff of Queen Anne's garden at Kensington Palace, 1708, shows two spirals with 'sharp-pointed cypresses' at the centre. These are clearly types of 'labyrinth', for two people and two dogs are seen walking in one of them. These are probably delineated by low box hedges a few centimetres high. But in his *Essay on Modern Gardening* of 1785, Horace Walpole describes the 'Siege of Troy' at Kensington, which, he reports, was a representation of military defence works. There, the yew and holly trees were cut 'to imitate the lines, angles, bastions, scarps and counter-scarps' of regular fortifications. Whether this labyrinth dated from the beginning of the eighteenth century is uncertain, but it may be associated with the fashion, current after the Duke of Marlborough's wars, to modify country estates to imitate the military fortifications of the time. In addition to the Kensington labyrinths, Kip's *Britannia Illustrata* of 1720 shows a number of other hedge mazes, at Wrest Park in Bedfordshire and at Badminton.

The Block Maze

An alternative variety of hedge maze popular at that period was the 'block', in which the pathway was made through an otherwise solid block of shrubs or a thicket, by 'plashing' the branches of limes or hornbeams together to make a continuous leafy wall. An alternative method was by filling the gaps between the paths with a mixture of evergreens and flowering shrubs. This type of labyrinth was known as a 'wilderness'. Unlike this, the 'standard' type of hedge maze has paths bounded by hedges of uniform thickness, called by Stephen

Switzer in his *Ichnographica Rustica* (1742), 'a labyrinth of single hedges or banks, after the ancient manner'.

The block type was popularized by the gardens at Versailles, where, towards the end of the seventeenth century, J. Hardouin-Mansart laid out a labyrinth for Louis XIV. In 1677 it was described by the fabulist Charles Perrault in his book *Labyrinthe de Versailles*, which was illustrated by Sebastien le Clerc. This was a block-type maze with rectilinear and curving pathways in which were located thirty-nine groups of hydraulic statuary supplied by water pumped from the River Seine by the '*Machine de Marli*'. This waterworks was the engineering wonder of its age, constructed by Swalm Renkin between 1675 and 1682, comprising fourteen water-wheels driving 253 pumps feeding the fountains and hydraulic statues through an underground labyrinth of piping. At the entrance to the maze was a statue of Cupid holding the clew. The Versailles labyrinth was destroyed in 1775.

At the end of the seventeenth and the beginning of the eighteenth century, block mazes were popular. In France, they existed at Choisy-le-Roi and Chantilly, both of which had spiral patterns which prefigure the design of Greg Bright's modern labyrinth at Longleat. The Choisy-le-Roi example was designed by M. Gabriel. In his late eighteenth-century book *Le Jardinier Solitaire*, Louis Ligier described this sort of maze: 'A labyrinth, is a place cut into several windings, set off with hornbeam, to divide them from one another ... The most valuable labyrinths are always those that wind most, like that at Versailles, the contrivance of which has been liked wonderfully by all that have seen it.' Some of the maze designs of Batty Langley, published in his *New Principles of Gardening* (1728) are derived obviously from the French model, being block mazes containing spiral and serpentine pathways, statuary and refuges. Other Batty Langley designs amalgamated traditional single-thickness hedge mazes with blocks of shrubs, a pattern which was followed in the nineteenth century by designers such as Nesfield. In the first half of the eighteenth century, block labyrinths existed at Trinity College in Oxford, at Belvoir Castle, Boughton and Exton Park.

The Destruction of Formal Garden Mazes

Although there was a considerable number of hedge mazes in English formal gardens, in the first part of the eighteenth century formal gardens were ravaged by the implementation of new ideas. Because of the fashionable association of mazes with the French formalized gardens of the Versailles type, the decline of such gardens spelt a decline for mazes too. From about 1720 onwards, 'landscape gardening', known on the Continent as 'le jardin anglais' ('the English garden') wiped out almost everything which had existed before, renaissance, mannerist, baroque and rococo. This means that all the mazes which once existed are gone, save for the Hampton Court example.

The origin of the reaction against formal gardens originated in European contacts with China, where the principles of geolocation or geomancy known as *Feng-Shui* were applied to the landscape for mystical reasons. In 1685 Sir William Temple published a curious work entitled *Upon the Garden of Epicurus*, in which Chinese landscape design, known in England as *Sharawadgi*, was first mentioned. Although the word *Sharawadgi* is of dubious provenance, perhaps from the Japanese, it was meant to refer to *Feng-Shui*. Ideas of *Feng-Shui*, without an inkling of its ethos or function, made a significant impact on European landscapes.

In 1712 Joseph Addison praised Chinese gardens, simultaneously denigrating European practice: 'Those who have given us an account of China,' he wrote in *The Spectator*, 'tell us that the inhabitants of that country laugh at the plantations of the Europeans, which are laid out by the rule and line; because they say, any one may place trees in equal rows and uniform figures. They choose rather to show a genius in works of this nature, and therefore always conceal the art by which they direct themselves. They have a word, it seems, in their language, by which they express the particular beauty of a plantation, that thus strikes the imagination at first sight, without discovering what it is, that has so agreeable an effect.' The supposed natural effect of *Feng-Shui*, whose results he had never seen, inspired Addison further: 'I would rather look upon a tree in all its luxuriancy and diffusion of branches, than when it is thus cut and trimmed into a mathematical figure: and cannot but fancy that an orchard in flower looks infinitely more delightful, than all the labyrinths of the most finished parterre.' Coincidentally, Addison had written an opera, *Rosamund*, about the maiden in the labyrinth. But with such words this arbiter of taste helped to turn away the next generation of landscape-designers from the pleasures and mysteries of mazes, and thus Bridgeman, Brown, Repton and their imitators swept away many an ancient maze in attempting to re-create the mystical Taoist landscapes of China on English soil.

Mazes in the Nineteenth Century

Although fashionable taste had moved away from formal gardens with labyrinths and towards naturalistic landscapes based on Chinese models, mazes still remained popular among many people. In the late eighteenth and for much of the nineteenth century, mazes flourished as adjuncts to the pleasure gardens and tea-gardens which could be found in almost every town. Because none survives now, the number and extent of them remain a little-documented subject. However, a considerable number are known, and many more must have existed. In London, for instance, White Conduit House in Islington; 'The Maze' in Chichester Place, Harrow Road; 'New Georgia', Turner's Wood, near The Spaniards, Hampstead, and Beulah Spa, on the South Bank, were all places where one could enjoy the pleasures of mazes. The Beulah Spa maze was referred to by Charles Dickens in his *Sketches by Boz*.

Mazes were not restricted to London pleasure gardens, either, being recorded from many parts of the nation. Rosherville Gardens at Gravesend had a maze as a tea-garden feature, whilst a copy of the Robin Hood's Race turf maze was a popular part of Poynter's tea-garden at Sneinton in Nottingham. It is the subject of the earliest-known photograph taken in that city. At Blofield, near Norwich in Norfolk, a maze existed in the grounds of a public house. No plan is preserved there, but the plan of the maze formerly at Whitefield House (later Overwater Hotel) in Uldale Parish, Cumberland, does survive. Designed by James McQueen, 'gardener, etc.', probably in the 1860s, this maze was rectangular, with a large 'goal'. It must have been typical of many which have gone unrecorded.

But it was in the gardens of stately homes and, to a lesser extent, in public parks that the great mazes of this period were built. In a less commercial and more stable climate, some of these have survived. Alfred Fox designed a curious non-rectilinear maze at Glendurgan, near Falmouth, Cornwall (map grid reference SW 772277) in 1833. Measuring 40.5 by 33 metres (133 by 108 feet), it is planted in laurel. It survives today in gardens owned by the National Trust, but it is only open to the public on some days during the summer time. Reputed to be one of the oldest hedge mazes was a copy of the Hampton Court maze at the High Rocks Hotel, near Tunbridge Wells in Kent. Planted in laurel, it measured 51 by 27 metres (146 by 88 feet). Other interesting Victorian mazes were made at Mistley Place at

Manningtree in Essex, at Arley Hall in Cheshire, at Debdale Hall at Mansfield Woodhouse in Nottinghamshire, and at Sudeley Castle in Gloucestershire. The maze at Arley Hall was hexagonal and composed of lime trees, an unusual choice of species for a hedge maze.

4.4. The maze at Chevening, the first which used the principle of islands to make its solution much more difficult.

Like the original Hampton Court maze, the early puzzle mazes could be 'solved' by the 'hand-on-wall' method. This involves following the left-hand wall consistently, in and out of dead ends, until one reaches the centre or exit. In 1820, however, Earl Stanhope, an eminent mathematician, designed a new type of maze. He designed at least three similar mazes, one of which remains at Chevening in Kent (though it is not open to the public). Stanhope was the first maze-designer to realize that it was possible to create a puzzle maze which could not be solved by the 'hand-on-wall' method. His new design located the 'goal' at the maze's centre in an 'island' inside the maze. If the 'hand-on-wall' method is used in this sort of maze, a person entering will be returned to the entrance. With 'islands', the maze-designer creates mazes-within-mazes, which could be removed without altering the essential pathway to the centre. The maze at Chevening is square and based loosely on Roman and medieval unicursal labyrinth patterns but incorporating Stanhope's new element – the 'island'. Like that at Hampton Court, this maze spawned many copies. The Chevening plan was copied at Beauport House, near Hastings, and also at Anerley, North Woolwich, and through them 'island' mazes became popular. McQueen's maze at Whitefield House, for example, was an 'island' maze.

Bridge End Gardens, at Saffron Walden in Essex, have an early Victorian puzzle maze which was allowed to deteriorate almost to the point of loss but which was then restored to its former glory. The gardens themselves, which are now a public park, date originally from the eighteenth century, but the maze was laid out in 1838–40, when yew saplings three or four years old were planted. The maze was designed by Francis Gibson, perhaps in collaboration with William Nesfield, and contained statues, a pavilion and a wrought-iron viewing platform. It was in good order in the early part of the twentieth century, being open to the general public for the admission fee of sixpence. Neglect from 1949 meant that by the early 1980s sycamore and elm saplings had become established, and the yew was overgrown, making the former maze into a ragged thicket. In 1983 it was decided to reconstruct the maze, and the existing yews and other trees were felled and uprooted by members of the British Trust for Conservation Volunteers. Examination of the tree-rings on the felled yews showed that they dated from 1835–6. It is probable that they originated then in a plantation and in 1838–9 were transplanted to form the maze. Over the next twelve years they grew quickly, and by 1852 they were being trimmed to make the appropriate maze hedges. For the next ninety-seven years the maze was trimmed and kept in good order. But after that, for the following thirty-five years, growth was unchecked. The self-seeded sycamores felled at the same time had thirty-five rings, dating them to 1949, when the maze was abandoned to nature. After felling all of the trees but two, which were left at the northern tip of the maze, to preserve a small part of the original, the ground was ploughed and covered with farmyard manure. In the autumn of 1984 the cleared area was sprayed with weed-killer, and the maze was relaid.

Tony Collins, an employee of the Planning Department of Uttlesford District Council, carried out some archaeological excavations to determine the original plan. According to local lore, the maze was supposed to be a copy of that at Hampton Court, but this proved to be incorrect. A plan of the maze, at variance with that on the 1877 Ordnance Survey map, had been supplied to the council by Minotaur Designs, who had in turn received it from the Caerdroia Project archives. Excavation proved that the Ordnance Survey map did not show the original design. Presumably it recorded the state of the maze in 1877, which had been altered at some time, knowingly or accidentally, from the original. Fortunately the Caerdroia Project's plan was proved to be the original, and the restorers used it to lay out the reconstruction. Archaeological excavation of the site, the only maze to be excavated so far, revealed a nineteenth-century brick kiln, from which the bricks used in the garden had come, as well as prehistoric flints which were nothing to do with either the garden or the maze, predating it by millennia. Remains of Victorian wine bottles and oyster shells indicated that the maze had been the location for picnics or parties at that time. Excavation also showed that the paths had been dug out to a depth of 15 cm (6 inches) and filled with medium-grade shingle. The paths had been worn down and reshingled at a later date, perhaps in 1918. As reconstructed, the maze at Bridge End Gardens is a worthy example of Victorian maze design and a tribute to those who worked on its reinstatement.

4.5. Plan of the Victorian hedge maze in Bridge End Gardens, Saffron Walden, Essex, reconstructed in the 1980s after thirty-five years of neglect.

4.6. Designs by William A. Nesfield. Top: Hedge maze at Somerleyton Hall, Suffolk (extant). Below: Hedge maze at the Royal Horticultural Society Gardens, South Kensington (destroyed).

William Andrews Nesfield, whose name has been associated with the Saffron Walden puzzle maze, was a retired naval officer who abandoned his second career as a painter in water-colours to pursue the design of gardens. Somerleyton Hall, near Lowestoft in Suffolk (map grid reference TM 494980), still contains a puzzle maze laid out by him in 1846. It measures 74.7 by 48.8 metres (245 by 160 feet) and is planted in yew. Its pathway is 402 metres (440 yards) in length, terminating at a small pagoda on an artificial knoll. It is a rather baroque shape, being based on a series of arcs centred upon five foci, the main one of which is the central circle at the 'goal'.

As well as designing the Somerleyton Hall maze, Nesfield also prepared plans for Kew Gardens, but his most famous maze design was that in the Horticultural Society's gardens at South Kensington. These were made on land bought from the profits of the 1851 Great Exhibition and leased to the Horticultural Society. They covered 23 acres (56.8 ha) which stretched from Exhibition Road to Prince Albert Road, now known as Queen's Gate, extending northwards to the site of the Royal Albert Hall. The gardens were divided into three sections, the 'ante garden' of which contained the maze, whose plan is illustrated here. At the 'goal' of his maze was a statue of Galatea, which replaced the fountain originally planned. Beyond the maze was the principal garden, with geometrical flower-beds, and the third division, a terrace with two bandstands and a conservatory. The garden is described in *Beeton's Book of Garden Management* (1861): 'The general effect of these gardens cannot fail to exercise a beneficial influence on the art of laying out ornamental flower-gardens.' In the 1880s the garden was destroyed by building development. The site of the maze is occupied now by the Science Museum. Also, when the 1851 Great Exhibition in London's Hyde Park had ended, amid protests and counter-arguments, the Crystal Palace was taken down as had been promised before the exhibition. It was re-erected at Sydenham, where a circular hedge maze was constructed in its grounds, later rooted out.

Another maze with Nesfield influence can still be visited. In 1886 a member of the Harington family designed a maze in the grounds of Worden Hall, in Leyland, Lancashire (map grid reference SD 537209). It was planted in beech and had a central mound as a goal, being a copy of Nesfield's Somerleyton Hall maze. It is now in Worden Park, the hall having been destroyed by fire in 1943. Tatton Park, at Knutsford, Cheshire (map grid reference SJ 744814), another copy of Hampton Court, was laid out around 1890 in beech. It still exists and measures 35 by 18 metres (114 by 60 feet).

Mazes in the Twentieth Century

A generation after the High Victorian period, the formalized floral and architectural elements of Victorian gardens were considered objectionable, and much was obliterated. Some of the objections to mazes were tied up with the important nineteenth-century concept of progress, which was enshrined in various doctrines by intellectuals such as Charles Darwin and Karl Marx. In his book *The English Flower Garden*, W. Robinson expressed the typical view of people whose views were coloured by this doctrine of progress: 'The Maze is one of the notions about gardening which arose when people had very little idea of the dignity and infinite beauty of the garden flora as we now know it.' Furthermore, influential gardeners such as Gertrude Jekyll shunned the maze, which could not be accommodated within their naturalistic ethos.

But not everyone agreed that the maze was *passé*. In this period the striking square maze at Hever Castle, near Edenbridge, Kent (map grid reference TQ 478452) was laid out by William Waldorf Astor. Completed in 1905, it marks the place where King Henry VIII courted Anne Boleyn and measures 22.8 metres (75 feet) along each side. In her 1911 book *Garden Design in Theory and Practice*, Madeline Agar wrote that in parkland, 'A maze is almost as great an attraction as a sheet of water, and might be introduced if room can be afforded.'

Between the world wars, building puzzle mazes was not very popular. In 1922 W.H. Matthews expressed the opinion that their day was past and that maze-building would never again become generally popular. 'Let us admit at once,' he wrote, 'that, as a favourite of fashion, the maze has long since had its day ... Like every other defunct mode, the topiary labyrinth is liable to temporary revivals by lovers of the antique, but there is little reason to hope or fear that it will ever again secure a position of any dominance in the affections of the gardener.' The few mazes built at this time bore out his pessimism.

Yet another copy of the Hampton Court design was laid out 1933–7 in privet at the Pleasure Beach, Blackpool, Lancashire. This was copied at the corresponding pleasure beach at Morecambe but was destroyed in 1987. (In 1979 a copy of the Morecambe maze was made at 'Pleasureland' at Southport in Lancashire.) In 1935 the maze at Hazlehead Park in Aberdeen (map grid reference NJ 895054) was laid

4.7. Victorian hedge mazes, Top: Plan of maze formerly at Whitefield House, Uldale Parish, Cumbria (after James McQueen, courtesy of Cumbria County Record Office). Below: Plan of maze at Hatfield House.

4.8. Labyrinth-bearing angel corbel designed by Mary Watts, 1896; Watts Memorial Chapel, Compton, Surrey. The labyrinth is that of San Vitale in Ravenna.

out in privet by Sir Henry Alexander.

The park was given to the citizens of Aberdeen by Sir Henry, and the maze, which measures 58 by 49 metres (190 by 160 feet) is still maintained. Directly and indirectly, the Second World War caused the destruction of a number of hedge mazes, and the enforced neglect of many others. Those at Totteridge Park, Debdale Hall and Arley Hall were lost through neglect. The military destroyed yet another, paralleling the obliteration of the Boughton Green maze in World War I. The circular hedge maze at Belton House, near Grantham in Lincolnshire, was cut down and a military building was constructed on its site.

After the war, little was done in the maze world. The Bridge End Gardens maze was abandoned in 1949, but the few notable examples which exist today were maintained. But in 1959 a 'Tree Maze' was constructed at Victoria Park in the North Bay district of the seaside town of Scarborough in north Yorkshire (map grid reference TA 038895). Possibly inspired by those at Blackpool and Morecambe, the Scarborough maze was built by the borough council as an attraction for summer visitors. Still extant, it measures 41 by 31 metres (135 by 100 feet), being planted in privet. However, its site is far from ideal. It is planted on a slope, and it was closed during the wet summers of 1987 and 1988. In 1963, inspired by the success of the first one, the Scarborough Borough Council planted another, this time on the other side of town, in the South Bay district (map grid reference TA 045875). This one, uniquely in a small clifftop urban square overlooked by large houses, was also rectangular and planted in privet, measuring 32 by 22 metres (105 by 72 feet).

In 1962, the year before the second Scarborough maze was commenced, two other hedge mazes were laid out. One was at Blackgang Chine on the Isle of Wight and the other at Chatsworth House in Derbyshire. The Blackgang Chine maze (map grid reference SZ 485768) was designed by John Dabell and planted in privet. It measures 27.5 by 24.5 metres (90 by 80 feet). It is floodlit at night during the summer. The Chatsworth maze was planted on the site of the Great Conservatory, Joseph Paxton's forerunner of the Crystal Palace (map grid reference SK 263697). Designed by D.A. Fisher, this maze is in yew and measures 40 by 35 metres (130 by 115 feet).

Despite these notable examples of the maze-maker's art, it is really to the 1970s and eighties that we must look for the renaissance of maze-construction which continues today.

5

Modern Labyrinths: The Return of Symbolism

From the middle of the 1950s until his death in 1975, the sculptor Michael Ayrton explored the theme of the labyrinth. Like many earlier mystics, he viewed it as supremely symbolic of the human condition. It is clear that his enthusiasm and deep understanding of the theme were the major instigating factors behind the present renewal of interest in labyrinths at all levels.

His investigation of the mythological aspects of the subject originated with a revelatory experience which he underwent in Italy at the Acropolis of Cumae on 11 May 1956. In myth, this was the landing-place of Daedalus after his flight from Crete, and historically it was the sacred *locus* of the oracle known as the Cumaean Sibyl, a great 'place of power' by any account. Ayrton entered the labyrinth-like cave system where the oracle had once pronounced her soothsayings, and felt that he had heard her voice in 'a hundred rushing streams of sound' through the openings in the rock.

After this numinous experience, Ayrton identified himself with Daedalus, 'the Maze-Maker'. His sculptures ranged through the Cretan legend of Theseus, including Daedalus, Icarus, the Cumaean Sibyl and the Minotaur, whom he saw as an image of the agonies of evolution out of the animal and towards the human condition. His first labyrinthine writing was *The Testament of Daedalus* (1960), which dealt with the legendary flight of Daedalus and Icarus out of Crete. Later in 1967, he wrote a book about Daedalus, *The Maze-Maker*, which he called 'a transposed autobiography' and his publishers called a novel.

In January of the following year, the New Zealander George

Wooller commissioned Michael Ayrton to cast a golden honeycomb for him, according to the technique that Daedalus had described in *The Maze-Maker*. Working with the goldsmith John Donald, he made seventeen attempts before finally achieving the perfect cast. Ayrton's masterpieces, two bronzes became the centre-pieces of his labyrinth, which was commissioned by the New York financier Armand G. Erpf. It was constructed at Arkville, in the Catskill Mountains in New York State. This monumental puzzle maze has walls of brick and stone 2.5 metres (8 feet) high, creating seven 'decision points'. Ayrton used 210,000 bricks in its construction, producing an enormous array of walls measuring 70 metres (200 feet) across. Its pathways measure 512 metres (1680 feet) in length. At the centre of its coils are two chambers. They both contain sculptures by Ayrton. One is of the Minotaur, the other is of Daedalus and Icarus. Daedalus is shown working at maze-making, whilst Icarus, winged, leaps upwards to fly from the labyrinth.

In *The Rudiments of Paradise* (1971) Ayrton gave a brief history of the labyrinth in the final chapter 'The Making of a Maze', from Knossos to Arkville. He noted that in his local town of Saffron Walden there were three mazes: in the church, the Town Maze on the common and the Bridge End Gardens maze. Unfortunately Michael Ayrton never had the chance to build a maze in Britain, but a small bronze replica of the Arkville Maze can be found on the memorial over his grave in the churchyard at Hadstock in Essex (map grid reference TL 559448).

Modern Thoughts on Maze Design

The recent renaissance of interest in mazes has led to new concepts in maze-making, of which some of the most important protagonists have been Greg Bright, Adrian Fisher and Les Wood.

In his book *Mazes and Mandalas* (1981) Les Wood suggests designs for two 'walk-in' mazes, one a hedge puzzle maze and the other a 'cryptomaze'. The meander maze is octagonal, without dead ends, all nodal points giving an even chance of success or failure.

Les Wood suggests that the most rapid way to build a maze is to use cyclone wire mesh suspended from three strands of wire threaded onto galvanized iron posts. Into this mesh, varigated ivy and flowering creepers can be woven, giving the impression of a hedge maze.

At Zürich airport, in the open area next to the cafeteria in the departures section, is a most unusual puzzle maze which uses this principle. It is composed entirely of galvanized steel mesh, into which some plants have been intertwined to give the impression of a hedge maze. It was designed by Stefan Rotzler and set up in 1985–6. In it, one walks on a floor of steel mesh, and the 'goal' has a mirrored floor.

Although such mazes are rapid to construct, both their appearance and their ecological appropriateness are open to question. To be successful, gardening in general, and labyrinth design in particular, requires to be conducted in a manner appropriate to the conditions at hand. This is the practice of geolocation, which includes the topography of the site, its orientation with regard to the diurnal and annual motions of the sun, the patterns of watercourses, and the prevailing winds.

There is a tradition which governs the location of features inside mazes. This is dealt with in *Ichnographia Rustica*, written between 1718 and 1742 by Stephen Switzer (*c.* 1682–1745), which describes the locational principles to be applied to garden statues. In his system, which was derived from traditional principles of geolocation, specific statues were related to specific classes of spaces: '*Jupiter* and *Mars* should possess the largest Open Centres and Lawns of a grand Design, elevated upon Pedestal Columnial, and other Architectornical Works ... *Neptune* should possess the Centre of the greatest Body of Water ... *Venus* ought to be placed among the *Graces, Cupid, &c.* And in all the lesser Centres of a Polygonar Circumscription, it would be proper to place *Apollo* with the *Muses* in the Niches ... Then *Vican* with the *Cyclops* in a Centre of less note, and all the Deities dispers'd in their particular Places and Order.' Such principles were applied to the location of statuary in hedge mazes. They should be taken into account when modern maze-designers attempt to re-create or simulate the mazes of this period. In *Ichnographia Rustica*, Switzer describes a 'Labyrinth of single Hedges or Banks after the ancient Manner' which echoes these principles.

The Modern Maze Resurgence

From the middle of the 1970s until the present day, there has been a great resurgence of traditional-style maze-building in Britain. Mazes of all types have been constructed by both public bodies and private individuals. Below are some of the more notable examples.

Surprisingly few have been made to commemorate national events. One exception is the maze at Springfields Gardens in Spalding, Lincolnshire (map grid reference TF 264243), which was built to commemorate the Silver Jubilee of Queen Elizabeth II in 1977. Designed by Peter Atkinson, it was planted in Leyland's cypress and measures 23 metres (75 feet) square.

One of the largest mazes in Britain, claimed at the time of construction to be the largest in the world, was laid out in 1978 by Greg Bright at Longleat House, Warminster, Wiltshire (map grid reference ST 807433). It is said to be Britain's first three-dimensional maze, having six wooden bridges, a system which allows a greater number of possibilities than in a maze on one level. It measures 116 by 54 metres (380 by 175 feet). Since its construction, it has been disputed whether this is indeed the largest. One in Japan is said to be bigger, whilst the more recent maze at Margam in South Wales is claimed to have a longer array of paths. One of the Milton Keynes mazes, which is not a hedge maze, however, is even longer.

A maze at Ragley Hall, Alcester, Warwickshire, designed by Maurice Rich, is square with block walls and dates from 1980. Another maze built in 1980 is at Traquair House, Peeblesshire. Designed by John Schofield, it measures 45 metres (147 feet) square and is planted in Leylandii. The Jubilee Maze at Symond's Yat West, near Ross-on-Wye in Herefordshire, dates from 1981, having been designed by Edward and Lindsay Heyes to commemorate the Queen's Silver Jubilee. It is octagonal with a 'temple' at the centre, measures 41 metres (135 feet) across and is planted in Lawson's cypress. Cawdor Castle, Nairnshire (map grid reference NH 847498), has a hedge maze dating from 1981 laid out in the form of a double-meander Roman labyrinth copied from one at Coimbra in Portugal.

Some modern mazes have been made for overtly symbolic purposes. None is more ironic than that at Canolfan Y Dechnoleg Amgen (the Centre for Alternative Technology), which can be found 4 km (2½ miles) north of Machynlleth in Powys. Designed by Pat Borer and constructed in 1982, this maze symbolizes the processes of government environmental decision-making!

Over the past few years, the maze-design and construction company Minotaur Designs has been busy constructing new mazes of various kinds, mostly in Britain. The earliest maze classified as a Minotaur maze was laid out in private grounds at Throop, Bournemouth, Dorset, in 1975. Called 'Embryo', it was designed by Adrian Fisher. Made of holly, it measured 32 by 22 metres (105 by 75 feet). The second Minotaur maze is a footprint-shaped hedge maze called 'Imprint' was made in yew by Randoll Coate in a private garden at Lechlade in Gloucestershire in 1975. It is shaped like a human footprint, with one toe in a river as a separate island, linked to the maze by a bridge. The whole maze contains symbolic representations of 'the fundamental symbols of man': the two genders, the Christian trinity, the four elements, the five senses, the ten planets (*sic*), the twelve signs of the zodiac etc. The next two mazes made by a Minotaur designer were at the Château de Belœil in Belgium, titled 'Pyramid', and at Varmlands Saby in Sweden, which was called 'Creation' (1977 and 1979 respectively); both were hedge mazes designed by Randoll Coate.

The Lappa Maze, at the Lappa Valley Railway, St Newlyn East, Cornwall (map grid reference SW 839558), was laid out in 1982. It consists of brick paths laid in grass and measures 49 by 31 metres (161

5.1. Plan of the unique unicursal hedge maze at Cawdor Castle, Scotland, a double-meander labyrinth (cf. the Harpham labyrinth, Fig. 3.2. which is a triple-meander).

by 101 feet). Its design is based upon the world's first steam railway locomotive, designed and built in 1804 for the Penydarran Tramroad by the Cornish engineer Richard Trevithick. The maze is laid out on a scale eight times the original size of the locomotive. The goal is the locomotive's flywheel crankshaft. The construction of this novel design seems to have set a precedent, as another 'locomotive' maze was built in 1984 at Springfield Park at Forest Hall near Whitley Bay in north Yorkshire. This is a design based on George Stephenson's 1829 locomotive *Rocket*.

Another form of symbolism can be found in the octagonal maze which was designed by Minotaur for the Duke and Duchess of Roxburgh and planted in beech at Floors Castle in Roxburghshire in 1983. Like several Minotaur designs, this maze contains within it images which relate to the character or history of the place. This one contains representations of the six different pieces in chess; a boar's head and unicorn from the achievement of the Duke; the portcullis of Westminster and the wheatsheaf from the Duchess's coat of arms; a holly leaf with red berries; and an exploding cannon. These last two images refer to an incident on 3 August 1460, when King James II was laying siege to the castle. The images are marked out by being planted in copper beech, visible from an octagonal pavilion at the centre of the maze.

Also in 1983, a copy of a maze known only from a painting was made at the Manor House at Chenies in Buckinghamshire. After the maze at Clifton Hall in Nottingham, recut in 1981, the Chenies maze was only the second 'reinstatement' of an ancient turf maze. It is to be hoped that it will not be the last.

In Britain, 1984 saw not the triumph of George Orwell's 'Big Brother' but the construction of an unprecedented number of mazes. If anything, 1984 was 'The Year of the Maze'. In that year Minotaur Designs built their 'Dragon Maze' at Newquay Zoo in Cornwall. In his book *After Man – A Zoology of the Future*, Dougal Dixon had visualized the possible results of 50 million years of evolution beyond the present, pessimistically, after the demise of our kind. Ten of these speculative 'future organisms' were produced as sculptures to be arranged as five groups of two, predator and prey. They were arranged in a hedge maze planted in *Eleagnus* in the form of a dragon with a coiled-tail entrance. It measures 64 by 29.5 metres (210 by 85 feet).

The most curious maze from Minotaur Designs was also made in 1984. Constructed at Thorpe Park at Chertsey in Surrey, it was built around a series of scale models of tall structures. These were 1:36 scale

models of the Telecom Tower in London, the Jefferson Memorial
Arch in St Louis, Missouri, and the Canadian National Tower in
Toronto. The maze, measuring 69 by 23 metres (225 by 75 feet) was
laid out in brick pathways patterned to imitate magnetic fields around
the structures. It is a flat 'three-dimensional' maze, where pathways
'cross over' one another, with 'bridges' in the brickwork.

Another maze from Minotaur Designs which dates from this time is
at the Bygrave Garden and Leisure Centre, next to the North Orbital
Road at St Albans in Hertfordshire. This maze, measuring 24.3 by
21.3 metres (80 by 70 feet), was designed to give a three-dimensional
'cube' effect. To enhance this illusion, it was planted in three different
varieties of bush. At each of the six vertices is a flagpole surmounted
by a golden ball, and at the centre is a raised pavilion giving views
across the maze.

Early in 1984 the *Sunday Times Magazine* acknowledged the
growing interest in mazes and held a competition for a maze to be built
at the Breamore Countryside Museum at Breamore House in
Hampshire (close to the ancient Mizmaze). Titled 'The Great British
Maze', the competition produced many interesting designs. The rules
stipulated a flat maze, not one with hedges, which ruled out some
good designs, including one by Hilary Parkinson and Richard Cave
which was based on the nine-men's-morris board. Various sorts of
design were entered: wheels, a square which spelt out the name
Breamore and mazes in the shape of animals, such as John Rowell's
entry in the shape of a cockerel. The winner was Ian Leitch, whose
design, 15.8 metres (52 feet) square, with brick pathways laid in grass,
was based upon traditional farmyard five-barred gates. At the centre
of this maze is a topiary ewe in yew!

A unique ecological-architectural experiment in the shape of a
hedge maze came into being in the Netherlands in 1984. In spring of
that year, Professor Peter Schmid of the Architectural Completion-
Milieu-Integration (AM) Research and Design Group of the
Department of Architecture and Building Sciences at the University
of Technology at Eindhoven set up a labyrinth in a specially
designated 'experimental area'. The labyrinth is of the medieval
Christian pattern, based on that at Chartres and almost twice its
diameter (23.5 metres, 25 yards). It was planted in willow saplings. In
a descriptive article and a lecture given at Labyrinth '86, Peter Schmid
gave his reasons for creating the structure. In such a labyrinth, the
walk to the centre is the longest possible one in a given space, and
geometrically it is the most balanced way of covering the ground. Both

elements are interesting architectural phenomena. The use of the Chartres-pattern maze was explained on the grounds of its interesting geometry; its traditional use through the centuries for various 'initiations'; its symbolic/magical functions; its use as a magic or spiritual game, and its use for ritual walking for concentration, meditation and contemplation. It was also, he said, a pattern for dancing with the purpose of accumulating vital energies in the dancer, still used by Continental gypsies, and finally it serves as a focus for geomantic and radiesthetic power, creating a special 'field of harmony'.

In Britain in May 1985, the Bath Festival Maze was opened to the public. The maze is located in the small park in Bath known as Beazer Gardens, which is located next to the River Avon at Pulteney Weir (map grid reference ST 753649). It was inspired by the 'labyrinth' theme of the Bath Festival in 1984, itself a manifestation of the renaissance of interest in things labyrinthine. That festival staged a major exhibition of Michael Ayrton's Daedalus-inspired labyrinthine art and a production of Michael Tippet's opera *The Knot Garden*. The maze is elliptical and measures 29.25 by 22 metres (96 by 72 feet).

One of the most unusual of the new generation of mazes can be seen in Victoria Park in southern Bristol (map grid reference ST 595716). It is of the medieval Christian design, being copied from a roof-boss in the nearby church of St Mary Redcliffe, which dates from the fifteenth century. The Victoria Park maze measures 7.6 metres (25 feet) in diameter and is constructed of brick. The main axis of the maze is oriented upon the spire of the church. Unlike any other maze in Britain, however, it is a 'water maze' in which the pathways of the maze are a continuous channel for water which flows from the centre to the outside. Obviously it is impossible to walk this maze, but the flow of water can be demonstrated by placing a leaf or twig in the central source and watching it flow through the labyrinthine gyres to the outflow at the maze's perimeter.

In 1985 Minotaur Designs constructed a Tudor Rose Maze at Kentwell Hall, a moated manor house near Long Melford in Suffolk (map grid reference TL 863479). Each summer Kentwell Hall is the scene of a re-creation of Tudor life. The building itself is renowned for its fine brickwork, some dating from the fifteenth century, and the only period not represented was the twentieth century. Patrick Phillips QC, owner of Kentwell Hall, commissioned Minotaur Designs to rectify this omission in the shape of a pavement maze laid in the courtyard between the outer ranges of the E-shaped building. It was built in 1985 to commemorate the 500th anniversary of the accession of the Tudor dynasty to the throne by force of arms. The Tudor Rose maze, composed entirely of brick paving in three colours, was laid by Michael and Malcolm Scott. Adrian Fisher's rose maze, designed originally for St Albans Cathedral but never executed there, was chosen, and Ibstock Building Products' design services team was commissioned to lay the maze. It was decided to lay the bricks on a concrete slab 15 cm (6 inches) thick, which was cast in five bays without allowance for movement. This allowed the slab to crack at random and settle before the pavers were laid upon it. It was levelled in such a way that there is a fall across the maze towards drainage channels which lead to the moat.

Because of the curving forms of the maze pattern, many bricks had to be cut, an estimated 17,000 cuts in all. In the most complex areas, bricklayers could lay only a hundred bricks a day, whilst in more simple parts of the maze they laid 600. Overall, 200,000 bricks were needed. The bricks used were 50 mm (2 inch) thick pavers. The pattern of the maze is a unicursal Tudor Rose, with allowance for crossings. The maze was picked out in three different colours of Ibstock bricks: Cheddar Golden, Gloucester Brown and Shortwood Red. There are fifteen plaques of diamond shape representing the flower's sepals. These bear Tudor motifs which include a prayer book representing the founding of the Church of England, a sailing-ship symbolizing the Age of Discovery, and a ruined abbey signifying the dissolution of the monasteries.

Fisher's original design for St Albans Cathedral was intended to be a proper pilgrimage maze in the tradition of medieval Christianity. Its theme was salvation, and each of the fifteen sepals symbolized one of the fifteen 'Mysteries' of esoteric Christianity. Now these fifteen points are part of a 'board game' played with people in Tudor period costume as playing-pieces. Also, at the centre of the Kentwell maze is a chequerboard of sixty-four squares as used for playing chess or English draughts. This was absent from the original St Albans plan. The maze was opened officially on 29 March 1985 by Viscount Coke of Holkham, and later that year the designers received the 1985 Heritage in the Making award from the English Tourist Board.

At the time of writing, there are three mazes in the new city of Milton Keynes in Buckinghamshire. The first was built in 1984–5 on the slope facing Willen Lake, near a Pagoda of Peace constructed by the Nitton Zan Myohoji sect of the Buddhist faith (map grid reference SP 880405). The Willen Bowl maze is of the turf labyrinth type, based

5.2. Willen, Milton Keynes. This plan is derived from that of the Town Maze at Saffron Walden (Fig. 2.3. b), with additional cross-pieces to make a puzzle maze.

in design upon the ancient Town Maze at Saffron Walden but with more rounded 'bastions' at the corner and with a wide gravel, rather than brick, pathway. Here the resemblance ends, for it is three times as large and has cross-pieces which alter the original unicursal design. It is the largest turf maze in Britain, measuring 105 metres (354 feet) in diameter, which makes the pathways about two miles (3.2 km) in length. It takes over an hour to walk the pathways in the traditional unicursal way, and understandably there are few traces of use there. Although it is an impressive structure, it is located on uneven ground, which makes certain parts of the labyrinth lower than other parts and spoils its overall appearance.

Not far away, another turf maze exists, in Campbell Park. This was designed by Mike Usherwood, and built during the winter of 1986–7. Its design is influenced by the medieval Christian labyrinth pattern. The third Milton Keynes maze is a hedge maze in Willen Park, laid out in winter 1985 and planted during winter 1986 as an attraction for the children who play in the park.

Like Milton Keynes, Warrington is a new town grafted onto an older, smaller settlement. The labyrinth, known officially as 'the reproduction turf maze', is in an area known as Parkfields, part of the Peel Hall 'Park System' (map grid reference SJ 630914). Access can be gained via residential culs-de-sac leading from Cinnamon Road, Enfield Park Road or Fearnhead Lane. This park contains 'landscape features' including a replica stone circle and a turf maze. The maze is circular and measures 18.5 metres (60 feet 6 inches) in diameter. It is not a standard unicursal design, for it has paths which allow rapid access or exit from the centre, and also choices in pathway, which is of gravel divided by turf banks – or rather, lawn beds. Unfortunately the design has square-ended turns, which are almost unknown from turf mazes, ancient or modern, being impractical both in terms of comfort for the walker and for ease of maintenance. The paths connected with the labyrinth form various patterns based upon antiquarian designs. One splits to become a giant hand, which appears to have been copied from that of the chalk-cut hill figure known as 'Helith' at Cerne Abbas, Dorset, whilst another goes between two modern standing stones towards an equally modern stone circle.

Doddington Hall in Lincolnshire (map grid reference SK 900697), 8 kilometres (5 miles) from the city of Lincoln, has a turf maze constructed by the owner in 1986. Jeff Saward considers it to be an adaptation of the labyrinthine device used by Bois-Dofin de Laval, Archbishop of Embrun, as figured in Claude Paradin's heraldic book *Devise Héroïques et Emblèmes*, published in France early in the seventeenth century.

The revival of mazes has continued and shows no sign of abating. In 1988 mazes were made at Russborough in County Wicklow, Ireland, at Leeds Castle in Kent and at Blenheim Palace in Oxfordshire. In 1989 an Italianate maze was created at Capel manor at Waltham Cross in Essex, and a maze commemorating C.L. Dodgson's creation, 'Alice in Wonderland', at Merrytown House in Dorset. At the time of writing, the maze seems to have regained its place as a feature in gardening, and the existence of a modern maze-building tradition will guarantee its continuation.

New Concepts in Maze Design

In the 1970s the new interest in mazes was manifested in new types of maze, derived from graphic design and the possibilities of colour and optical illusion. Greg Bright's designs, mazes based on Op Art and hard-edge abstract painting, took design in a new direction. Similarly Les Wood's 'crypto' mazes and Adrian Fisher's 'colour mazes' redefined the nature of the maze.

Cryptomazes were designed on the principle that at each decision point there is a direction sign which makes the maze-follower turn in a specific direction. In this way, although there are no dead ends, the possible number of paths is increased greatly.

Similarly, colour mazes are based on the concept of increasing the possibilities of a maze without dead ends. It is the modern version of Ariadne's 'clew'. The basic principle of these colour mazes is similar to the floor-guidance system in some large hospitals, except that one must follow coloured pathways in sequence. For instance, if the pathways are coloured red, yellow and blue, they must be followed in that order: on leaving a yellow path at a node, a blue one must be chosen; on leaving a blue path, a red one, and so on until the goal is reached.

The Largest of Them All?

Margam Country Park at Port Talbot in South Wales has what is claimed to be the largest hedge maze in Britain, or alternatively the world. It is in the old kitchen garden at Margam Mansion, the ancestral home of the Talbot family after whom Port Talbot was named. When it was planted in 1982, using 4,000 Leylandii saplings, Dr Terence Stevens, the Margam Parks director, stated: 'The maze at Longleat Safari Park is said to be the world's longest, with 1½ miles of paths, but we have beaten that with an extra quarter-mile of access paths.'

The claim that the topiary castle maze at Margam has the longest pathways stands no longer, for now the Willen Park Peace Pagoda maze at Milton Keynes would appear to have the longest path, over 2 miles (3.2 km) in length. In addition, being a modified unicursal design, it is possible to walk all of the Willen maze's paths, which, with a puzzle hedge maze, is undesirable.

But the question of the largest labyrinth in Britain, or even the world, is clouded by the status of Glastonbury Tor. More correctly termed Tor Hill, this prominent landmark is a remarkable hill which rises 159 metres (521 feet) above the otherwise-flat fenlands of the Somerset Levels. On its surface is the most curious and debatable of any ancient labyrinth, the prominent terraces, ridges or 'strip-lynchets' that encircle the whole hill. The first historic record of the enigmatic terraces on Glastonbury Tor can be seen in an illustration by Newcourt and Hollar to William Dugdale's *Monasticon Anglicanum* of 1654.

The usual explanation for these terraces is that they were made in the Middle Ages by peasants who needed to cultivate as much land as possible. But, as evidence for another theory, the Arthurian author Geoffrey Ashe has claimed that hills terraced like the Tor are not the normal products of English agriculture of the medieval period.

Another theory is that the terraces are completely natural, being the 'freak' result of soil creep and erosion. Cattle-tracks are another possibility that has been advanced, whilst yet others suggest that they were made so that ox-carts could be brought to the summit for the construction of the series of churches which have stood on top of the hill. In 1934 the 'New Age' writer Dion Fortune suggested in her book on mystic Glastonbury, *Avalon of the Heart*, that these terraces were the remains of an ancient ritual pathway. She claimed that the track which winds around the 'cone' of the tor was indisputably human in origin. But she did not see it as a labyrinth, for there was no labyrinth tradition either in the local folklore or within the Glastonbury occult milieu at that time.

The labyrinth idea was brought to the public's attention first in 1968 by Geoffrey Russell, who had been an enthusiast since experiencing a labyrinth pattern in a dream in 1944. He suggested that the prominent ridges on Tor Hill were actually the remains of a three-dimensional Classical labyrinth. This theory was published in a booklet entitled *Glastonbury – A Study in Patterns*, issued by the Research Into Lost Knowledge Organization in 1969. Although Geoffrey Russell claimed that the labyrinth which he had detected was a human artefact, constructed in the remote past, he never published an accurate plan showing how the labyrinth path relates to the terracing. He connected the spiral appearance of the tor's lynchets with the ancient Celtic tradition of Caer Sidi, the fairy or spiral castle. Within Caer Sidi was the magic cauldron of Ceridwen, an entry-point to Annwn, the underworld. The legend of St Collen associated with the tor has elements which reinforce this theory.

Unlike many suggestions emanating from 'Earth Mysteries', this

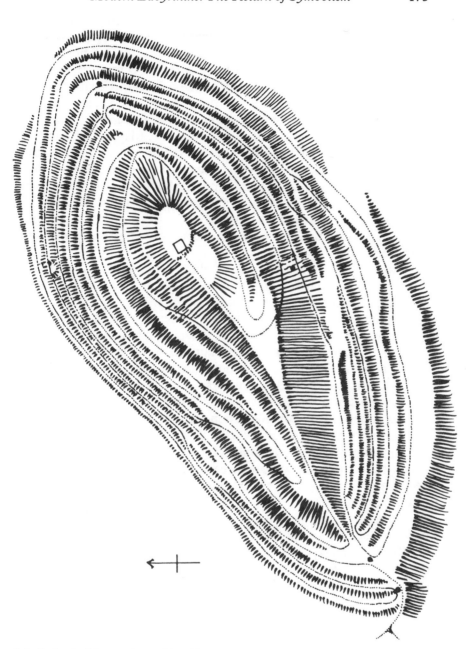

5.3. Labyrinthine pathway identified in 1969 on the terraces of Glastonbury Tor. The path is shown dotted, but where it does not follow the terracing, it is shown continuous.

idea was not dismissed out of hand by archaeologists. Philip Rahtz (see Ashe, *Caerdroia, Bibliog.*), who excavated sites on top of Tor Hill from 1964 to 1966, thought that it was 'worth consideration'. 'If the maze theory were demonstrated to be true,' he continued, 'it would clearly be of the greatest relevance to the origins of Glastonbury as a religious centre.' Little more was done about this alleged labyrinth until 1979, when Geoffrey Ashe published *The Glastonbury Tor Maze*, in which he showed how, in distorted form, the Classical labyrinth fits the terraced terrain of Tor Hill. This was the first definite statement of the maze, which earlier had been little more than a suggestion. Since then, this labyrinth has passed into Glastonbury folklore and has become part of the 'New Age' mythos of the town. In 1984 the National Trust, which owns the site, erected new information panels which mentioned that the labyrinth theory was a possible explanation of the terracing.

However, proving the theory that the lynchets comprise a deliberately fashioned labyrinth necessitates the existence of seven complete circuits of the hill with appropriately defined vertical connections. The nature of these connections poses the greatest difficulty, for their definition on a sloping surface is much more difficult than on a flat one. There appears to be little evidence that these indistinct vertical connections are human artefacts. In 1984 Russell Scott investigated this in detail, considering the topographical requirements of a Classical labyrinth. After much research, he came up with the only possible solution, which was different from the pathway published by Geoffrey Ashe.

The pathway accepted by walkers today has several places which do not fit the topography very well. On the first two double turns, the paths use the same part of the terrace, whilst higher up the fourth and fifth ring have to make abrupt kinks and changes of level. Finally, on the approach to the summit, the path has to cut obliquely across the terrace wall on its final two turns before reaching the relatively flat area before the final ascent to the summit (Fig. 5.3).

However, despite these structural anomalies, there is no question that a labyrinth of some sort (whatever its origin, natural or artificial) exists on Glastonbury Tor *now*. The debate, which continues, is over its nature. There have been theories that the maze was built deliberately, whilst others have suggested that it is fortuitous, a coincidence recognized quite recently and then formalized. But whatever its cause or origin, without doubt it *is* the largest labyrinth in the world, even though it has been recognized as such only since 1968.

Modern Stone Labyrinths in the British Isles

Close to the site of the original St Agnes Troy Town, in the Scillies, reconstructed in 1989, is another stone labyrinth. It is located to the east of the site of the original one, around the headland (map grid reference SV 878078). Its design is unlike any hitherto seen in Britain, being based upon the German design with an entrance and an exit of the type extant as the Rad at Hanover in Germany and the former maze at Kaufbeuren. (This, however, is an ideal design for stone labyrinths.) It measures 9.2 metres (30 feet) in diameter and was built in August 1986 by Nick Mann, Anne Morgan and others as an attempt to take tourist pressure away from the earlier one, and thus preserve it. Unfortunately, since then the unauthorized 'reconstruction' of the original St Agnes labyrinth has damaged the ancient site.

Elsewhere in the Scillies, there are a number of stone labyrinths on the north point of the island of St Martin's (map grid reference SV 923170). Their exact origin is unknown, but according to local tradition the first ones were constructed during the Second World War by airmen stationed there. Others have come and gone since, and new ones are built with stones taken from the old ones, so the construction of mazes there is a living tradition.

In contrast with the transience of the St Martin's labyrinths is a 'modern' Welsh one which is intact after almost two decades. Located on the Gower Peninsula of Wales at Three Cliffs Bay, near Pennard, is a boulder labyrinth constructed in 1972, known as 'the Fairy Ring'. It is located on the flats by Pennard Pill (map grid reference SS 539882) and measures 8.8–9.4 metres (29–31 feet) in diameter. Two other Welsh examples, built by Chris Turner and colleagues, existed to the west of Gower, at Ginst Point, Laugharne (map grid reference SN 325079). The first, constructed at Hallowe'en in 1982, was square, of the design of the St Catherine's Hill turf maze near Winchester. It measured 10 metres (33 feet) square but was destroyed by storm-driven high tides in February 1983. This was followed by a Classical labyrinth 7 metres (23 feet) across, built at Easter 1983 and destroyed by the weather in April 1984. Another coastal labyrinth was a large Kaufbeuren-type maze in Ireland. This was laid out in stones at the top of the beach at Camp, in County Kerry, in August 1988 by a visiting 'international labyrinth team' composed of the author, Rosemarie Kirschmann, Mona Miksicek and Ursula Schmitz. Like the Welsh examples, this was destroyed by storms in the winter of 1988–9.

Other small stone labyrinths include fragments of a labyrinth of unknown date or origin on Ilkley Moor in Yorkshire (map grid reference SE 126451) and one at Ardnave Point on the island of Islay (map grid reference NR 292749), built by Jeff and Deb Saward. In Ireland, a small Classical labyrinth was built by Nigel Pennick and Eleonore Schmid in August 1988 near the summit of the holy mountain of Knockarea in County Sligo (map grid reference G 627346). With the current interest in labyrinths, more are bound to be constructed, creating a puzzle for future historians.

Modern Temporary Labyrinths

The ancient Welsh tradition of *Caerdroia* is carried on today by individuals who, for various reasons, make mazes for immediate use. Materials I have used have included bricks, pebbles, pine cones, tree bark and sawdust.

Since the mid-1970s it has become customary to lay out mazes at 'alternative' fairs and free festivals. They were present at most of the series of Albion Fairs held in East Anglia. For example, the Faery Fair at Lyng, Norfolk, July 25–6 1981, had a maze laid out by Jeff Saward in flintstones to the pattern of the former Fairy Hill maze at Asenby, Yorkshire. Seven years later, the Harvest Festival fair held at Rougham, near Bury St Edmunds, Suffolk, had a copy of the Boughton Green maze laid out with sticks and string.

On a less impromptu level, a temporary but highly symbolic Beatles Maze was constructed for the 1984 International Garden Festival at Liverpool. Devised by Minotaur Designs (which then comprised Adrian Fisher, Randoll Coate and Graham Burgess), it was a unicursal brick pavement maze which consisted of pathways in the overall shape of an apple laid in a pool of water. The apple was the symbol of the company once owned by the Liverpool rock music group The Beatles. The apple design, known as *Mokum*, symbolizes the New Jerusalem in esoteric Jewish tradition in the Netherlands, and the city of Amsterdam. In the centre of the apple, the 'goal' was a 15.5 metre (51 foot) long 'Yellow Submarine', alluding to one of the most famous Beatles songs.

The paths were arranged to symbolize a pair of ears listening to the music. At the centre, the path gave way to stepping-stones, which had tails to resemble musical notes. At the beginning, the path contained four parallel rows of bricks along the centre, symbolizing the four members of the group. But where the path passed a statue of John

Lennon who was assassinated in New York in 1980, the central line narrowed to three parallel rows of bricks. Each path ended with a head shape of a water bird, a flamingo and a swan, whose heads were surrounded by pink and white water-lilies respectively. When the Garden Festival ended, this fascinating maze was destroyed.

In August 1986 I laid out and directed the construction of the first permanent stone labyrinth in North America at the Ojai Foundation, near Oxnard, California. It was of the Classical labyrinth design, laid on a specially prepared bed of sand. At the centre of the 'cross' was a special conglomerate boulder, selected as a 'mother stone'. The labyrinth was dedicated with a long ritual which included music and dancing.

Almost simultaneously, at the 1986 Glastonbury CND Festival held on Worthy Farm at Pilton in Somerset, a very similar stone labyrinth was constructed by Jeff and Deb Saward. It was a seven-circuit Classical labyrinth laid out in stones. The outer circuit contained eight small cairns which contained night-lights which were lit at dusk, allowing walkers to traverse the gyres by night. At the centre was a post which served as a sundial gnomon which enabled small cairns marking midsummer sunrise and set to be added to the periphery of the maze.

In 1987 I was an invited participant in the traditional crafts section of the annual art fair Art in Action, held at Waterperry House, Oxfordshire. Over a four-day period, using standard British house bricks laid on mown grass, I constructed a number of temporary labyrinths. All the standard designs were used, ranging from the simplest three-circuit Classical labyrinths to the medieval Christian and standard Roman designs. Among these designs was one which, to my knowledge, had never before been made large enough to walk through. it was the square variant of the Classical labyrinth, known only from a Romano-Celtic site at Saint-Côme-et-Maréjols in the south of France, which is only about a metre across. Interestingly, this pattern aroused some of the most interesting comments, causing its walkers more problems than one might expect. To my knowledge, the Art in Action event is the only occasion at which a series of full-size, walkable labyrinths has been constructed in this way.

Labyrinths and Earth Mysteries

The relatively new subject of 'Earth Mysteries', which arose in the 1960s and which was formalized in the 1970s, deals, among other things, with traditions and realities of subtle forces in the earth. These forces were recognized as a reality by the people of pre-scientific, pre-industrial cultures and were visualized in terms of non-human yet sentient beings which were called gnomes, sprites, trolls, yarthkins and dragons. Sacred places were defined as locations at which this force could be felt by people sensitive to such things. This mystic earth force studied in Earth Mysteries has been described as that subtle 'fifth element' which powers all things. It is a reality in all pre-industrial cultures, being known all over the world under many different names. In Celtic lands is was called *nwyfre*, and it is through this tradition that Earth Mysteries research has been able to draw some intriguing conclusions. Some of the nature of this subtle force is explained in the collection of ancient Welsh writings known as *Barddas* (the element of Bardism), which tells of five elements: '*Calas; fluidity; breath; uvel* and *nwyvre*. From *calas* is every corporeity, namely, the earth and every thing hard; from *fluidity* are moisture and flux; from *breath* are every wind, breeze, respiration and air; from *uvel* are all heat; fire and light; and from *nwyvre* every life and motion, every spirit, every soul of man, and from its union with the other elements, other living beings' (Barddas, Landovery, 1861).

The *nwyvre* is a power expressed in the form of the mythological dragon-like being which is depicted widely in European medieval art. It has the head of a predatory animal, with ears, joined to a reptilian body which has one pair of forelegs. Its back bears wings, and its rear part is a prehensile, snake-like body and tail.

An Icelandic representation of Jörmungand, the World Serpent which lies at the bottom of the ocean, encircling the world, is shown in this form. Similarly the leviathan in the French medieval manuscript known as *Hortus Deliciarum (The Garden of Delights)*, which shows God the Father fishing for this beast, is depicted as a *nwyvre*. Here God is using a crucified Christ as bait to hook the monster! *Vouivres* exist as stone carvings in many churches, including the cathedrals of Strasbourg and Zürich, where their spiralling tails are prominent features.

The connection between the *nwyvre* and the labyrinth was pointed out to me by Paul Devereux in 1986. He noted that the Belgian Earth Mysteries researcher Pierre Mereaux, in his work at Carnac in Brittany, had investigated the relationship between *nwyvre* and geomagnetic fields and had shown that the placement of the Breton standing stones at Carnac are associated with scientifically measurable geomagnetic patterns. Some dowsers have been shown to be sensitive to minute electromagnetic variations at ancient sites, which may account for the patterns they detect. Devereux notes that if Mereaux is correct, the labyrinth pattern itself may be more than a dance path made on the ground. Made at the right place, where earth forces are active, he suggests, it could provide the optimum contact between the biological fields of the human organism and the earth's geomagnetic field. This interaction could affect the electromagnetic impulses in the brain, bringing an altered state of consciousness and, through it, spiritual enlightenment. 'Wise women' such as Kate Turner used their carved labyrinths to alter their states of consciousness by following the pattern, and this too would assist the integration of the human bodily fields with those of Mother Earth.

Unlike any other human symbol, the labyrinth has caught the attention of historians, anthropologists, folklorists, artists, architects, geomants, dowsers and psychologists. A universal figure, it remains as potent a symbol of spiritual experience as it was the first time some unknown person traced it in the sand. As ever, it remains a link between our inner, personal life and that of the Earth, from which we come and to which we return.

Gazetteer of Notable Mazes and Labyrinths in the British Isles

This list is of the most notable mazes and labyrinths which can be visited in the British Isles. It lists the place's name and its map grid reference, and remarks on the maze's design, its dimensions and the construction date, where known. As far as is known, at the time of writing, these mazes and labyrinths are open to the public during normal visiting hours.

England

AVON

Bath: Beazer Gardens, near Poulteney Bridge, ST 753649. Oval maze, stone paths laid in grass. 29.5 by 22 metres (97 by 73 feet). Constructed 1985.

Batheaston: Parish church, ST 777679. Pavement labyrinth of square 'St Bertin' design. 5 metres (16 feet 6 inches) diameter. Laid in 1985.

Bristol: Parish church of St Mary Redcliffe, ST 591732. Roof boss of medieval Christian labyrinth design. 20 cm (8 inches) diameter. fifteenth century.

Bristol: Victoria Park, ST 595716. Brick labyrinth of medieval Christian design, with pathways as water channels. Circular, 7.6 metres (25 feet) in diameter. Constructed 1984.

BUCKINGHAMSHIRE

Milton Keynes: Willen Peace Pagoda area, SP 880405. Gravel paths in grass, circular with 'bastions'. 105 metres (345 feet) diameter. Built 1875.

CAMBRIDGESHIRE

Bourn: Parish church of St Helena and St Mary, TL 325563. Pavement maze in red and black tiles. 4.5 by 2.3 metres (15 by 12 feet). Built 1875.

Ely: Cathedral. TL 541803. Pavement labyrinth, square with corner 'bastions'. 6 metres (20 feet) in diameter. Built 1870.

Hilton: The Village Green, TL 293663. Turf maze with Sparrow's Monument at the middle. Circular, 17.6 metres (55 feet) in diameter. Made in 1660.

CHESHIRE

Knutsford: Tatton Park, SJ 744814. Puzzle hedge maze in beech. 35 by 18 metres (114 by 60 feet). Planted *c*. 1890.

CORNWALL

Glendurgan, near Falmouth: SW 772277. Hedge maze in laurel. 40 by 33 metres (133 by 108 feet). Planted 1833.

Newquay: Lappa Valley Railway, SW 839558. Maze in the shape of a railway locomotive, pathway of brick, laid in grass. Overall dimensions 49 by 31 metres (161 by 101 feet). Constructed 1982.

Newquay Zoo: SW 860612. Puzzle maze in eleagnus in the shape of a dragon 64 metres long (210 feet). Constructed 1984.

Tintagel: Rocky Valley ruined mill rock face, SX 073894. A pair of carved Classical labyrinths, 23 cm (9 inches) in diameter. Date disputed.

DERBYSHIRE

Chatsworth House: SK 263697. Puzzle hedge maze in yew, 40 by 35 metres (131 by 115 feet). Planted in 1962.

DORSET

Isle of Portland: Portland Sculpture Park, SY 685727. Stone labyrinth where pathway is on the stones, 7 metres (23 feet) diameter. Constructed 1985.

ESSEX

Hadstock: Churchyard, TL 559448. Tombstone of Michael Ayrton (1921–75), bearing bronze labyrinth designed by the artist. Erected 1975.

Saffron Walden: The common, TL 543385. The Town Maze, modified medieval Christian design with corner 'bastions'. 46 by 33.5 metres (150 by 110 feet), pathway of bricks in grass. Date unknown, but pre-1699.

HAMPSHIRE

Breamore: Mizmaze Hill, SU 142203. The Mizmaze, medieval Christian design circular turf maze. 26.5 metres (87 feet) diameter. Date unknown, presumed thirteenth century.

Breamore House: SU 153192. The Great British Maze, winning design of *The Sunday Times* maze competition, 1984. Brick path in grass. 16 metres (52 feet) square.

Itchen Stoke: St Mary's church, SU 560335. Brick labyrinth, 1866. 5.5 metres (15 feet).

Winchester: St Catherine's Hill, SU 484278. The Mizmaze turf maze, path as a groove between turf banks. Square, 21.3 metres (70 feet) along each side. Pre-1710.

HEREFORD AND WORCESTER

Symond's Yat, near Ross-on-Wye: SO 554174. Octagonal puzzle maze in cypress. 41 metres (135 feet) square. Planted 1981.

HERTFORDSHIRE

St Albans: Bygrave Garden and Leisure Centre. Hexagonal puzzle maze. 24 metres (80 feet) in diameter. Planted 1983.

HUMBERSIDE

Alkborough: Julian's Bower, overlooking Trent and Humber confluence, SE 880218. Turf maze, circular medieval Christian design. 13.4 metres (44 feet) in diameter. Date unknown.

Alkborough: Parish church, SE 882219. Medieval Christian labyrinth design inlaid in the floor of the church porch. 1.8 metres (6 feet) diameter. Laid in 1887. There is also a labyrinth in the stained glass window at the east end of the church.

Alkborough: Village cemetery, SE 880214. Celtic cross tombstone of J. Goulton-Constable, with inset small labyrinth design. Erected 1922.

Kingston-upon-Hull: City Hall. Roman labyrinth mosaic from Harpham. 3.35 metres (11 feet) square. Early fourth century CE.

Kingston-upon-Hull: King Edward Street. Brick pavement labyrinth, Christian pattern, square 13.2 metres (43 feet 3 inches). Built 1987.

ISLE OF WIGHT

Blackgang Chine: SZ 485768. Puzzle hedge maze in privet. 27.5 by 24 metres (90 by 80 feet). Planted 1962.

KENT

Edenbridge: Hever Castle, TQ 478452. Puzzle maze in yew. 23 metres (75 feet) square. Planted 1905.

LANCASHIRE

Leyland: Worden Park, SD 537209. Puzzle maze in beech, copy of Somerleyton Hall, Suffolk, maze (q.v.). Planted 1886.

Warrington: Parkfields Estate, SJ 630914. Circular turf maze, pathway in gravel. 18.5 metres (60 feet 6 inches) across. Constructed 1984.

LEICESTERSHIRE

Wing: By the roadside close to the village recreation ground, SK

895028. Turf maze, circular, medieval Christian design. 15 metres (50 feet) in diameter. Date unknown.

LINCOLNSHIRE

Lincoln: Doddington Hall, west of Lincoln, SK 900697. Circular turf puzzle maze, with pathways in gravel. Diameter 23 metres (75 feet). Constructed 1986.

Spalding: Springfields Gardens, TF 264243. Puzzle hedge maze in Leylandii. 23 metres (75 feet) square. Planted 1977.

LONDON

Warren Street, WC1: Playground, TQ 293821. Pavement labyrinth in red and black bricks. 1960s.

NOTTINGHAMSHIRE

Nottingham: Clifton Hall, SK 542355. Turf maze, circular, medieval Christian labyrinth design. 10.3 metres (34 feet) in diameter. Cut 1981.

OXFORDSHIRE

Henley-on-Thames: Greys Court, SU 727835. The Archbishop's Maze, with brick paths laid in grass, basically circular. 25.9 metres (85 feet) diameter. Made in 1981.

SCILLY ISLES

St Agnes: Troy Town Farm. SV 876078. Two stone labyrinths. One, the Troy Town, is the oldest in the British Isles. 4.8 metres (16 feet) in diameter. Built 1729, reconstructed 1989. The other, 9 metres (30 feet), was built in 1986.

St Martin's: SV 923170. A series of labyrinths, ever-changing. Begun *c* 1940.

SOMERSET

Glastonbury: Tor Hill, ST 512382. Hillside 'strip lynchets' or terracing. Distorted Classical labyrinth design. 518 by 244 metres (1,700 by 800 feet). Identified as a labyrinth in 1969.

SUFFOLK

Near Long Melford: Kentwell Hall, TL 863479. Tudor Rose Maze laid in bricks in the courtyard of the Hall. 21 metres (70 feet) in diameter. Constructed 1985.

Near Lowestoft: Somerleyton Hall, TM 494980. Puzzle maze in yew. 75 by 49 metres (245 by 160 feet). Planted 1846.

SURREY

Compton, near Guildford: Watts' Memorial Chapel, SU 956474. Four labyrinth carvings on roof corbels and one on the altar of the chapel. Built 1896–1900.

Richmond: Hampton Court Palace, TQ 157687. The oldest hedge maze in Britain. 68 by 25 metres (222 by 82 feet). Planted *c.* 1690.

WILTSHIRE

Warminster: Longleat House, ST 807433. Puzzle maze in yew. 116 by 53 metres (380 by 175 feet). Planted 1978.

YORKSHIRE

Blackstone Edge, next to the Roman road: SD 973172. Stone labyrinth. No known date; probably 1970s.

Near Whitley Bay: Forest Hall. Puzzle maze in the shape of steam locomotive, gravel path in grass. 30.5 metres (100 feet) in length. Built 1984.

Dalby, Howardian Hills: By the side of the B1363 road, SE 626719. The City of Troy, turf maze, Classical labyrinth pattern. 8 by 6.7 metres (26 by 22 feet). Recut in 1900.

Ilkley Moor: SE 126451. Stone labyrinth, ruined. No date, but probably 1970s.

Leeds: Temple Newsam House, SE 357321. Brick path maze, 35 by 28 metres (114 by 92 feet). Constructed 1976.

Scarborough: Victoria Park, TA 038895. Tree Maze puzzle maze in privet. 41 by 30 metres (135 by 100 feet). Planted 1959.

Scarborough: The Esplanade, TA 045875. Tree Maze puzzle maze in privet. 32 by 22 metres (105 by 72 feet). Planted 1962.

Ireland

DONEGAL

Burt: St Regnus's Church, C 365212. Cast labyrinth designs as plaques and door handles. 1967.

DUBLIN

Dublin, National Museum, Kildare Street: The Hollywood Stone, Classical labyrinth carving, incised on a boulder. 76 cm (30 inches) in diameter. Date uncertain; said to be 2000 BCE, but possibly *c*. 550 CE.

MEATH

Rathmore: Church of St Lawrence, N 753670. Medieval Christian labyrinth carved on a stone slab on the interior of the south wall of the ruined church. Fifteenth century?

SLIGO

Knockarea, near Sligo: G 627346. Classical stone labyrinth. 4.2 metres (14 feet) diameter. Constructed 1988.

Scotland

ABERDEENSHIRE

Aberdeen: Hazlehead Park, NJ 895054. Puzzle hedge maze in privet. 58 by 49 metres (190 by 160 feet). Planted 1935.

ISLAY

Ardnave Point: NR 292749. Stone labyrinth. 3.6 metres (12 feet) diameter. Constructed 1986.

NAIRNSHIRE

Cawdor Castle: NH 847498. Hedge maze in holly, reproducing a Roman mosaic design, square. Planted 1981.

PEEBLESSHIRE

Traquair House: NT 331355. Puzzle maze in Leylandii. 45 metres (147 feet) square. Planted 1980.

ROXBURGHSHIRE

Kelso: Floors Castle, NT 711347. Puzzle maze in beech. 58.5 metres (192 feet) square. Planted 1983.

Wales

WEST GLAMORGAN

Port Talbot: Margam Country Park, SS 806862. Hedge maze. 87 by 85 metres (286 by 280 feet). Planted 1984.

Pennard, Gower Peninsula: SS 539882. The Fairy Ring stone labyrinth, Classical design. 9.4 by 8.8 metres (31 by 29 feet). Constructed 1972.

Glossary

Annwn: The underworld of Celtic mythology

Bastion: On a turf maze, the raised turf pathway or divider

Baulk: A corner projection on a circular or square maze

Boulder labyrinth: Alternative name for a stone labyrinth i.e. one in which the pathways are defined by 'walls' composed of rounded stones, usually in single rows

Caerdroia: Literally 'the city of turns', Welsh name for shepherds' turf mazes

Caer Sidi: The 'fairy castle' of Celtic mythology

Centre: The middle or 'goal' (q.v.) of a maze, usually used when the maze is symmetrical in form

Chakra-Vyūha: The Indian labyrinth pattern, used as a yantra (q.v.) to focus the concentration during childbirth.

Chartres-type: Labyrinth of the medieval Christian pattern (q.v.), as at Chartres Cathedral

Classical labyrinth: Unicursal (q.v.) labyrinth form, sometimes called 'the Cretan maze' after its use on the coins of Knossos

Clew: A ball of string, especially as used in labyrinth myth

Colour maze: Maze in which the path to take is defined by colours laid in the pavement

Cretan maze: *See* Classical labyrinth

Cross, corners and dots pattern: The basic pattern for the simple construction of a Classical labyrinth

Cunning man: Male practitioner of folk-magic and healing

Cup and ring marks: Enigmatic circles and depressions carved on standing stones and rock outcrops

Dalle: Paving-stone, especially one from Saint-Omer

Decision-point: A place in a maze at which the path divides and the walker has to make a choice of which way to go. Sometimes called a 'node'

Dedal: Old English word for a maze, after Daedalus, creator of the Cretan labyrinth (also Dédale)

Dowsing: The ability to detect water, minerals or other features below the ground surface by means of a rod, pendulum or other disclosing-instrument

Earth Mysteries: The multi-disciplinary study of traditions and practices of the human interaction with the Earth. Uses a 'holistic' of 'general systems' approach to decipher evidence left by pre-industrial cultures

Etruscan Discipline: Method of Etruscan and Roman town-planning based on a fourfold division of the land delineated by a grid of lines running north–south and east–west

Fylfot: Swastika-like pattern related to the Classical labyrinth

Geolocation: Location of a human artefact such as a building, with regard to the topography and prevailing conditions, such as the winds

Geomancy: The detection of various subtle qualities of the land and place, and the modification of those qualities so as to harmonize human activity there with the inherent natural character of the place

Goal: The centre of a maze, the place which people attempt to reach

Grimborg: Mythical hero of the Swedish labyrinth legend

Gyre: A 'turn' of a labyrinth, especially circular

Hedge maze: Puzzle maze (q.v.) composed of planted hedges too tall to see over

Hiberno-Saxon: Style of art from the first millennium CE, characterized by interlacings and distorted animal motifs

Island: Area within a maze, with a continuously linked section of barrier not linked with the perimeter

Irrgarten: A maze or labyrinth (German)

Jallad Khan: Hero of the Afghan labyrinth legend

Jörmungand: The Norse world serpent, an aspect of nwyvre (q.v.)

Julian: Patron saint of innkeepers, patron of the maze 'bower'

Julian's Bower: A traditional English turf maze name, probably related to St Julian

Knot garden: A garden laid out in regular geometrical patterns, often using inlay materials such as coloured sands, chalk or coal along with the plants

Kota: Literally 'the fort', Indian labyrinth pattern

Kolam: Indian protective pattern, drawn on steps etc

Labyrinth: Anglicization of the original Greek word, related to *labrys*, the sacred double-axe sacred sign of Greek pagan religion. Interchangeable with maze, but used more frequently to refer to stone and pavement examples

Luaithrindi: Magical patterns drawn on shields or the ground in the heroic period of Irish legend.

Manas-Chakra: The Indian version of the Classical labyrinth

Maze: Interchangeable with labyrinth, but used more frequently to designate puzzle mazes (q.v.) and turf mazes (q.v.)

Medieval Christian labyrinth: Originating around the millennium, generally circular, divided into four quarters with an ingenious pattern of paths comprising thirty-five separate movements from the outside to the goal

Minotaur: Mythical beast, half-man, half-bull, which lived in the labyrinth of Knossos

Mokum: The New Jerusalem in Dutch–Jewish tradition, symbolized by the apple

Multicursal: Having many pathways, with 'dead ends'

Node: Decision point (q.v.)

Nwyvre: The life-force or subtle element, depicted as a two-legged dragon with a coiling, serpentine tail

Omphalos: Literally 'the navel of the world', place or stone marking a geomantically powerful location

Önd: The subtle energy dealt with in Earth Mysteries research (Norse) (*see also* Nwyvre)

Otfrid-type: Development of the Classical labyrinth (q.v.) attributed to Otfrid von Weissenburg (*c.*790–875)

Pavement labyrinth: Labyrinth laid indoors in a floor, or outdoors in a paved area, composed of stones, tiles or mosaic, usually unicursal (q.v.)

Petroglyph: A rock carving of a character or symbol

Puzzle maze: Multicursal maze in which the aim is to reach the centre without getting lost

Qi: The subtle energy dealt with in Chinese geomancy and the oriental martial arts (*see also* Nwyvre)

Reniform: Kidney-shaped

Retronuevo: The principle of taking the best qualities of the past and using them in a new manner appropriate to the present

Rune: A character from the Germanic-Norse alphabet

Sigil: A character, such as a letter of the alphabet, or planetary sign, with a specific meaning whilst not being a *symbol*

Smågubbar: Malevolent spirits ensnared by labyrinths in the Swedish fishermen's tradition

Stone labyrinth: One in which the pathways are defined by pebbles or boulders placed on either side of the pathway

Theseus: Hero who killed the Minotaur in the Greek labyrinth legend

Thule: A Norse diviner, from the place-name, meaning 'the place where one is forced to turn back', i.e. one who returns from the otherworld, or from within the labyrinth

Troytown: General: a turf or stone maze; Cornish dialect: a house in disorder

Turf maze: Unicursal labyrinth (q.v.) with paths defined by cutting the turf. The maze-walker walks either along the top of the baulks or in a groove between them, often lined with gravel to make a pathway

Unicursal: Having a single pathway with no 'dead ends'

Yantra: Magical diagram from Indian Tantric tradition which expresses a magical principle in its design

Yarthkin: A harmful earth spirit in the East Anglian tradition (cf. Smågubbar, q.v.)

Bibliography

1 Ancient Rock and Stone Labyrinths

Anati, Emmanuel, *Evolution and Style in Camunian Rock Art* (Capo di Ponte, 1976)

Anon., 'Sanfte Renovation des Hauses zum Irrgang. Ein vieldeutiges Hauszeichen' *Neue Zürcher Zeitung*, 9 October 1987

Aspelin, J.R., 'Steinlabyrinthe in Finland', Zeitschrift für Ethnologie, Vol. IX (1877), p. 439

Ayrton, Michael, *The Rudiments of Paradise* (London, 1971)

Baine, George, *Celtic Art: The Methods of Construction* (London, 1951)

Banks, M.M., 'Tangled Thread Mazes', *Folk-Lore*, Vol. XLVI (1936), pp. 78–80

Bord, Janet, *Mazes and Labyrinths of the World* (London, 1974)

Breeks, J.W., *An Account of the Primitive Tribes and Monuments of the Nilagiris* (1873)

Brooke, S.C., 'The Labyrinth Pattern in India', *Folklore*, Nos. 63–4 (1952–3), pp. 463–72

Cirlot, J.E., *A Dictionary of Symbols* (London, 1971)

Cleaver, Alan, 'Holy Wells: Wormholes in Reality?' *Source*, No. 4 (1986), pp. 28–9

Cohen, Daniel, 'Notes from Crete', *Caerdroia*, No. 16 (1985), pp. 4–5

Courtney, Margaret Ann, *Cornish Feasts and Folklore* (Penzance, 1890)

Critchlow, Keith, 'Chartres Maze – a model of the universe?' Architectural Association Quarterly, Vol. 15, No. 2 (1973)

Deedes, C.N., 'The Labyrinth', *Further Studies in the Relationship between Myth and Ritual in the Ancient World*, ed. Hooke, Samuel H. (London, 1935)

Eilmann, Richard, *Labyrinthos* (Athens, 1931)

Elderkin, G.W., 'Meander or Labyrinth', *Journal of American Architecture*, Vol. XIV (1910), pp. 185–190

Elworth, F.T., *The Evil Eye* (London, 1895)

Freudenthal, A.O., 'Öfversigtaf Ostra Nylands fornlemningar' (*Finska fornminnesföreningens Tidskrift*, Vol. 1 (Helsinki, 1874), p. 67

Furnival, F.J., and Pollard, A.W. (eds.), *The Macro Plays, III* (London, 1904)

Gibson, Ackroyd, 'Rock-carvings which link Tintagel with Knossos: Bronze Age Mazes discovered in Cornwall', *Illustrated London News*, 9 January 1954, p. 46

Goodwin, Arthur, *The Technique of Mosaic* (London, 1985)

Hadingham, Evan, *Circles and Standing Stones* (New York, 1976)

Haigh, A.E., *The Attic Theatre* (London, 1898)

Hamkens, Haye, 'Trojaburgen', *Germanien*, Vol. 2 (1934), pp. 359–65. Translated by Michael Behrend and published as pp. III–VI of *Trojaburgen* by Caerdroia Project & Institute of Geomantic Research, Benfleet & Bar Hill (1982)

Hildburgh, W.L., 'The place of confusion and indeterminancy in mazes and maze-dances', *Folk-Lore*, Vol. 55, pp. 133–49

Hooke, Samuel H., *The Labyrinth* (London, 1935)

Kern, Herman, *Labyrinthe: Erscheinungsforme und Deutungen 5000 Jahre Gegenwart eines Urbilds* (Munich, 1982)

Kimmis, Jim, 'The Hermetic Labyrinth', *Caerdroia*, No. 15 (1984), pp. 25–7

Knight, W.F. Jackson, 'Myth and Legend at Troy', *Folk-Lore*, Vol. XLVI (1936), pp. 98–121

Knight, W.F. Jackson, *Cumaean Gates: A Reference to the 6th Ænid (of Vergil) to the Initiation Pattern* (Oxford, 1936)

Kraft, John, *'Götlands Trojeborgar'*, *Götlandskt Arkiv* (1983), pp. 59–90

Kraft, John, 'Stone Labyrinths – An Introduction'. *Caerdroia*, No. 17 (1985), pp. 12–18

Kraft, John, *The Goddess in the Labyrinth* (Åbo, 1985)

Krause, Ernst, *Die Trojaburgen Nordeuropas* (Glogau, 1893)

Layard, John, 'Maze Dances and the Ritual of the Labyrinth in Malekula', *Folk-Lore*, No. XLVII (1936), pp. 123–70

Layard, John, 'Labyrinth Ritual in South India: Threshhold and Tattoo designs', *Folk-Lore*, No. XLVIII (1937), pp. 115–82

Leather, Ellen Mary, *The Folk-Lore of Herefordshire* (1912)

Lenormant, François, *Chaldean Magic* (London, 1878)

Lethaby, W.R., *Architecture, Mysticism and Myth* (London, 1891)

MacWhite, Eoin, 'A New View on Irish Bronze Age Rock-Scribings', *Journal of the Royal Society of Antiquaries of Ireland*, 76 (1946), pp. 58–80

Madge, S.J., *Chapel, Kieve and Gorge of St Nectan, Trevillet* (Millcombe, 1950)

Matthews, W.H., *Mazes and Labyrinths, Their History and Development* (London, 1922)

Maynard, G.N., 'The Ancient Labyrinth or Maze at Saffron Walden with some Notes on the Antiquity of Mazes in General', *The Essex Naturalist*, Vol. 3 (1889), pp. 244–7

Merne, John G., *A Handbook of Celtic Ornament* (Cork, 1974)

Moyre, Ernest J., *Raising the Wind. The legend of Lapland and Finland Wizards in Literature* (East Brunswick, 1981)

Muller, F., '*De beteekenis van het Labyrinth*', *Med. der Koninklijke Akad. van Wetenschappen, Afdeeling Letterkunde*, 78 (1934), Series B, No. 1

Nance, R. Morton, 'Troy Town', *Journal of the Royal Institute of Cornwall*, Vol. 71 (1924), pp. 262–79

Nance, R. Morton, 'The Plen an Gwary or Cornish Playing Place', *Journal of the Royal Institute of Cornwall* (1935), pp. 190–211

Ore, Oystein, 'An Excursion into Labyrinths', *The Mathematics Teacher*, 1959, p. 367

Orpen, G.H., *Journal Roy. Soc. Ant. Ireland*, LIII, p. 177

Orpen, G.H., *Journal Roy. Soc. Ant. Ireland*, XLI, p. 183

Pennick, Nigel, *Sacred Geometry* (Wellingborough, 1980)

Pennick, Nigel, 'The Labyrinth and the City', *Caerdroia*, No. 10 (1982), pp. 9–11

Pennick, Nigel, 'Solar Patterns and Labyrinths', *Caerdroia*, No. 12 (1983), pp. 4–5

Pennick, Nigel, *Earth Harmony* (London, 1987)

Pennick, Nigel, *Einst War Uns die Erde Heilig* (Waldeck-Dehringhausen, 1987)

Purce, Jill, *The Mystic Spiral* (London, 1974)

Réville, Albert, *Lectures on the Origin and Growth of Religion* (London, 1884)

Richardson, L.J.D., The Labyrinth, Proceedings of the Cambridge Colloquium on Mycenaean Studies, eds. Palmer, Leonard R., and Chadwick, John (Cambridge, 1965)

Ross, Charles, *Soft Tech* (London, 1978)

Rouse, W.H.D., 'The Double Axe and the Labyrinth', *Journal of Hellenic Studies*, Vol. XXI (1901)

Rudbeck, O., *Atlantica* (1695–8)

Russell, G.N., *The Irish Times*, 16 December 1964

Saward, Deb, 'The Sun Dances', *Caerdroia*, No. 17 (1985), pp. 21–3

Saward, Jeff, 'The Chaldon Labyrinths'. *Caerdroia*, No. 10 (1982), pp. 12–20

Saward, Jeff and Deb., 'Cup and Rings'. *Caerdroia Project Newsletter*, No. 4 (1980), pp. 12–13

Saward, Jeff and Deb., 'Tintagel', *Caerdroia Project Newsletter*, No. 4 (1980), pp. 6–8

Saward, Jeff and Deb., *Caerdroia*, No. 12 (1983) *Geranos*, pp. 23–9

Saward, Jeff and Deb., 'Labyrinths of Ireland', *Caerdroia*, No. 14 (1984), pp. 4–9

Scott, Russell, 'Maze Musing', *Caerdroia*, No. 11 (1982), pp. 9–14

Screeton, Paul, *The Lambton Worm and Other Northumbrian Dragon Legends* (London, 1978)

Seligmann, S., *Der Böse Blick* (Berlin, 1910)

Stjernström, Bo, '*Sörmlandskustens labyrinter*', *Sörmlandsbygden* (1981), pp. 127–44

Stjernström, Bo, *Kust Labyrinter: Dokumentation och Klassificering* (Tyresö, 1982)

Stjernström, Bo, *Kust Labyrinter* (Örnsköldsvik, 1982)

Turner, Chris, 'Maze Design: An Analysis', *Caedroia*, No. 7 (1981)

Van der Ven, D.J., '*Niederländische Windelbahn- und Reigentänze*', *Germanien*, Vol. 10, 1942, pp. 122–43

Villiers-Stuart, Patricia, 'Bend Me a Maze (Here is the Key)', *Glastonbury – Ancient Avalon, New Jerusalem*, ed. Roberts, Anthony (London, 1977)

Visdal, Miroslav, '*Za Tajemstvim Labyrintu*', *Cteni*, No. 1 (1980)

von Baer, C.E., 'Stone Labyrinths in the Russian North', *Bull. Hist. Phil. de L'Acad. de St. Petersbourg*, Vol. I, 184. Translated by Michael Behrend and published in *Caerdroia*, No. 11 (1982), pp. 4-7

von Richthofen, B. Freiherr, '*Kaukasische Holzgefässe der gegenwart als vorgeschichtliche überlieferung*', *Germanien*, 1942, Vol. 10, pp. 226–30

von Zaborsky, Oskar, *Urväter-Erbe in Deutscher Volkskunst* (Leipzig, 1936)

Waldo-Schwartz, Paul, *Art and the Occult* (London, 1977)

Winter, Heinrich, '*Radmählen*', *Germanien* (1940), Vol. 8, pp. 291–6

Wirth, Hermann, *Die Heilige Urschrift der Menschheit*, Vol. 3 (Leipzig, 1936)

2 Ancient Turf Mazes

Allcroft, A. Hadrian, *Earthwork of England* (London, 1908)

Anon., *Census of India*, Vol. XXXIV (Mysore, 1901)

Aubrey, John, *Remaines of Gentilisme and Judaisme* (London, 1696-7)

Bailey, *Annals of Northamptonshire*

Behrend, Michael, 'Julian Bowers', *Caerdroia*, No. 15 (1984), pp. 4–7

Behrend, Michael, 'The Mazes of Nottingham', *Caerdroia*, No. 11 (1982) pp. 22–30

Blackner, John, *History of Nottingham* (1815)

Boyes, John H., 'Saffron Walden Maze, *Essex Journal*, No. 8 (1973), pp. 88–9

Breeks, J.W., *An Account of the Primitive Tribes and Monuments of the Nilagiris* (London, 1873)

Briscoe, J. Potter (ed.) *Old Nottinghamshire* (London, 1881)

Brown, W.R. (aka Urbs Camboritum), *Cambridge Daily News* (1890s). Reprinted in Cambridge Cameos series (Cambridge, n.d.)

Brusewitz, G., *Anteckingar under vandringar i sodra Halland sommaren 1865* (Halmstad, 1953)

Burne, C.S., *Shropshire Folklore* (London, 1883)

Callois, Roger, Man, Play and Games (London, 1962)

Camden, W., *Britannia*, ed. Gough (1789)

Coate, Randoll, and Fisher, Adrian, *A Celebration of Mazes* (St Albans, 1982)

Davis, Olive, 'Mazes and Labyrinths', *Stella Rosita*, No. 5 (1988), pp. 6–7

Davis, Olive, 'Mazes in England', *Stella Rosita*, No. 6 (1988), pp. 5–7

Deedes, C.N., op. cit.

Deering, Charles, *History of Nottingham* (Nottingham, 1751)

De La Pryme, A., *Diary* (Surtees Society, 1870)

Dickinson, P.G.M., 'Mazes', *Day Out*, Vol. 2, No. 7 (1965), pp. 30–32

Dickinson, P.G.M., 'Earth-cut, Church and Topiary Mazes', *Hunts. Local History Society Journal*, Vol. 1, Part 3 (1967), pp. 33–9

Dickinson, P.G.M., and Garnett, W. 'The Hilton Maze', *Archaeological Journal*, Vol. CXXIV (1967), p. 241

Dunn, Chris, 'The Long and Winding Path of Hilton', *Hunts. Post*, 8 January 1976

Dunne, Mrs, 'Mrs Dunne's Recollections', *Trans. Thoroton Society*, Vol. 19 (1915), pp. 143–4

Eiselen, Ernst, *Der Wunderkreis, neu entworfen und beschrieben* (Berlin, 1829)

Ferguson, R.S., 'A Labyrinth on Rockcliffe Marsh', *Cumberland & Westmorland Antiquarian & Archaeological Soc. Trans.*, VIII (1883–4), pp. 69–73

Fisher, Adrian, and Coate, Randoll, 'Way-Out Mazes'. *Amateur Gardening*, 26 December 1981

Garnett, W., 'Retracing the Hilton Maze'. *Archaeological Journal*, Vol. CXXIV (1967), p.241–5

Gordon, E.O., *Prehistoric London, Its Mounds and Circles* (London, 1925)

Gowland, T.S., 'Mazes at Ripon and Asenby', *Yorkshire Archaeological Journal*, Vol. XXXV (1943), p. 343

Grigson, Geoffrey, 'Mazes in the Wanton Green', *Country Life*, 13 September 1962

Gudenberg, Wolff, '*Kaufbeuren*', *Germanien* 1937, p. 315

Haken, Die Windelbahn zu Stolp Pomm. Archiv. d. Wissenschaften und des Geschmackes, Vol. III (1784), p. 49 ff

Halliday, Robert, 'Cambridgeshire Mazes'. *Cambridgeshire Life*, July 1967, pp. 23–4

Hallmann, Frithjof, 'London's Labyrinth Lore', *Caerdroia*, No. 15 (1984), pp. 23–4

Hallmann, Frithjof, *Labyrinthe und Trojaburgen. Mannus-Bibliothek NF* Band 29 (Bonn, 1988)

Hamkens, op. cit.

Hennicke, Franz, *Die Trojaburg bei Graitschen, eine nordische Sonnenkultdarstellung in Thüringen. Kreuz und quer durch Thüringen*, Vol. 2 (1926), pp. 33–8

Hitching, Francis, 'Patterns of Life', *The World Atlas of Mysteries* (London, 1978)

Hutchins, John, *The History and Antiquities of the County of Dorset*, 3rd edition (London, 1861)

Jackson, Dan, 'Journeys into Anglia'. *Cambridge Evening News*, 23 May 1983

Johnson, W., *Folk-Memory* (London, 1908)

Jünemann, Joachim, '*Das Labyrinth vom Dransberg*', *Unsere Heimat*, No. 44, May 1969

Jünemann, Joachim, *Radiaesthetische Aufschlüsse an einstigen Kirchen, Burgen und Kultstätten im Landkreis Göttingen* (Dransfeld, 1986)

Kern, Hermann: op. cit.

Knauth, C.C., *Alt Cellische Chronica* (Leipzig, 1721)

Kraft, John, 'Wunderberg and Jerusalem', *Caerdroia*, No. 13 (1983), pp. 11–19

Kraft, John, 'German Turf Labyrinths'. *Caerdroia*, No. 14 (1984), pp. 11–18

Kraft, John, 'Turf Labyrinths in Southern Scandinavia', *Caerdroia*, No. 15 (1984), pp. 14–22

Kraft, John, *Labyrintnamn – från Troja till Trelleborg. Sydsvenska Ortnamnssällskapets Årsskrift* (Lund, 1986)

Krause, Ernst, op. cit.

Layard, John, 'Maze Dances and the Ritual of the Labyrinth in Malekula', *Folk-Lore*, Vol. XLVII (1936)

Lega-Weekes, Ethel, 'Gallants' Bowers', *Transactions of the Devonshire Association*, Vol. 61 (1929), pp. 237–48

Leonhardt, K. Fr., *'Das Rad in Eilenriede, sein Ursprung und seine Bedeutung'*, *Hannoverische Gesch.-blätter Sonderheft* (1938), pp. 65–76

Liebeskind, Paul, *Die Trojaburgen in Thüringen. Zeitschrift d. Gesch. -u Altertumsver. f. Zeitz. u. Umgebung* (1921–2)

Lotze, Wilhelm, *Geschichte der Stadt Dransfeld* (Munich, 1878)

MacMhuirich, Cailean (Murray, Colin) (ed.), *The New Celtic Review*, Samhain 1981

Manning, Owen, and Bray, William, *The History of Surrey*, Vol. III (London, 1814)

Massmann, H.F., *Wunderkreis und Irrgärten für Turnplätze und Gartenanlagen* (Leipzig, 1844)

Matthews, W.H., op. cit.

Maynard, G.N., 'The Labyrinth or Maze at Saffron Walden', *Essex Field Club Proceedings*, 1889

Morrell, R.W., *Nottinghamshire Holy Wells and Springs* (Nottingham, 1988)

Mössinger, Friedrich, 'Baumtanz und Trojaburg' in *Germanien*, Vol. 8. (1940), pp. 282–9

Mössinger, Friedrich, 'Haferrad und Trojaburg', *Germanien*, Vol. 6 (1938), pp. 90–1

Mountaine, D. (T. Hyll), *The Gardener's Labyrinth* (1579)

Mullard, Jonathan, *Caerdroia Salopia: The Lost Turf Mazes of Shropshire* (Telford, 1983)

Murray, *Hand-Book for Northamptonshire and Rutland* (1901)

Orange, James, *History of Nottingham*, Vol. 1 (1840) pp. 370–1

Pennick, Nigel, *Geomancy* (Cambridge, 1973)

Pennick, Nigel, *Caerdroia* (Trumpington, 1974)

Pennick, Nigel, *European Troytowns* (Bar Hill, 1981)

Pennick, Nigel, 'Comberton, Cambridgeshire', *Caerdroia*, No. 5 (1981) p. 9

Pennick, Nigel, *Labyrinths: Their Geomancy and Symbolism* (Bar Hill, 1984)

Pennick, Nigel, and Devereux, Paul, *Lines on the Landscape: Leys and Other Linear Enigmas* (London, 1989)

Plassmann, Otto, 'Die Trojaburg als Torzeichen, *Germanien*, Vol. 8 (1940), pp. 289–90

Roberts, P., *Cambrian Popular Antiquities* (London, 1815)

Robertson, Seonaid, *Rosegarden and Labyrinth* (London, 1963)

Robinson, David N., 'Julian's Bower', *Lincolnshire Life*, Vol. 9 (1969), p. 28

Rutz, E., 'Das Windelbahnfest der Stolper Schuhmacher', in F. Ücker-Stettin, *Pommern im Wort und Bild* (1904), p. 374ff

Saward, Deb, 'Troytowns in Germany'. *Caerdroia Project Newsletter*, No. 2, (1980), pp. 4–6

Saward, Jeff, *Caer Sidi* (Benfleet, 1979)

Saward, Jeff, *The Saffron Walden Turf Maze* (Benfleet, 1981)

Saward, Jeff, *The Caerdroia Field Guide* (Benfleet, 1987)

Saward, Jeff and Deb, 'German Troytowns', *Caerdroia*, No. 13 (1983), pp. 20–30

Saward, Jeff and Deb, 'Germany Update', *Caerdroia*, No. 20 (1987), pp. 30–33

Schrader, Georg, *Oratio de lande Hannoveræ* (Hanover, 1650)

Shore, T.W., and Nisbett, H.C., 'Ancient Hampshire Mazes', *Hampshire Field Club Proceedings*, Vol. III (1896), p. 257

Sieber, Siegfried, *Trojaburg-Maigraf-Zunftfest. Mitteld. Blätter für Volkskunde*, Vol. II (1927), pp. 61–7

Sieber, Siegfried, '*Eine Trojaburg in Pommern*', *Germanien*, 1936

Stares, Judith, 'Amazed in a Rectory Garden', *The Observer*, 5 August 1969, p. 10

Stukeley, William, *Itinerarium Curiosum* (London, 1776)

Sumner, George Heywood, *The Ancient Earthworks of Cranborne Chase* (London, 1913)

Throsby, John (ed.) Thoroton, Robert, *Antiquities of Nottinghamshire*, Vol. 2 (3 vols. 1790–6) pp. 171–2

Trollope, Edward, 'Ancient and Medieval Labyrinths', *Archaeological Journal*, Vol. XV (1858), reprinted as *Ancient and Medieval Labyrinths* (Caerdroia Project & Institute of Geomantic Research, Benfleet & Bar Hill, 1981)

Tyack, George S., 'Mazes', *Ecclesiastical Curiosities*, ed. Andrews, William (London, 1989)

Valentine, Mark, 'A Lost Maze', *Caerdroia*, No. 12 (1983), p. 11

Valentine, Mark, *The Holy Wells of Northamptonshire* (Northampton, 1984)

Van der Ven, D.J., op. cit.

Voigt, G., '*Das Windelbahnfest zu Stolp*', *Pommernheimat*, Vol. 2 (1928)

Wade W.G., *The Antiquary*, April 1981

Wetton, G.N., *Guide-Book to Northampton* (1849)

Whellan, William & Co, *History, Gazetteer and Directory of Northamptonshire* (London and Peterborough, 1849)

White, *Directory of Nottinghamshire* (1832)

Williams-Freeman, J.P., *Field Archaeology as Illustrated by Hampshire* (London, 1915)

3 Pavement and Church Labyrinths

Backman, E., *Den religiosa dansen inom kristen kyrka och folkmedicin* (Stockholm, 1952)

Carmichael, A., *The Sun Dances* (London, 1960)

Charpentier, Louis, *The Mysteries of Chartres Cathedral* (London, 1972)

Coles, Sarah, 'Itchen Stoke Church Maze', *Caerdroia* (1989), p. 29

Critchlow, Keith, op. cit.

Daszewski, Wiktor A., *Nea Paphos II, La Mosaïque de Thésée, études sur les mosaïques avec representations du labyrinthe, de Thésée et du Minotaure* (Warsaw, 1977)

Devereux, Paul, 'The Thornton Maze', *Caerdroia*, No. 9 (1982), pp. 29–31

Durand, J., *Les Pavés Mosaïques en Italie et an France. Annales archéologiques*, XIV-XVII (1855-7)

Eichberg, Henning, '*Labyrinten. Om de krumme liniers kultur*', *Cras*, No. LIII (1988) pp. 68–89

Fisher, Adrian, 'Bourn Maze', *Caerdroia Project Newsletter*, No. 6 (1981), pp. 11–13

Fulcanelli, A.H.S., *Le Mystère des Cathédrales* (Paris, 1971)

Gailhabaud, J., *L'Architecture du Vme au XVIIe siècle* (Paris, 1858)

Géruzez, J.B.F., *Description Historique de la Ville de Reims* (Reims, 1817)

Goodwin, A., *The Technique of Mosaic* (London, 1985)

Haigh, op. cit.

Hallmann, Frithjof, *Labyrinthe und Trojaburgen. Mannus-Bibliothek NF*, Vol. 29 (Bonn, 1988)

Kern, Hermann, *Labyrinthe, Erscheinungsformen und Deutungen 5 000 Jahre Gegenwart eines Urbildes* (Munich, 1982)

Kraft, John, 'The Cretan Labyrinth and the Walls of Troy: An Analysis of Roman Labyrinth Designs', *Opuscula Romana*, Vol. XV (1985), pp. 79–86

Lethaby, William R., op. cit.

Luckwald, Hans A., '*Vom Ringkreuz*', *Germanien*, Vol. 1, 1933, pp. 371–6; Vol. 2, 1934, pp. 21–4

Luszczkiewicz, Władyslaw, '*Labirynt Kadedny we Wloclawku nad Wista*', *Wiadomosci Numizmatyczno-Archáeologiczne*, Vol. 3 (1898), pp. 426–33

Maisch, R., *Greek Antiquity*

Markham, Gervase, *The English Husbandman* (London, 1613)

Matthews, William Henry, *Mazes and Labyrinths* (London, 1922)

Pennick, Nigel, *The Ancient Science of Geomancy* (London, 1979)

Pennick, Nigel, 'Pavement Labyrinths', *Caerdroia Project Newsletter*, No. 6 (1981), 20–26

Pennick, Nigel, 'Chartres', *Caerdroia*, No. 7 (1981), pp. 4–6

Pennick, Nigel, 'The Tor – A Calvary Mount?', *Caerdroia*, No. 14 (1984), pp. 26–8

Pennick, Nigel, 'Octagonal Geography', *Caerdroia*, No. 15 (1984), pp. 8–11

Pennick, Nigel, 'Indian Board Games, Pavements and Labyrinths, *Caerdroia*, No. 21 (1987), pp. 25–8

Pernety, Dom, *Dictionnaire mytho-hermetique* (Paris, 1787)

Ruskin, John, '*Our Fathers Have Told Us*'. Sketches of the History of Christendom, for Boys and Girls Who Have been Held at its Fonts. Part I. *The Bible of Amiens*. Orpington, 1884.

Rypson, Piotr, 'The Labyrinth Poem', *Visible Language*, Vol. XX (1986), pp. 65–95

Saint-Hilaire, Paul de, *L'Enigme des labyrinthes* (Brussels, 1975)

Santarcangeli, P., *Le livre des labyrinthes* (Paris, 1974)

Saward, Deb, 'The Sun Dances', *Caerdroia*, No. 17 (1985), pp. 21–3

Saward, Deb, 'British Pavement Labyrinths', *Caerdroia*, No. 19 (1986), pp. 27–9

Saward, Jeff, *The Caerdroia Field Guide* (Benfleet, 1987)

Stirling, William, *The Canon: An Exposition of the Pagan Mystery Perpetuated in the Cabala as the Rule of All the Arts* (London, 1891)

Trollope, Edward, 'Notices of Ancient and Mediaeval Labyrinths', *Archaeological Journal*, Vol. 15 (1858), pp. 216–35

Tyack, George S., 'Mazes', *Ecclesiastical Curiosities*, ed. Andrews, William (London, 1899)

Walcott, M.E.C., *Sacred Archaeology* (London, 1868)

Wallet, E., *Description d'une crypte at d'un Pay mosaïque de l'Église Saint Bertin à St Omer* (Paris, 1834)

4   The Origin and Development of Puzzle Hedge Mazes

Addison, Joseph, *Rosamund* (opera, *c.* 1712)

Agar, Madeline, *Garden Design in Theory and Practice* (London, 1911)

Aleff, Margaret, and Aleff, Peter, *The Labyrinth Game* (Henrietta, New York, 1984)

Cecil, Hon. Mrs Evelyn (Alice Mary Tyssen-Amherst), *A History of Gardening in England* (New York, 1910)

Collins, Tony, and Bosworth, John, 'A Victorian Maze Restored', *Caerdroia*, No. 16 (1985), pp. 13–28

Defoe, Daniel, *Tour Through Great Britain*

Fisher, *et al*, op. cit.

Harvey, John, *The Medieval Garden* (1981)

Hyll, Thomas (Didymus Mountaine), *A Most Brief and Pleasant Treatyse Teachynge How to Dress, Sowe and Set a Garden* (London, 1563)

Islip, Adam, *The Orchard and the Garden* (London, 1602)

Kip, J., *Britannia Illustrata* (London, 1720)

Langley, Batty, *New Principles of Gardening* (London, 1728)

Law, E., *History of Hampton Court Palace* (London, 1900)

Lawson, William, *A New Orchard and Garden* (London, 1618)

Leland, John, *De Rebus Britannicis Collectanea* (ed. Thomas Hearne, Oxford, 1715)

Macartney, Mervyn, *English Houses and Gardens of the Seventeenth and Eighteenth Centuries* (1908)

Mountaine, Didymus (Thomas Hyll), *The Gardener's Labyrinth* (London, 1579)

Mössinger, Friedrich, '*Baumtanz und Trojaburg*', *Germanien*, Vol. 8, 1940, trans. as *Treedance & Troytown* M. Behrend in *Trojaburgen*, Benfleet & Bar Hill 1982.

Nevison, J.L., *The Embroidery Patterns of Thomas Trevelyon*, Walpole Society, Vol. XLI (1966–8), pp. 1–38

Pennick, Nigel, 'The End of the Road to Jerusalem', *Caerdroia*, No. 13 (1983), pp. 4–8

Pennick, Nigel, 'The Royal Game of Goose: A Labyrinthine Byway', *Caerdroia*, No. 18 (1986) 23–4

Pennick, Nigel, *Games of the Gods* (London, 1988)

Pennick, Nigel, 'Thomas Trevelyon's Labyrinth', *Caerdroia* (1989), p. 28

Perrault, Charles, *Labirinthe de Versailles* (Paris, 1677)

Robinson, W., *The English Flower Garden*

Singleton, Esther, *The Shakespeare Garden* (London, n.d. – *c*. 1932)

Strong, Roy, *The Renaissance Garden in England* (London, 1979)

Switzer, Stephen, *Ichnographia Rustica* (London, 1742)

Temple, Sir William, *Upon The Garden of Epicurus* (London, 1685)

Thurston, Herbert, *The Stations of the Cross* (London, 1914)

Tyack, George S., 'Mazes', *Ecclesiastical Curiosities*, ed. Andrews, William (London, 1899), pp. 186–205

Wolseley, Viscountess, *Gardens, Their Form and Design* (London, 1919)

5 Modern Labyrinths: The Return of Symbolism

Anon. 'The Labyrinth With 3000 Rooms', *The Hotspur*, 18 February 1967

Anon. 'Dr Runcie's dream has come true', *Church Times*, 31 December 1981

Antonowicz, Anton, 'Amazeing: A puzzle to send you right round the twist', *Daily Mirror*, 29 May 1989, pp. 16–17

Artaud, Antonin (trans. Hirschmann, Jack), *Artaud Anthology* (San Francisco, 1965)

Ashe, Geoffrey, *The Glastonbury Tor Maze* (Glastonbury, 1979)

Ashe, Geoffrey, 'The Tor Maze', *Caerdroia*, No. 14 (1984), pp. 19–21

Atha, Matthew, 'Labyrinth on Ilkley Moor', *Northern Earth Mysteries*, No. 36 (1988), pp. 19–21

Ayrton, Michael, *The Testament of Daedalus* (1960)

Ayrton, Michael, *The Maze-Maker* (London, 1967)

Ayrton, Michael, *The Rudiments of Paradise* (London, 1971)

Boeckler, G.A., *Architectura Curiosa* (1664)

Caine, Mary, *The Glastonbury Zodiac – Key to the Mysteries of Britain* (Torquay, 1978)

Devereux, Paul, 'The Path of the Nwyvre', *Caerdroia*, No. 20 (1987), pp. 26–9

Dugdale, William, *Monasticon Anglicana* (1654)

Fisher, Adrian, 'The Design of Modern Puzzle Mazes'. *Caerdroia*, No. 19 (1986), pp. 6–8

Fortune, Dion, *Avalon of the Heart* (London, 1934)

Lonegren, Sig, 'Labyrinth Meditations', *Caerdroia*, No. 20 (1987), pp. 17–21

Mac Mhuirich, Cailean (Murray, Colin) (ed.), *The New Celtic Review*, March 1980

Macmillan, R.F., 'The Milton Keynes Labyrinth', *The Mathematical Gazette*, Vol. 72 (1988), No. 462, pp. 319–22

Mann, Nick, *Glastonbury Tor, a Guide to the History and Legends* (Glastonbury, 1986)

Mann, Nick, 'A New St Agnes Troy Town', *Caerdroia*, No. 20 (1987), pp. 24–5

Mereaux, Pierre, *Carnac – un porte vers l'inconnu* (Paris, 1981)

Mollison, Bill, *Permaculture: A Designer's Manual* (Tyalgum, Australia, 1988)

Pennick, Nigel, 'Uses for New Square', *Cambridge Evening News*, 1983

Pennick, Nigel, 'The Tor – A Calvary Mount?', op. cit.

Pennick, Nigel, 'The Ball of String – A Clue to the Labyrinth', *Caerdroia*, No. 19 (1986), pp. 22–5

Pennick, Nigel, 'The Ojai Labyrinth', *Caerdroia*, No. 20 (1987), pp. 14–16

Russell, G., in *Glastonbury – A Study in Patterns* (Research into Lost Knowledge Organization, 1969) pp. 16–19

Saward, Jeff, 'Maze or Myth?', *Caerdroia*, No. 14 (1984), pp. 29–32

Saward, Jeff and Deb., 'The Bristol Water Maze', *Caerdroia*, No. 16 (1985), pp. 28–30

Saward, Jeff and Deb., 'Labyrinth Layout', *Practical Geomancy*, 1 (1985), pp. 22–5

Schmid, Peter, 'A Turfed Labyrinth: The first in the Netherlands', *Caerdroia*, No. 16 (1985), pp. 31–40

Scott, Russell, 'A 3-D Labyrinth?', *Caerdroia*, No. 14 (1984), pp. 22–5

Stares, Judith, 'Amazed in a Rectory Garden'. *The Observer*, 5 August 1969, p. 10

Tromp, S.W., *Psychical Physics* (London, 1949)

Turner, Chris, 'Ginst Point', *Caerdroia*, No. 20 (1987), pp. 12–13

Williams ab Ithel, J., *Barddas; or a Collection of Original Documents Illustrative of the Theology, Wisdom and Usages of the Bardo-Druidic System of the Isle of Britain* (Llandovery, 1862)

Wood, Les, *Mazes and Mandalas* (London, 1981)

Index